HUNTING
MONSTERS

HUNTING MONSTERS

An Officer on the Trail of the World's Worst War Criminals

ÉRIC EMERAUX

sh.

**SUTHERLAND
HOUSE**

TORONTO, 2023

Sutherland House
416 Moore Ave., Suite 205
Toronto, ON M4G 1C9

First edition, September 2023

If you are interested in inviting one of our authors to a live event or
media appearance, please contact sranasinghe@sutherlandhousebooks.com
and visit our website at sutherlandhousebooks.com for more
information about our authors and their schedules.

We acknowledge the support of the Government of Canada.

Manufactured in India
Cover designed by Lena Yang
Book composed by Karl Hunt

Library and Archives Canada Cataloguing in Publication
Title: Hunting monsters : an officer on the trail of the
world's worst war criminals / Éric Emeraux.
Other titles: Traque est mon métier. English
Names: Emeraux, Éric, author.
Description: Translation of: La traque est mon métier : un officier sur les traces
des criminels de guerre. | Includes bibliographical references and index.
Identifiers: Canadiana (print) 2023017728X | Canadiana (ebook) 20230177328 |
ISBN 9781990823053 (hardcover) | ISBN 9781990823190 (EPUB)
Subjects: LCSH: Emeraux, Éric. | LCSH: Detectives—France—Biography. |
LCSH: Criminal investigation (International law) | LCSH: War crimes investigation. |
LCSH: War crimes. | LCSH: War criminals.
Classification: LCC KZ7390 .E44 2023 | DDC 363.25/938092—dc23

ISBN 978-1-990823-05-3
eBook 978-1-990823-19-0

To my wife and two sons who have accompanied me on this long and winding road, in service of our military and gendarmerie.

"To whom could I dedicate this book, if not the victims of those for whom Death is a Profession."—Robert Merle, La Mort est mon Métier

To whom could I dedicate this book, if not to those around the globe who contribute, up close or at a distance, to the fight against impunity.

Gendarmerie [john-dar-muh-ree]. A French military structure heavily involved in police work and investigation, possessing its own elite units. In the United States, this would be similar to a combination of the Army and the FBI, with aspects of Homeland Security. The more direct translation, *National Guard,* is obviously not appropriate.

Gendarme [john-darm] (same *j* as above). A person serving in the gendarmerie.

CONTENTS

CONTENTS

FOREWORD

Eric Emeraux is that rare individual who so combines empathy, competence, and courage that he can accomplish tasks impossible for others. As a law enforcement attaché in Sarajevo and a police commander of the French Office to Combat Crimes Against Humanity in Paris, he immersed himself in the world of victims, bystanders, and perpetrators of mass atrocities. He feels the suffering of the survivors and personally commits to bringing their tormentors to justice. But at the same time, he seeks and gains an understanding of all the actors' motivations to enable tracking of the perpetrators in their own communities. It is the insights that he gains and shares that separate his book from others about the chase for the bad guys. He reminds us that the same blood flows in our veins, the same passions could motivate us to tolerate tyrants, to become perpetrators or silent accomplices.

Emeraux's leadership in the successful tracking and arrest of Felicien Kabuga is the capstone of his career and his account of it concludes his memoir. Kabuga was chair of board of the most powerful messenger of hate, RTLM radio, and the alleged financier of the Rwanda genocide, an organized campaign that hacked to death 800,000 men, women, and children over 100 days of 1994. Kabuga used his resources and benefited from officious indifference to give the world the slip for twenty-seven years. I personally recall the detailed requests the Rwanda tribunal sent to European law enforcement agencies and the responses received after many months showing compliance to the letter, but never the initiative to look around corners or to follow the leads that their observations revealed. Emeraux tells us the secret of success: he made the case his own. It was as if his own neighbors had been murdered and the killer was on the loose. Because Eric

Emeraux joined the chase, Kabuga was arrested and is today facing his victims across a courtroom in The Hague.

—Stephen Rapp successfully prosecuted the leaders of the Rwandan "media of hate" and Liberian President Charles Taylor at United Nations-backed tribunals. He was later US Ambassador-at-Large for Global Criminal Justice in the Obama Administration.

PREFACE

The 20th century was riddled with atrocities that "defy the imagination and offend the human conscience."[1] It compelled the international community to create tools that allow victims of human barbarism to see their tormentors brought to justice. Yet the 21st century is following the same path: destruction, massacres, atrocities, acts of torture, and other crimes against humanity have come in waves, motivated by the timeless human instincts toward predation and perversity.

The recurrence of these crimes, time and again in different parts of the world, does not make it easier to capture and punish their perpetrators. Bad people continue to act with impunity. Thus, the government of France in 2013 created OCLCH, the Office Responsible for Combating Crimes Against Humanity.[2] It is staffed with seasoned professional investigators, men and women driven by the same conviction: whoever the criminal, whatever the crime, and whenever it occurred, justice must be served.

Our investigations, exceptionally long and painstakingly documented, are dedicated to busting war criminals, sometimes with an arrest, and in all cases with a concrete establishment of culpability, true to history and to the victims of their crimes. While the criminals pursued by the OCLCH share common characteristics, similarities between the investigations are almost nonexistent. Unique terrains, conflicts, principals, suspects, and facts all come into play. The criminal may have acted on behalf of a state, in the context of a civil war, or even a genocide; he may have already been captured or he may be on the run.

Our mission demands that we adapt to circumstances and, above all, overcome our primary disadvantages: not only are we far from the scenes of the crimes we investigate, but time has passed since their commission. We have to turn back the clock, interrogating witnesses and meticulously collecting material evidence, laboriously and carefully reconstructing events and seeking to establish unequivocal truths. It is never easy but, as I hope you'll see in these pages, it is entirely possible.

The reader will understand that, for reasons of confidentiality, due process, and the protection of witnesses, some names, locations, times, and other circumstances have been modified.

1

FUGITIVE

"Reconciliation in the Balkans cannot exist so long as the denial of the crimes remains"

—Carla Del Ponte

February 14, 2018. 2:00 p.m.

I park my car on a side street in Saint-Denis, France. On standby. The rest of the OCLCH team is in place, ready for the arrest.

A glance in the rear-view mirror finds the Saint-Denis Basilica. Its ancient clock marks the passing hours. It's a long wait for us, but for Bosnia-Herzegovina, it's been twenty-six years since that terrible day in Višegrad.

Hora fugit, stat jus. Time passes, but justice remains. The motto of the OCLCH.

Paris's feeble winter sun reflects off the dashboard. A Glock is jabbing into my side. I have to remember to fix that later.

Our target has been dead in our sights for six days. We are working with Groupe d'Observation et de Surveillance d'Ile de France (GOSIF). There is no way we can let him escape. Bosnia-Herzegovina would not forgive us, and I wouldn't forgive myself.

For six days, we've followed him as he moonlights, doing small jobs here and there. We receive regular updates on his movements from Daniel, the deputy head of the strategy division to whom I've entrusted operational management of this file.

I take out my phone and tap on the keyboard to bring up Interpol's "red notice" page. Red notices are issued for fugitives wanted either for prosecution or to serve a sentence. They request law enforcement agencies worldwide to locate and provisionally arrest a person pending extradition, surrender, or any other legal action. They also allow for the questioning of the person concerned on national territory. I enter the name Goran Popovic. The file appears. It won't be on the site for much longer.

The team has been in place since 6 a.m. this morning. It is hidden, watching through remote cameras in the "submarine," an unmarked van specially outfitted for surveillance operations. The team consists of two police officers and two gendarmes: two women, two men.

Daniel reported to me a few hours earlier that the target has not moved.

2:05 p.m.

It shouldn't be long now. I start the engine and welcome the freshness of the air conditioning against my face. Questions rattle through my mind, the same silent tensions that always precede an arrest.

For our target, this will be the end of his peaceful little life in France. A return trip to Bosnia-Herzegovina awaits him. He'll be judged there, under the eyes of his victims.

The sun disappears behind large threatening clouds. The radio is playing a new electro number. I Shazam the track for later. Kavinsky's "Nightcall."

2:10 p.m.

My cell rings. It's the attorney general's office. I pick up. The advocate general gives me the green light to arrest Popovic. He will be detained until he can be handed over to Bosnia authorities for extradition.

"The authorization should be in your inbox."

"Perfect." I respond. "I'll call you back as soon as we wrap it up."

I hang up, cut the radio, and walk over to join the team. I give Daniel a nod. "We got the green light."

Everyone gets out of the vehicle and straps on Kevlar, because you never know. One of the officers grabs a battering ram. It is still cold, with a growing mass of gray and black clouds. It smells like a storm is coming on.

We head down the street with determined steps. Daniel breaches the front door of the building. We follow in single file down a dark and narrow corridor, without a word, and emerge into a courtyard. Everything is calm; so much the better.

A second entryway takes us to a winding staircase. Two climb two floors and arrive at the door of Bogdan and Marjorie Popovic's apartment. I question Daniel with my eyes. He grabs the battering ram.

"Wait," someone whispers. "Maybe we can call."

"What is Bogdan's number?" I ask.

Daniel checks: "07-xx-xx-xx-x8."

I dial.

Everybody listens. We hear footsteps within the apartment. Someone picks up. Silence. Then more footstep and the door opens. A young man presents himself, dressed in black, like a security guard.

"Mr. Bogdan Popovic?"

"Oui."

"Federal police, Office Responsible for Combating Crimes Against Humanity. Is your father inside?"

"What is this about?"

"Are you the son of Mr. Goran Popovic?"

He does not answer but turns his head toward a room in the apartment.

I ask him another question to which I already know the answer and in that moment, Daniel pushes Bogdan aside and the rest of the team quickly enters the premises. An old man, stunted, almost emaciated, stands in the doorway to his room, arms flailing, eyes wide. One of the gendarmes grabs him. The other closes the window in case he tries to jump. Every contingency is planned for.

I look to the right and to the left. Everything is under control. I turn to Goran.

"Mr. Popovic?"

"Da!"

"You are under arrest. You will be extradited to Bosnia-Herzegovina."

The old man looks dazed, uncomprehending. He looks at his son who translates into Serbian.

"What is this story?" asks the son. "My father is innocent." They both look angry now. "You are making a mistake. Show me your documents."

Without saying a word, I bring up the authorization on my phone. He reads the text carefully.

"What does this mean? Why are you arresting my father?"

"The charges will be disclosed by the authorities in Bosnia-Herzegovina."

Daniel intervenes, "Tell your father to prepare a bag with his clothes, toiletries, and medication."

An officer helps the old man gather his personal effects. I watch him, withered, in a white tank top with holes and sky-blue striped pajama bottoms. He still has the same little beard that I noticed in the photos of him from 1992. His mind seems elsewhere. Perhaps already back in Bosnia-Herzegovina.

As we head for the door, Bogdan loses it.

"To that shit country! Bosnia! It's not even a real country! Just a bunch of people who don't want to live together, run by a gang of Mujahideen! If we had known in 1995, we would have finished the job and eradicated them all. My father will never be judged objectively. They want to make him an example. The whole country is a sham. All the Muslims used to be Christian, and for a handful of rice they converted and sold their souls to the Ottomans. We Serbs did not! We liberated the Balkans from the yoke of the Ottomans and that gives us the right to the land. Nothing's changed there. To send him back is to kill him."

I say nothing in return. The diaspora is often more radical than those who stayed in the Balkans. I've heard this same speech, over and over again for the past five years. A country divided into the Republika Srpska (Serb Republic) and the Federation of Bosnia and Herzegovina, with each ethnicity doing everything in its power to obstruct the other. In short, *Absurdistan*.

"So long, *moj drug.*" In his tongue, "buddy."

Recognizing the language, Bogdan's eyes follow me suspiciously.

Goran is handcuffed and surrounded by our personnel. He looks haggard as we head down the stairs. When we emerge in the street, I notice that the sun is trying to make an appearance.

I call the head prosecutor and let him know the operation went well and that we'll be arriving soon. Thank and congratulations. I breathe a little.

4

A video camera meets us on the street. It's a small gesture to our colleagues at GOSIF who've worked nonstop for six days. A record of a job well done.

I start the car, turn on the flashing lights and hit the play button: Archive, "Pills (Live in Athens)." I turn up the volume and head toward the Court of Appeals, Paris.

In the rear-view mirror, I glance at Goran, not saying a word, staring into the void. I wonder what's going through his mind. What does a war criminal, caught by the police, think in this moment on the road to accountability? About that day in June 1992 when, according to the Bosnian justice system, he committed the unspeakable?

My own thoughts are with Lejla, Amina, and Bakira—the women of Višegrad—and the victims of the human animals unleashed on their small country.

An hour and a half later, our vehicles turn off Boulevard du Palais onto the Quai de l'Horloge. The two large allegorical figures representing Law and Justice come into view, framing the building's gold clock. The scene reminds us of the purpose of what we do: *Machina quae bis sex tam juste dividit horas Justitiam servare monet leges que tueri.* "This machine, that so justly divides the hour into twelve parts, teaches us to protect justice and defend the laws."

Same Day, 3:30 p.m., Court of Appeals, Paris

I climb the stairway in the old building. Each step bears the impressions of centuries of justice. I have a meeting with the prosecutor who green-lit our operation. Our primary point of contract on the case, he reports directly to the Attorney General of Paris's Court of Appeals, the office that approves these special investigations into fugitives officially condemned by foreign governments for human rights violations, genocides, or war crimes. Three flights up, the prosecutor greets me with a smile.

"Colonel, excellent work once again. The diplomatic world can breathe a sigh of relief."

The magistrate lays out the remainder of the plan concerning Goran.

He's to be processed through extradition. A few moments later, he'll be enroute to the detention center in Fresnes.

All goes according to plan. On Sunday, February 25, 2018, Goran Popovic is surrendered to Bosnian authorities. At 10 a.m. the following day, he's presented to the war crimes in Sarajevo. For me, that's where it ends, a story that finished back where it started in June 2013.

2

THE PATH OF AN
ALPINE HUNTER

The wisdom of our ancestors bestows upon us a principle whereby no one is above the law. The gendarmerie that enforces the law gives it life, and should make the most persevering efforts to ensure that this judiciary presumption becomes a practical and concrete reality, especially in what concerns the participation legislation has conferred upon them regarding the execution of its prescriptions.

Cochet de Savigny, *Mémorial de la gendarmerie*

I hadn't planned on becoming a hunter of war criminals like Goran Popovic. I was born in the Vosges, a mountainous region in Northeastern France. Naturally, I've always had a thing for the mountains. At eighteen, I made up my mind to join the Chasseurs Alpins,[1] the elite mountain infantry of the French army. I enlisted at the High Mountain Military School[2] in Chamonix in October, 1982. After two years of training, I was assigned to the 11th Battalion of the Chasseurs Alpins. My goal was to join the cross-country skiing units in Barcelonnette.

I hadn't counted on the colonel, number two in the battalion, who strongly encouraged me to consider a career as an officer. In 1987, I left the Southern Alps and made my way to Bretagne, attending the military academy in Coëtquidan. Throughout my two rather unpleasant years there, I had one thought in mind: return to the mountains.

That happened in 1990 when, as a lieutenant, I joined the intelligence section of the 7th Battalion in Bourg-Saint-Maurice—the ski scouts, a descendant of the *Maquis alpins*[3] that had wreaked havoc on the Germans during the Second World War.[4] Our section was part of the Human Research Units of the 27th Alpine Division (URH 27). Our mission in time of war is to infiltrate, hole up, and inform command on enemy positions.

War, of course, is always knocking on someone's doorstep, usually just a few thousand miles from our own. In August 1991, it was in the former Yugoslavia, where a bloody conflict broke out among the Serbian, Bosnian, and Croatian populations.

In February 1992, the United Nations decided to send fourteen thousand blue helmets (peacekeepers) as part of UNPROFOR (the United Nations Protection Force). On the French side, our army made plans to deploy ground troops in the war zone.

One morning, the colonel who commands the 7th battalion called me into his office. He offered me a position as head of the URH team assigned to infiltrate Sarajevo.

It was tempting, but I had other plans. For weeks, I had been busting my ass on the National Gendarmerie competition. My objective was to join the search-and-rescue unit of the High Mountain Gendarmerie Platoon (PGHM). It was part of a promise I had made to myself a few years earlier when I was trying to keep a fellow soldier after falling ten meters from a rock bar. When the PGHM helicopter from Briançon touched down to evacuate my friend, I knew that he'd live (unfortunately, as a quadriplegic).

So that was the plan. Afterward, perhaps, a tour in law enforcement.

The colonel knew my intentions, but wanted to keep me onboard. Hence the offer.

"When do you need to know by?"

"I need a response immediately."

"Well, if I'm on the spot, the answer is no."

Silence.

"Alright. I don't blame you."

Just like that, the dice were thrown.

Fortunately, I passed the competition for the gendarmerie, without knowing that it was going to bring me back, twenty years later, to Sarajevo.

After swapping the uniform of the Chasseurs Alpins for that of the gendarmerie, I continued my career in the mountains, first as the head of a squadron of mobile mountain gendarmerie in Pamiers, in Ariège, then with a search-and-rescue squad in Hautes-Pyrénées, and finally with a company based in Annecy, in Haute Savoie. It was twenty years in command of a wide range of units, professional experiences that I was happy to share with young officers by joining the *École des officiers de la gendarmerie nationale* in Melun, near Paris.

Law enforcement was always on deck. In August 2003, I joined the judicial police.[5] I was assigned to an investigative section in Montpellier. Homicides and organized crime in a city that gets lost in the shadow of Marseille's corruption, but has no shortage of its own cases. Between 2007 and 2008, my team investigated nine homicides and dismantled a myriad of trafficking operations: arms, narcotics, and priceless works of art. This included the famous Air Cannabis case implicating high-profile Corsican criminals in a network that used a helicopter to import massive amounts of cannabis resin from Morocco via Spain to France.

My five years as head of the Montpellier investigations section were quite an adventure, culminating with my 2008 transfer to Lyon as deputy general for all matters relating to the judicial police in the Rhône-Alpes-Auvergne region. It wasn't a move I'd expected.

For some time, I'd made it known that I was interested in a foreign assignment. Based on my expertise, I expected to be transferred to West Africa to combat narcotics trafficking but that fell through.

Finally, on August 1, 2012, I receive a transfer to the French embassy in Sarajevo to serve as an internal security attaché. My mission was to facilitate police and judicial cooperation between France and Bosnia-Herzegovina. On the menu were arms and explosives trafficking (Bosnia-Herzegovina reportedly had a stockpile of over 750,000 arms illegally held by civilians and easily transportable by car into France); human trafficking and exploitation; counter terrorism; and the arrival of radical Islam in certain parts of the country.

I wouldn't be bored.

My family arrived in the capital at the end of July. My wife, two sons, and I would discover the city, the divided country, the culture, and the Balkan people.

Sarajevo is said to be a city that either spits you out or swallows you up. For us, the experience was more like "Sarajevo, mon amour."[6]

3

THE AVENGERS

"Only the victims and their executioners know who's buried. The first are dead, the second are walled in silence."
—Éric Stover and Gilles Peress, *Les Tombes*

June 2013—Sarajevo

I have been living in this country for almost a year now and I never tire of walking the streets of Sarajevo. The Turkish and Austrian-Hungarian ambience. Hrvatin Street. Certain houses still carry the scars of war. As do certain minds.

But things no longer jump out at me. Habit quickly erased my astonishment. I come out on the bridge spanning the Mijaska River, just in front of the Vijesnicá: a majestic library, originally designed as a hotel by the great Czechoslovakian architect Karel Pařík, and built in 1891 under the reign of the Austrian-Hungarian Emperor. It was partially destroyed by shell fire on August 25, 1992, during the siege of Sarajevo. The goal had been to annihilate history, erase culture. The preamble to genocide.

Over 700 original manuscripts went up in smoke. Before the attack, the library contained 1.5 million books, 155,000 of them the only copies in existence. Through sniper fire and flames, Sarajevo's citizens and library personnel rushed in and saved what they could.

Today the building stands as a symbol of art and culture's victory over war. It is being renovated with European funding. The reopening is scheduled for June 28, 2014, to commemorate the hundred-year anniversary of the assassination of Archduke François Ferdinand.

I circled the library and entered Baščaršija, a neighborhood in Old Sarajevo where the mornings are always full swing. The city is awakening. Flaky *burek* are warm in the markets and I can see steam rising from the *ćevapčići,* those little grilled beef and veal sausages that Bosnians love so much—they're served around the clock. Some Sarajevians are already relaxing in the sun, drinking their coffee. Savoring life, perhaps, or just contemplating the passage of time.

Easy, or *polako* in the local tongue. It is the reigning word in this country. It is meant as praise to slowness, a counterintuitive notion to those of us accustomed to compressing time and space. Just thinking about it brings a measure of tranquillity as I turn down Maršala Tita, a central artery of the city. I pass a synagogue on the left, a Catholic church, an Orthodox church, a mosque. Sarajevo, the Jerusalem of the East.

On the sidewalk, I step around the divots left by mortar shells, starbursts of a thousand branches, filled with red paint. They're called the Roses of Sarajevo. More stigmata.

On my right, grocers are setting up their fruit and vegetable stalls on the Markale market, the target of two deadly bombardments. The first attack, on February 5, 1994, left sixty-eight dead and 144 wounded. The second on August 28, 1995, killed thirty-seven and wounded ninety. The fin of a mortar shell remains embedded in the ground, encased in glass. A plaque serves as a reminder of the horror and the names of the victims.

I continue on my journey, listening to music through headphones. I pass the monument dedicated to the memory of the 1,000 dead children, victims of bombardments and snipers during the siege of the city, one of the deadliest after that of Leningrad. Reports indicate that an average of 329 shells hit per day. The blockade of the city by Serbian forces was total: shipments of food and medicine, water, electricity, and heat were cut off, along with shipments of food and medicine. The Serbs never tried to take the city. They were numerically inferior to the forces of the Bosnian army, composed of Bosniaks but also of Bosnian Serbs and Bosnian-Croats. They simply laid siege, weakening it with a continuous bombardment, never leaving the hills.

It was the tragic second attack on the Markale market, following the massacres and genocide in Srebrenica in July 1995, that triggered the

NATO bombing campaign, Operation Deliberate Force. It mobilized 400 planes and 5,000 soldiers from fifteen nations for a month.

The aerial attacks, combined with artillery fire from French army units and U.S. Navy Tomahawk fire on a Bosnian-Serb communications tower, caused the Bosnian-Serb authorities to surrender in mid-September 1995. Negotiations followed, paving the way to the Dayton Accords two months later, ending the war in Bosnia-Herzegovina.

I walk through a small park with a few Ottoman tombs. At the top of the park near the French embassy, my destination, are four statues. Four ghosts. This monument was erected in memory of the ninety-six international soldiers who died for the restoration of peace. I always have a thought for these colleagues who died far from their homes. Might have been my fate.

Today's plan is to head to Višegrad with Jasmina, my interpreter, to meet a woman I'll call Lejla. I'm working on a tip that came from a local police officer, Asim Sadikovic, a French-speaking officer, in love with France, passionate about his job. He's a very enthusiastic and colorful character who reminds me of Benigni in the movie *La vie est belle*. He informed us that a woman named Lejla wants to share information about a war criminal currently residing in France.

I sit outside the embassy in a Nissan four-by-four waiting for Jasmina. She looks pale. Not entirely there. Trouble sleeping? She jumps in the passenger side and greets me with a handshake.

"Good morning, Colonel."

"Dobro jutro, kako ste?" I answer, trying to demonstrate my progress with the language.

"Doing well, thank you."

Jasmina is from Central Bosnia. She works for the French Embassy as an interpreter in the internal security branch. In short, she goes where I go. Since the death of her sister, she travels to Travnik every weekend to take care of her mother and nephew, for whom she is responsible. Like the majority of Bosnians, regardless of ethnicity, the civil war continues to impact her life.

After filling up with fuel, we leave the city through one of the narrow gorges that surround it and head toward East Bosnia. A few minutes later, we pass through a tunnel and meet the red, blue, and white stripes on Republika Srpska's flag, which marks our crossing of the border. One country, two flags: the first, imposed by the international community, belonging to Bosnia-Herzegovina, the other representing Republika Srpska or the Serb Republic. One national anthem, however. Glorious, and purely instrumental—the lyrics were a point of contention among the various ethnicities. As are the schools. Sometimes the principle is *one roof, two schools*, with two separate entrances.

Divide well to handle well. It's easy and it works every time. Those in power wave the nationalist red flag and the people come charging heads down, not thinking of their own interests. The local political parties run this charade, distributing employment, fixing votes, filling their pockets with a five-figure payoff. They're appointed for life. The usual corruption.

The car continues through the steep gorge. In the distance, the brown Mijaska River drifts by, as does Pale, the ancient capital of Republika Srpska. I glance at Jasmina and see her mood is darkening. She doesn't like this trip. Too many bad memories. Revisiting a past that's not far enough behind. Suffering, loss, rape, and murder. She knows the stories.

I put on a CD by the local singer, Dino Merlin, who fills the cabin with a blend of Eastern European and electro waves. In the Balkans, music is particularly in tune with life and the times. In the bars, bands form spontaneously and everyone sings along. It's enough to give you chills. Even during the worst moments of the siege, in darkness and candlelight, the Bosnians sang to fortify their spirits, to endure life and face death.

While driving, my gaze falls on these mountains which bear a strange resemblance to mine, the Vosges. We cross villages frozen in time, mostly in the 1960s. Bales of straw, cattle, farm buildings with their steep roofs to evacuate the snow. All of this spread out over lush plains, touching forests that extend past the horizon.

After two hours winding through mountain roads, we're finally alongside the Drina River, its green waters forming a large part of the border between Bosnia-Herzegovina and Serbia.

The light is beautiful, a sky of azure. Coming out of a bend, our city appears with its majestic Mehmed Paša Sokolović Bridge, one of the two monuments of the country classified as World Heritage by UNESCO. Constructed in the 16th century by the Turk Vizier Mehmed Paša Sokolović, it is both impressive and symbolic, uniting the two banks of the Drina.

The stone bridge was made famous by Nobel Prize-winning author Ivo Andrić's 1945 novel *The Bridge on the Drina*, a story about tolerance between cultures. Times have changed. Andrić paints a picture of a city where daily life and principal historic events revolve around a space at the bridge's center, the *kapia*, where people gather to converse, drink, and smoke. "It seems that under the ample arches of the white bridge flows and pours not only the green Drina, but also all this harmonious and perfectly domesticated landscape, with all that it shelters, and also the southern sky above it."

Yet many massacres took place on this bridge in 1992. Some 3,000 Bosnians, including 600 women and 199 children, were assassinated. Many were simply lined up and shot, their bodies thrown into the green water.

We park not far from the bridge. With my diplomatic plates, I don't go unnoticed. Jasmina is more and more sullen. We notice faces behind the windows, staring out at passers-by.

At first glance, Višegrad is a quiet and peaceful town, home to 6,000 souls. A nice place for a stroll, especially on a sunny day like today. But there's a disquiet to it. A façade of paradise desperately covering a shameful past. Although there's too much past and it's too hideous to mask.

In 1991, on the eve of war, the city's population was 6,900. The surrounding canton, made up of 162 localities—rural areas, villages, often monoethnic—housed around 11,000. The primary business is cattle breeding but there are various other industries, including a thermal-electric plant at the city's edge, military barracks, and several wood treatment plants. The ethnic distribution is roughly 50 per cent Bosnian (primarily Muslim), 38 per cent Bosnian-Serb (primarily Orthodox), a rump of Bosnian-Croatians (primarily Catholic), and a scattering of Roma and Jews. Everyone in the region went to the same schools, offices, and sports clubs. There was a collective life organized around events that transcended ethnicity and religion, whether departure ceremonies for conscripts, balls and galas, or other professional and recreational endeavors. But they had separate political parties,

SDS for Bosnian Serbs, SDA for Bosnians, and HDZ for Bosnian Croats, and there were very few intermarriages.

Jasmina seems to have regained some of her color. I wonder if it is the heat. I take out my wireless and call our contact.

"Good morning, I'm calling on behalf of Asim."

"Yes, of course. Let me give you my address."

"Are you sure you want us coming to your house?"

"Absolutely. I've got nothing to hide, unlike some people. And I'll be safer here than anywhere else."

"Well, that's not standard procedure, but if that's what you'd prefer, we'll be there in a few minutes."

The house is impressive, styled in that magnificent Bosnian fashion, immaculately white with a traditional iron-ring door knocker. I glance up in time to catch a face disappear behind the second-story window, latticed to allow a view of the street without fear of exposure. These particular windows open to a completely enclosed balcony projecting roughly a meter into the street.

I knock. A few seconds later, the door opens. A woman, about five-foot-six, slender, in her fifties, aging well.

"Hi, I'm Lejla. I called you."

She extends her hand and gives me a firm handshake. Her eyes are khaki green, soft but mysterious. A kind of veil, difficult to decipher. She wears light makeup and a suit that matches her eyes. I hold her gaze for a moment and then break away.

"Follow me, please. And thank you for coming to me. Besides, today is a bit special."

"Oh, good?"

"Yes, you will see."

We follow her into a courtyard, paved with pebbles. Purple wisteria climb the white walls. Lejla walks toward the main house and pushes open a wooden door. As per Bosnian custom, we removed our shoes. On the ground floor, a slightly raised porch leads to a stone staircase that leads in turn to an upper gallery. In the corner of this living room is an immense white wood-burning stove adorned with round green tiles.

Music resonates from the adjacent room, probably the one in which I caught the face in the window. Instruments mixed with vocals. I recognize the sound. These are songs of mystical poetry, the classic repertoire of the Sufi brotherhoods established in Bosnia since the 15th century. The repertoire has been transmitted orally from one generation to the next in a selective and somewhat secretive way within the brotherhood.

With a melancholic smile, Lejla invites us into the lounge. The heat is overwhelming. The room is traditionally furnished with a low divan covering almost half the floor plan. In the center stands a beautiful table intricately engraved in the Konjic style. Underneath, a red and green kilim, the famous Turkish carpet woven in Mostar—a legacy of four centuries under Ottoman rule.

Lejla seats us on the divan and offers us strong Bosnian coffee. This is standard hospitality: coffee first, conversation after. After the long drive, we gladly accept. Surveying the room, I spot a picture of Tito[1] and nod to Jasmina. She looks without saying a word. Tito nostalgia.

Several black-and-white photographs are enthroned on a sideboard. Inside the black frames, a dark-eyed man with an emaciated face; and a child; and a young boy around twelve-years-old. Black ribbons hang on the corners. Jasmina watches me silently.

Lejla returns with a tray carrying three small cups or *fildžani*, a long-handled coffee pot or *džezva*, and a small cake.

She sits down, glances at the photos, and begins.

"I've asked you to come because I think I can help you locate a war criminal, someone responsible for certain horrors in Višegrad near the start of the war."

"Please," I respond, setting my glass aside.

"Are you familiar with the history of this town?"

"Not really. I'm still a bit new to your country."

"Would you like me to give you some background?"

"Of course."

Jasmina sinks into her seat. Yet again I'm asking her to translate the untranslatable. Lejla lets out a long sigh. The Sufi songs have silenced.

"Very well. As you know, war broke out in early April 1992 following the declaration of independence of Bosnia-Herzegovina. On the 6th, several units of the Serbian army entered the territory of the municipality of Višegard—the same day that the siege and shelling of Sarajevo began. An armored column approached our city from Serbia. It took eight days to arrive. As it had done to villages it passed on the way, the column fired heavy artillery on our Muslim neighborhoods, which could be identified by their minarets. Višegard fell on April 14 but by then it was almost empty. Resident were terrified by the gunfire, both Serbs and Muslims. They fled."

"Did you stay?"

"Yes, with my husband and my son."

I took a look at the photos on the sideboard. They seemed to be watching us.

"The tanks and heavy artillery pieces rolled in with a great noise. Small mobile groups detached from them. Among these groups of regular soldiers of the JNA [Yugoslav People's Army] were local volunteers. These were often young militants of the SDS, recruited on the spot through the local branches of national party. They were our neighbors. They showed soldiers the way to Muslim houses."

Lejla gets up, walks over to the sideboard, and returns with a document.

"Do you know what Biljana Plavšić, ex-president of Republika Srpska, said? She was the only to have pleaded guilty to war crimes during her appearance before the ICTY in The Hague.[2] Here is her statement:

> In reviewing the evidence against me, I have come to believe and accept the fact that many thousands of innocent people were the victims of an organized and systemic effort to drive Muslims and Croats from the territories on claimed by Serbians. At the time, I had easily convinced myself that what was at issue was our survival, our self-defense. In fact, it was much more. The leaders, of which I was a part, of course, targeted countless innocent people. Arguing about the need to defend oneself to survive does not in any way justify these acts. Why didn't I see it before? And how is it possible that our leaders and those who followed them committed such acts?

Lejla paused and then continued to read:

> By thinking this way, we who were part of the leadership violated the first duty of every human being: the duty to control oneself in order to respect the human dignity of others. It is unfortunate that we had to come to this horrible point to understand this essential point. The Serbian leaders have created a fiction around their disappearance. This allowed them to justify their role as protectors, the last guard. I call them the besieged . . . they created a kind of castle whose ramparts were made of hate . . . Their fiction was banal and incessant, built over time, from generation to generation, with a common thread: the fear of the other, which becomes a permanent threat. It insinuates itself into each mind with cliches, quasi-historical explanations, sometimes jokes.

Jasmina speaks up. I look at her, surprised. She says:

"Sometimes they'd say: "Oh, these Muslims, they need to be killed like flies." And we laughed. They only said it for fun. But in the end, they did what they'd been saying for years. And the hardest part was admitting that our own neighbors had thought about all this beforehand. We saw the writing on the wall, in nearby cities and towns, but it just didn't sink in.[3] By the time we opened our eyes, it was too late. Our neighbors wanted to kill us, or point us out to those doing the killing, all following this logic of self-preservation legitimized by their political leaders.

"Everyone knew where we lived. We went to school together, sat next to each other, shared our snacks. In certain villages, strangers started appearing in the streets, dressed as civilians. They were gathering information from locals, who were answering to their political leaders. Then the weapons started arriving, in certain houses, certain bars. The Yugoslavian Army dismissed all non-Serbian troops and ranking officers, and kept all its weapons. They used the local branches of nationalist parties to recruit those volunteers."

Lejla resumes: "So the volunteers of Višegrad guided the military groups coming in from Serbia. They had information on every village: the inhabitants of each house, their gender distribution, number of livestock, each farm's wealth in both goods and labor."

"General orders were to shoot off automatic weapons upon arrival, push some people around, start giving out orders. They kicked in doors, 'requisitioned' cars and tractors, murdered and kidnapped. They made sure to grab from the men all the hunting rifles and other weapons. Finally, they pillaged and set fire to some of the houses, while advising people to leave the area as quickly as possible. A volunteer or militiaman could participate in a 'cleaning,' masked with a balaclava or with a face covered in paint, and return the next day to his bakery if he was a baker, or to his taxi if he was a driver. The goal was to frighten and subjugate a population for the purposes of ethnic cleansing."

"And then there were the paramilitary groups, like Arkan's Tigers or the Black Wolves. They're bonded by rituals, baptized in groups in collective Orthodox ceremonies where they make pledges and pray before a priest and icons of Jesus Christ. The priests themselves are sometimes present before the stages of battle, for absolution. Patrimonial ties, tested by crime."

For a brief instant, I wonder what the running count is—the number of times that nationalism and religion, mixed in with a bit of obedience and fear, have resulted in ethnic cleansing and genocide.

"Some were appointed voivodes [dukes]," Lejla continues, "and turned into real little kingpins. They put their followers at the service of local police or army units. Their currency was redistribution of pillaged goods and women."

Lejla looks away. It doesn't take a genius to figure out what she's been through. I do not interrupt her. It's getting hotter in the room. Lejla gets up to open a window, under the piercing gaze of the figures in the photographs, framed in black.

She begins to speak again and Jasmina continues translating:

"Here, we had the Lukićs, Milan and Sredoje, with their paramilitary group, The Avengers.[4] Vengeance for what? We'll never know. Milan was born in 1967, Sredoje in 1961. They're cousins, their fathers were brothers. Their two families came from the same village, Rujište, in the canton of Višegrad. The third ringleader was Mitar Vasiljević, a local waiter and a drunk. He's the *kum* to Milan's child. It's a particular Serbian and orthodox tradition, which entails strict obligations of respect and solidarity."

Someone knocks at the door. Lejla looks at us and gets up.

"I've taken the liberty of inviting a guest."

The next minute, a short-haired blond woman enters the room. Chiseled face. Solid. She extends her hand to me.

"Hello, I'm Amina. I'm the one who asked Lejla to call you at the embassy. Are you French?"

"Yes, why?" I said, smiling.

"Because you have more of the build of the people here . . . Well, I mean all the French people I met during and after the war, they were more stunted."

Jasmina smiles. I'm not sure how to take it. I decide to go for compliment. It is true that here in the Balkans, under a certain weight, one does not get a say.

Lejla says, "I asked Amina to join us because she runs a women victims' organization, an NGO that fights for human rights and researches war criminals."

"Pleased to meet you. Civilian contributions are extremely valuable in bringing justice to victims."

"I'm glad to hear you say that because here it's not the norm," says Amina.

"I was just explaining our story so that the Frenchman can have a clear understanding of things," says Amina.

"Perfect. Please continue."

"On April 10, 1992, during the first days of the war, Milan Lukić returned to Bosnia from Germany.[5] His cousin, Sredoje Lukić, and Mitar Vasiljević had remained in Višegrad. Sredoje had become a policeman in this municipality.

"From April to May, they formed this militia, The Avengers. It had five to fifteen people, depending on their needs. According to certain protected witnesses who testified at his trial, Milan Lukić was driving around Dušče, a small village on the outskirts of Višegrad, around 4 o'clock in the afternoon on May 18, 1992. He was chasing down the only new German car in the area: a red Volkswagen Passat that belonged to Dzemal and Behija Zukic, a symbol of their success. They had brought it back from Germany after years of hard work as immigrants. Lukič wanted the car. The Passat would become his emblem."

Amina cuts in: "They called him the man who moved very fast and silently. A cat. He wanted to make his mark in the canton. Mark his territory."

Lejla goes on: "Milan Lukić overtook the Passat on the road, forced it to stop and made the occupants get out of the vehicle. He insulted them, asked for their keys and papers, and drove away in the Passat. An hour later, Lukić and his men went to the Zukic home. They massacred Behija, cut off her head, and carried off her husband and young son, Faruk. They were never seen again. On the 19th, one of Behija's neighbors received a call from the town hall warning that an ambulance was coming to pick up her body and that it must be prepared. Horrified, the neighbor managed to place the decapitated body in a blanket. When the ambulance arrived, other neighbors accompanied the body to the morgue. Milan Lukič was there waiting. He was wearing camouflage clothing and a beret with the double-headed eagle of the Serbian nationalists. His face was painted black. He had the red Passat, the car stolen from Behija. He was accompanied by his cousin Sredoje and a former policeman who was a member of their group. When the nurses took the body, Lukič started laughing out loud, cynically. On the afternoon of the 20th, Behija was buried in the Muslim cemetery with another Muslim couple who had just been murdered. At the end of the ceremony, a van appeared along with the red Passat. Fifteen men present at the funeral were forced into the van. They were never seen again."

Lejla gets up to refill the pitcher with fresh water. Water, often of excellent quality, is a special pride of Bosnia, although they're not bashful about sometimes importing it from Croatia.

Amina continues in a grave voice: "Then there were the Drina executions on June 7, 1992. Milan Lukič's operation swept through the villages methodically. All the exits were blocked with control points manned by the police, army, or militia. It was terror. The men who were summoned to the police station never returned. In the city, people took to basements, usually in the buildings next door. Each night, men, women, and children would flee into the wood to sleep."

"From then on, every day and every night, houses and mosques were set on fire and cemeteries were desecrated. During the day, the less able women stayed with the children and elderly, tending to the livestock and gardens. The men looked for refuge in one apartment after another, from one farm to the next. If it was too risky to stay in Višegrad, it was just as risky to leave. They were massacring people in cars and buses."

Lejla stands up. Walks out of the room.

Jasmina watches me closely.

Amina glances at the photographs on the buffet, their presence now palpable.

"On June 7th, around 4:30 p.m.," says Amina, "Lejla's husband, Samir, left the farm. He came back to hug their thirteen-year-old son Dino before returning to the forest. Samir had started to organize a Muslim defense against the militia. Four men arrived. Their leader, Milan Lukič, approached, armed with a sniper rifle and silencer, and demanded that Samir show his papers. Samir had his precious 'authorization to leave the city' document on him. Milan Lukič took it in his teeth and, looking Samir straight in the eyes, began tearing it into pieces. He then grabbed Samir and handed him over to one of his soldiers while Lejla looked on, begging Lukič to let him go."

"Lejla and Lukič knew each other well. They went to the same school. She was very pretty in her day. Lukič, with a whistle, ordered her to be evacuated. She was taken to the Vilina Vlas Hotel, which Lukič had made into his headquarters. Her son, Dino, was shaking from head to foot. Dino and Samir were locked in a house with eleven others who had been taken prisoner. Milan Lukič ordered them to stand in a semicircle, place all their objects of value in the center of the room, and remove their shoes and socks. He grabbed their money and wedding rings. Dino and Samir, and a man named Meho were loaded into the red Passat. The ten others who remained in the house were never seen again. Their bodies were not even found."

"The same day, Višegard's old mosque was burned to the ground. The second mosque, by the Rzava Bridge, was burned as well."

"The prisoners were driven to the edge of the Drina River. Samir immediately recognized his friend Mitar Vasiljevic among the militia and soldiers."

"Milan asked the prisoners in the car: 'Who knows how to swim?' Meho approached the river, and Samir and Dino were forced to follow him."

"Meho would survive the assassination attempt and later testify at the trials in The Hague. "

"Samir called out to his friend Mitar: 'For Christ's sake Mitar, what are you doing?'"

"A soldier asked Milan Lukič: 'How should we shoot them?'"

"The response: 'One by one.'"

"The men fell into the river as they were hit by bullets. Meho managed to dive under water and miraculously succeeded in hiding himself under Samir and Dino's bodies. He later made his way to dry land."

"That day was the end of the world for Lejla. She lost her husband and son. Afterward, she became an anonymous sex object. It's taken her a long time to piece herself back together. Just like me."

Jasmina takes down a huge glass of water. I follow suit.

Amina resumes: "The month of May was a dangerous time for women and young girls. They were being abducted in larger and larger numbers and taken to the Vilina Vlas Hotel. Women, young girls, young teenagers, were locked up, raped, and killed. Several dozen of their bodies would later be found buried in the cellar of the hotel. But most of them just disappeared. Two hundred are dead. Lejla and I are survivors. Since then, our life has been about making them pay, doing what's necessary to bring them to justice."

It crosses my mind to respond with something to the effect of "I understand." But actually no. I don't.

Lejla returns.

Amina continues: "After that, everything let loose. On June 10, 1992, there were mass killings in the Varda factory, during the Bayram celebrations, the Eid el-Kebir of the Arab-speaking countries. And on the 14th, Koritnik. It is a village not far from here, composed of several hamlets of Serbian and Muslim families. On June 10, 1992, a group of Serbian neighbors attacked the village with heavy artillery, inciting panic and confusion. They pillaged, stole cattle, tractors, and carted off furniture. It was from there, toward the middle of June, that we began to organize a resistance by gathering in the forests, arming ourselves when possible."

Lejla explains: "Samir was one of the resistance leaders. Someone surely ratted him out."

"On June 13th," Amina continues, "the Serbian Army (VRS) arrived in Koritnik with local militiamen. They entered houses, ordering everyone to gather in the square. The instructions were clear. The Muslims were to leave the village at 8 a.m. the following morning, bringing a two-day supply of food and a few personal items. 'This is ethnic cleansing. You will be taken to Kladanj and exchanged. You will live in Serb houses there, and they will come to live in your houses here. It is the only practical way. We cannot live together so each ethnic group will live in territories that we will make uniform.'"

"At 8 a.m. the following morning, two male neighbors took charge of the group of villagers preparing to depart. Seventy people, primarily women, both young and old, and children, including a baby born in the woods two days earlier. Some left their keys with their neighbors, only to later see them entering their houses to pillage what remained. The two men led the group toward the village of Greben for their evacuation by bus. But there was no bus. The group continued its march to Višegrad and was led to the Red Cross building. But it was closed. It was a Sunday."

"The group was then taken over by Mitar Vasiljević, dressed in the army uniform with a black leather cowboy hat. He gave a speech explaining that Serbs and Muslims can no longer live together, that they must separate, and said that the next morning a convoy of buses would take this group and others to Kladanj. He tried to reassure the people, addressing some of them by their first names. While waiting for their transportation, they would have to spend the night in a house in the Muslim quarter, on Pionirska street. It was a house opposite the school. It belonged to Jusuf Memic, the teacher. The house was empty. It was about 3:30 p.m. People were pushed into the Memic house. Women and children from a previous round-up were already there. Mitar continued to reassure people, showing them an 'official' paper saying that they would be exchanged. Two hours later, Milan and Sredoje Lukić, Mitar Vasiljević, and a man named Popovic, the latter living in a village one kilometre from Šeganje, enter the house, carrying automatic weapons."

Lejla interrupted: "It is for Popovic that I brought you here. He lives in France."

Amina continued with her account: "It is now about 5:30. Milan gathered everyone in the same room. He asks them to deposit their gold, jewelery, watches, and money in a cloth on the table, with the promise of a bullet in the head for anyone who hides anything."

"All the women were called in groups of two or three to a room 'to control them.' In one of the rooms, Popovic, twenty-five years old, curly-headed and bearded, forced the girls and women to undress, to dance naked, to contort themselves. A fifteen-year-old girl refused to obey and he ordered the other women to tear off her clothes. The ordeal lasted an hour and a half. When the search was over, Popovic came back down. He pointed out three girls to Milan Lukič. They were taken away and together with another young girl, Jasmina, who had been abducted from her home by Milan Lukić, they were raped at the Vilina Vlas hotel."

"The three girls returned an hours later in a deplorable state. Mute. Their faces and bodies had bite marks on them. The four men then left the house, leaving the group in the care of soldiers with the regular army."

"When the men returned, they were drunk. It was just after 10:00 p.m. They ordered everyone to exit Jusuf's house and move next door to another house. The children had fallen asleep. They had to be woken up. Up until this point, some still believed that an exchange would take place following morning."

"As the people entered the new house, they were seized by a strong smell and noticed that the carpet was thick with a sticky substance. Moments later, Milan threw an explosive device into the room. The soldiers outside starting shooting into the house through the windows to keep people from jumping out. Everything went up in flames. Two women managed to throw themselves and their fourteen-year-old sons out a window. An old man, Huso Kurspahic, was blasted out of the house."

"All of the others, a large portion of the population of Koritnik, disappeared in smoke. Screams, screams, and the smell of burning flesh spread through the neighborhood. A few survived to testify before the Court of the International Criminal Tribunal for the former Yugoslavia in The Hague, as well as the son of the man who had been ejected, who told his son about the scene before he died. Fifty-nine people were burned alive. A few weeks later, another sixty people, mostly women and children, were similarly murdered in nearby Bikavak."

Silence. I ask, "How were they caught?"

"Vasiljevic was picked up in Germany in 2000. . . . As for Milan, he left Bosnia-Herzegovina in 2003, following a settlement of accounts among organize crime groups. He was arrested in 2005 in Argentina after two years on the run, then transferred to the International Criminal Tribunal for the former Yugoslavia. During their trial, which began in July 2008, the Lukić cousins denied their involvement in the crimes in Višegrad. Milan Lukić even brandished the Koran from the witness dock. In the end, on Monday, July 20, 2009, Milan Lukić and his cousin Sredoje Lukić were sentenced, respectively, to life imprisonment and twenty-seven years in prison."

Lejla gets up and opens the sideboard drawer again under the gaze of the portraits to pull out another document.

"Do you know what the president of the tribunal, Patrick Robinson, said?"

I nod no.

She read:

In the too long, sad, and pitiful history of man's inhumanity to man, the fires on Pionirska Street and Bikavac are at the top of the scale. At the end of the twentieth century, a century marked by war and bloodshed on an immeasurable scale, these horrific events stand out for their violence, especially using fire, for their obvious premeditation, for the callousness and brutality of those men who locked their victims in the two houses. In doing so, they trapped them in a hell of flames, burning them alive and inflicting an unheard of degree of pain and suffering.

Amina speaks again: "Thank you for coming to us and for taking the time to listen. This is our story. We are marked for life in our flesh. Now all we have left is the fight for justice. The fight against impunity. Until the end and until our dying breath."

Lejla says to me: "Popovic has taken up residence in your country. He lives there quietly, cozily."

"How do you know?"

"We got an anonymous tip."

"Anonymous? If you don't know where exactly he is, it's going to be complicated but I can ask to investigate. If he is living under an assumed name, I can't guarantee anything but I will do my best."

"We don't have precise information yet," says Lejla, "but I'm looking for him and, believe me, I will find him."

Lejla and Amina stand up as one: "Sir, thank you again for your help. We are counting on you. You know, three thousand people died here. Many have never been found."

They hold out their hands to me and lead us back to the front door. Before leaving us, Amina asks, "do you want to see the house?"

"Yes, of course."

"Good. Let's meet there. I warn you, today is a commemoration."

A few minutes later, we walk over to Pionirska Street. A young teenager accosts us. Shaved hair, khaki pants, black t-shirt.

"Hello," he says. "Where are you headed?

"We've come to see the Pionirska house."

"Ah! The Lukić house. They are going to destroy it. To make a road. City hall decision. We won't think about it anymore."

Jasmina contains herself.

"Yes, just like that, we erase. And move on. In twenty years, we can start again with a new generation. A new game."

Incomprehensible.

"You know, some people around here consider the Lukičs heroes?"

"And you? What do you think?"

"Me? I'm looking forward to one thing: leaving this country and not looking back. Heading up to Germany to make a living."

"Great idea. At least it'll prevent you from being manipulated by nationalist bullshit."

Jasmina has stopped translating.

At the corner of the street, we join a kind of procession of about fifty people. Men, women, and children, in a slow march. The women at the head of the line display signs with the faces and names of the victims in the Piornirska house. And a date: June 14, 1992.

There are Bosnian flags. White roses everywhere. Grave faces. Silence.

We find Lejla and Amina in front of the house. They have put on veils and are praying with open hands. Crying dry tears.

We wait for the ceremony to finish before approaching them

"They're planning to demolish the house?"

"Yes. It was scheduled for December 2013, but we were able to stop the process. Not without difficulty. The police harassed our spokeswoman, Bakira Hasečić. But she's strong. This is her fight."

"Will you follow us to the bridge?" they ask us. "We're going to throw our roses in the Drina to honor those who were assassinated on or around the bridge. Their bodies were thrown in the river."

An hour later, we're standing on the aqueduct, watching the Drina's green waters flow gently underneath. My mind wanders back to Ivo Andrić's novel, *The Bridge on the Drina*. The sound of crying and Amina's voice pull me back.

"Three thousand people were massacred here. A lot of the bodies just disappeared, which has been characteristic of Bosnia's ethnic cleansings. According to the International Committee of the Red Cross, between 28,000 and 30,000 people disappeared in Bosnia during the war.[6] To this day, one third of them have not been found."

In 2010, it was decided to empty Lake Perucac in order to clean the Bajina Bašta dam on the Drina. This is how Lejla found the remains of her husband and son. In the sludge at the bottom of the lake and on its shores, human remains were discovered. Two and a half months later, at the end of October 2010, the team dispatched to the site had exhumed 396 skeletal remains, making it possible to reconstruct, at least in part, the bodies of ninety-seven separate people. These are our dead. They were identified through DNA and the work of the Bosnian Institute of Missing Persons, which is linked to the International Commission on Missing Persons in The Hague.

Lukić would get Muslims on a bridge, including children, force them to jump into the water, and then fire a burst of automatic weapons at them.

I turn my eyes to Lejla, who is staring into space.

It is time for us to return to Sarajevo. I step toward Amina and Lejla. Another handshake. Two piercing glances.

"You won't forget us?"

"No, I promise."

Deep down, however, I'm wondering how I'll ever mobilize my colleagues for such a large investigation. It will be like looking for a needle in a haystack, especially if our target has changed his identity—Bosnian-Serbs have two passports, one Serbian and one Bosnian, just like Croats.

Silence on the way back. Only the melancholic voice of Božo Vrećo floats through the cabin. With his beard, deep black eyes, and backless dresses, he has a queer esthetic reminiscent of Conchita Wurst. He sings Sevdah, a traditional local folk music.

Lost in my thoughts, eyes riveted to the asphalt, I think of questions that have haunted me since childhood, especially with regard to the Nazi horror. They've haunted me more since moving here. By what mechanisms, by what manipulations, can one people try to destroy another? What are the conditions and processes that lead to mass murder? How do some "ordinary" men become, in spite of themselves or of their own free will, "ordinary" mass murderers when they are placed in a specific context?

Jasmina seems to read my mind and breaks the silence. "It's as if the dogs decided to wipe the cats off the face of the earth."

Silence.

"Yes, that's right, but to get there, there is a whole process that is mostly rooted in favorable sociological and economic soil. Also, there's always a bit of an imaginary 'we' story."[7]

Jasmina turns to me. "An imaginary 'we'?"

"Yes, a kind of matrix built around an ideal of purity with ethnic, religious, historical, nationalistic notions. It crystallizes a common identity to which people adhere. The 'we' is conceived by intellectuals, philosophers, religious people who juggle myths or religious texts in order to anchor it and to give it powerful legitimacy.

"One must always be wary of those who have an ideal of purity," Jasmina says. "In general, they want to mask their own depravity, sickness, or deviance."

"Yes, exactly. Also, most of the time, they identify women, homosexuals, or Jews as the first dangers to this purity. Especially since the 'we' has another characteristic."

"What is that?"

"It has suffered. It is part of a common past of pain and suffering caused by 'others,' who are identified as the enemy. Foreigners, sometimes, but also, and especially, fellow citizens. Neighbors of a different ethnicity or religion become threatening and can represent the devil. But also those of the same ethnicity or religion who for reasons of personal ethics are opposed to this mechanical premise of mass murder."

"You are describing what I have experienced."

"For the architects, the construction of the 'other' is just as important as that of the 'we,' especially in regard to the ferocity of the former and the ability to eliminate the latter. The ideal is to dehumanize the other, opening the door to murder. Carefully prepared infusions of fear, consumed daily, conceptualized as a plot and gradually transformed into hate. Extreme paranoia is diffused through media and propaganda. The other must be eliminated before they have a chance to eliminate us. The final equation becomes 'your death equals my life.'[8] Genocide by anticipation. Fear and emotion blind people. The more powerful and devious the other is supposed to be, the harder the 'we' must fight to defend themselves."

We pass over the plateau of Romanjia, unfolding into endless plains, interwoven with small pine forests. The sheep and cattle graze. We pass the typical villages of Bosnia-Herzegovina with their wooden farmhouses, frozen in time. In the distance, the sun lowers, light giving way to the shadow of night.

I keep talking: "Politicians surf these waves of hatred for electoral advantage, playing on emotions and bipolarity—the divisions that loom so large in our lives. Nowadays, the hatred is encouraged by social networks and their daily streams of fake news, by tampering with images and texts. They develop a form of Newspeak, reducing language in a manner that stupefies people. Eventually it's one little tweet and that's it."

"The more we reduce the number of available ideas and reduce the richness of language, the less we think, the more we function on impulse and emotion, and the more we can be manipulated. History is shot through with demonstrations of this process. The Nazis, the Hutus, the Serbs—there's no need to go way back in time. In his proclamation of June 29,

2014, at the Al-Nuri Mosque in Mosul, Abu Bakar al-Baghdadi proposed the restoration of the Ottoman caliphate that had been dissolved in 1924. He simply created a 'we' with the aim of restoring a community of believers. Then he proposes an ideal society governed by the sharia, seeking purity. Finally, he exhorts Muslims to free themselves from the humiliation and injustice they suffer in a world ruled by a system dominated by Jews and crusaders. In short, he invents the 'other' and the suffering that has been inflicted on a daily basis to the 'we.' This is the birth of the Islamic State, which has exterminated the Yezidis launched a propaganda campaign with loads of Hollywood-caliber films streaming online to recruit young militants drunk on videos and doublespeak."

At the exit of the road to Pale, I leave the Republika Sprska and the first minarets of Sarajevo finally appear.

What a day. It is time to go home and take a shower. Cleanse.

But before that, I stop at the embassy to write France with my official application for an investigation.

For ten months, nothing happens. I work on one file after another. Arms trafficking, human trafficking, including the creation of the first joint investigation team on the so-called "little subway robbers" networks. There are visits to France and training missions in Bosnia with French investigators. But I can't forget the voices of Amina, Lejla, and the others. All the others.

April 3, 2014—Sarajevo

My cellphone rings. The face of my new assistant, Warrant Officer Cédric Plassart, pops up on my screen. Cédric arrived in Sarajevo last summer. Big fellow, 6'4", strong build, athletic, looks you in the eye. Military energy, with a frankness and loyalty to the corps. He learned to speak fluent BHS(Bosnian Hrvat Serb) during a prior tour in Kosovo, where he was completely immersed in Northern Serbian territory. It didn't take long for me to rely on him across the board. When you open doors, there are some you let follow behind you, and others you wouldn't dare because you're watching your own back. Cédric belongs to the first category.

"Colonel, good news, Goran Popovic was just arrested in France, in Creil, in Oise."

"Damn? Who made the arrest?"

"A judicial police office, the Central Office for Combatting Crimes Against Humanity."

"Really? Never heard of them."

"Yeah, it was created six months ago, in November 2013. It's attached to the national gendarmerie."

"This is fucking good news!"

"How's that?"

"The arrest and the creation of this office. Now we have someone to talk to."

4

DETECTION

"As long as I can, as long as I'm in good health, I will see as many war criminals behind bars as possible. As long as I'm alive, we will pursue them."

—Bakira Hasečić

April 4, 2014, Sarajevo. French Embassy,
Department of Internal Security

I receive a call from the chief of staff of the attorney general, Samir H., a sort of mini vizier who wants to sit in for the caliph.

"Pukovnik.[1] Bravo, France! Did you see the papers? We're thrilled with this news, and with the work of the embassy and the French police. This is a great day for Bosnian justice and for the victims of Višegrad."

"Thank you, Samir. Do you know how they found him?"

"It was Amina, the head of the women victims NGO."

"How?"

"Facebook. She found a conversation between him and his wife, sometime during the summer of 2013. He wrote, 'Are you my neighbor, the wife of Daco?' She replied in the affirmative. Then she deleted her Facebook profile. Too late. They had already taken a screenshot of his page and pieced together photos and selfies to locate where she was living, a town called Crieli. So she identified where he lived."

"Good job!"

"Yeah. They took the information to an investigator at Poursuites, a Geneva-based NGO that chases international war criminals. It employs

34

five investigators who go on-site and collect witness testimonies and other evidence that it transmits to special magistrates. The NGO launched an investigation to confirm the wife's whereabouts."

Samir tells me that Amina also brought this information to the attorney general's office in Bosnia-Herzegovina. On March 3, 2014, a Sarajevo court issued an arrest warrant for Goran Popovic based on the evidence pertaining to June 1992 crimes against humanity in Višegrad. Then the prosecutor in charge of crimes against humanity at the Paris prosecutor's office was handed responsibility for executing the arrest on behalf of Bosnia-Herzegovina.

Amina didn't waste any time in finding him. It looked like a successful case. In fact, it wasn't. Three years later, Popovic is still not extradited.

April 13, 2017—French Embassy, Sarajevo

Ambassador Élisabeth Marion walks into my office looking serious, not her usual cheerful self. The president of the women victims' NGO is scheduled to arrive. It's Amina. She wants to know why Goran Popovic has yet to be extradited. I do, too, for that matter. Amina holds me personally accountable. Rightly so.

I dial Pierre Grand, our liaison magistrate in Belgrade.

"Hello Pierre, how is Belgrade?"

"Fine. We are waiting for spring. What can I do for you?"

"It's about Popovic. Do you know where we are?"

"Wait a moment. I'm looking at the file."

Pierre puts down the phone. A few seconds of silence followed by the sound of a cupboard opening and he picks back up.

"Popovic has appealed both the arrest and extradition decisions. He has been released and placed under judicial supervision. He denies the facts. His lawyer argues that his client has been living in France with his wife and two children since May 1998 and that he had guarantees of representation. He asserts that Popovic is the victim of an identity error. 'Goran Popovic cannot be a party to the facts.' According to him, the Bosnian authorities are mistaken. He points out that the name that appears on transcripts at the court in The Hague is 'Aleksandar Popovic' and not 'Goran Popovic.'"

I look on the Internet and find the lawyer's statements: "My client can therefore in no way have been a member of a paramilitary militia commanded by Milan Lukič. He held a job as a mechanic in Višegrad's largest repair shop. This gross confusion on the first name is deliberate, part of the resurgence of nationalism that the country is experiencing. The authorities wish to send a message to the Muslim community by arresting a major war criminal."

"OK. What's next?"

"If the court of appeal confirms his extradition, he'll have another chance to appeal. If that's rejected, he can bring his case to the court of cassation."

"And then?"

"If the court of cassation rejects the appeal, then usually the prime minister will issue an extradition order. However, Popovic can also make an appeal to the council of state. And there you have it."

"Alright . . . thanks. I'll let the ambassador know. What happens after that? Will it stop?"

"The appeal to council of state will be final."

And that's exactly how it plays out. On May 26, 2016, The Paris Court of Appeal confirmed the extradition of Goran Popovic to Bosnia-Herzegovina. The victims and their families, including Leglaj and Amina, traveled to Paris to confirm his identity. The Bosnian authorities investigated the famous Aleksandar Popovic, who happens to be a distant cousin, but he was able to demonstrate that he was not present at the time of events.

Popovic appealed the decision. His appeal was rejected. He then turned to the court of cassation, where he was rejected again.

While this was going on, Amina returned to the embassy numerous times to check on the progress of the trial. Our paths cross one last time on July 11, 2016, in Srebrenica, at the annual commemoration organized by The Mothers of Srebrenica, held at the same time every year at sites where the genocide occurred. Victims' remains that have been exhumed from mass graves and identified by DNA are buried the same day.

Amina approached me as I stood with other members of the international community in front of the Muslim coffins draped in green cloth.

"Hello Pokovnik."

"Hello Amina."

"What's up?"

"Things are moving along as planned, Amina. This is French law. That's how it goes."

"I know. I wrote an open letter to your president, François Hollande."

"Did he respond?"

"Not yet. But I'll write another if needed. I also requested another meeting with your ambassador."

"You're right to do it. Don't let it go, Amina."

Two months after Amina's follow-up meeting with the ambassador, on May 23, 2017, Prime Minister Édouard Philippe issues Goran Popovic's extradition order. As expected, in the weeks following, his lawyer files an appeal to the council of state. In autumn, I pack my bags for Paris to take command of the Central Office for Combatting Crimes Against Humanity (OCLCH). I'll never forget Lejla and Amina, nor that June 2013 day on the bridge in Višegrad.

On February 14, 2018, my thoughts were with them while I directed Goran Popovic's final arrest. His final appeal had failed.

Case closed. Finally. Time often moves too slowly for victims. Understandably.

August 16, 2018—Paris

I take a look through my inbox. I've set up Google Alerts to notify me of everything to do with genocides, crimes against humanity, and war crimes. Popovic's name appears regularly. As does "Daco," accused of participating in the Lukić massacres. His trial has just begun in Bosnia-Herzegovina.

This evening, with a sort of nostalgia, I put on Danis Tanović's film *No Man's Land*, winner of a César Award for best feature film and an Oscar for best foreign language film in 2002. It is a war chronicle with a healthy dose of Bosnian humor, which is distinct and often dark—a sort of natural defense mechanism that allows Bosnians to overcome daily challenges. Humor and singing.

No man's land. How many times have particular men decided that others could no longer live on theirs? *Like if dogs decided that cats no longer had the right to live*, as Jasmina put it. In the film, the Bosnian Army, its ornate flag of three lilies waving, faces the Bosnian-Serb Army. Both sides are entrenched. One of the Bosnian soldiers takes advantage of a break in the fighting to read a newspaper.

"Well shit!" he says.

"What? What's wrong!?" asks his comrade.

"Rwanda! What a mess."

5

OPEN SEASON ON WAR CRIMINALS

"Where policemen don't exist, there's a certain race of honest people who are capable of anything."

—François Mauriac

October 2017, OCLCH

I am moving into my new space at the headquarters of the Office Responsible for Combating Crimes Against Humanity. When they offered me the position, I did not hesitate. I had been thinking that I would continue my career in the field of organized crime, or maybe homicide, after Sarajevo. A phone call from Paris changed everything.

"We have a new position in mind for you."

For the gendarmerie's human resources director, it seemed a logical career progression for me, and I said nothing to dissuade him. I had been immersed for five years in a society that had experienced a ruthless civil war, marked by genocide, crimes against humanity, and war crimes. Those are experiences that stay with you.

I'd seen the devastation unleashed on bodies and the minds, families and communities. Years later, incomprehension and suspicion linger, especially when justice is not served. Wounds remain open. Anger smolders. All it takes is one ill-intentioned politician to blow on the coals and a bloody history will be rewritten. That's always a problem: the public interest undermined by the private interests of increasingly ill-intentioned politicians.

Justice must prevail in these situations. Without it, we're back at arms a generation down the line.

Created in 2013, the OCLCH is the newest of the gendarmerie's bureaus. Our mission is threefold. To investigate the gravest of crimes: genocide, crimes against humanity, war crimes, torture, and enforced disappearances;[1] to investigate hate crimes, in which the victim is associated with a particular social group, often defined by race, religion, sexual orientation, disability, ethnicity, nationality, age, sex, gender identity, or political party; and to search for fugitives or to make arrests for extradition purposes, as with Goran Popovic or Mario Sandoval in Argentina.

It's a vast mandate.

Opening investigations into international crimes which are, for the most part, committed on foreign soil, naturally raises questions regarding France's jurisdiction. Our laws permit investigations in three instances: when the perpetrator of a crime committed abroad has French nationality; when the victim of a crime committed abroad is French; and, thanks to universal jurisdiction,[2] when the alleged perpetrator of a crime committed abroad is habitually residing in France. The concept of habitual residence requires that a suspect have either moral or material interests in the given state. In cases of torture or enforced disappearance, the mere presence of a suspect in the state suffices. All of this is quite helpful in tracking down people who've come to France from abroad carrying heavy secrets, thinking they've put themselves in the clear.

Our office was conceived in 2012 following broader movements in Europe and the international community in response to the bitter observation that the loss of millions of men, women, and children to unimaginable atrocities was not something we'd left behind in the 20th century. These same thoughts inspired the 1998 Statute of Rome, a treaty that established the International Crimes Court (ICC), which began operations in 2002.

France ratified the treaty and committed herself, as the homeland of human rights, to never allow perpetrators of atrocities to take refuge in her territories, to pursue them relentlessly as far as jurisdiction permitted, and to seek retribution for victims of human barbarism. It was recognized that a new specialized branch of the justice system would have to be created to effectively fulfill these objections. Our office comprises about a dozen law-enforcement professionals, investigators, prosecutors, and special assistants. It has been integrated since July 2019 with the prosecutor's office of the national anti-terrorism office.

How are investigations initiated and entrusted to the OCLCH?

A preliminary investigation can be opened on the basis of simple suspicion, perhaps sparked by witness testimony, public documents, or press articles. For instance, the details of a list of sanctions published by an economic minister might raise the eyebrows of a public prosecutor who would be in touch with us to initiate an investigation.

We might also come across information in the course of our own operations that leads to an investigation. Also, Article 40 of the code of criminal procedure states that "any constituted authority, any public officer or civil servant who, in the exercise of his duties, acquires knowledge of a crime or an offense is required to notify the public prosecutor without delay. Thus in 2015, as we will see later in the case of Syria, France's minister of foreign affairs reported to the public prosecutor in Paris that crimes of torture had likely been committed by the Syrian regime and documented by a Syrian military police photographer.[3]

In the same vein, since 2015 legal reforms of the right to asylum, the director of the French Office for the Protection of Refugees and Stateless Persons (OFPRA) is required to report to the anti-terrorist prosecutor's office any person excluded from asylum pursuant to Article 1F of the 1951 Convention Relating to the Status of Refugees.[4] This measure is intended to prohibit asylum for any person suspected of crimes against the peace, crimes against humanity, war crimes, or actions contrary to the goals of the UN.

If, in the latter case, OFPRA accepts that an individual has a well-founded fear of persecution if returned to his or her state of origin, the individual cannot be expelled from France, consistent with international human rights law. Out of 150 investigations we have underway, more than fifty involve individuals who have been excluded from asylum by OFPRA. There are many perpetrators of foreign atrocities who wash up in France and other European nations amid the flow of refugees from war zones, eager to obtain asylum by lying about the crimes in their past.

Investigations can also be opened on the basis of documentation assembled by NGOs and independent researchers. Their evidence may come from victims, descendants of victims, and related groups that meet the criteria set out in the code of criminal procedure. [5]

Finally, certain cases are opened in cooperation with foreign or international authorities. Our role is sometimes investigative and other times to arrest, extradite, or hand over a fugitive criminal. Once requests have been transmitted through diplomatic channels, they are transmitted to magistrates in the crimes against humanity and war crimes offenses unit, who in turn pass them along to our offices to take action—hearing witnesses, searches and seizures, wiretaps, depositions of persons held in police custody, etc.

The establishment of the OCLCH in 2013 was a long time coming. It began in the 1980s with the creation of a special investigative unit of the Paris gendarmerie. Leaders of the unit shared a passion for history and directed their efforts to tracking down both Nazi war criminals and French citizens that had collaborated with German occupational forces.

Their first case involved Paul Touvier, a former civil servant who had collaborated with the Vichy regime and was sentenced to death at France's liberation. He managed to escape and remained at large, living under a false identity. President Georges Pompidou granted him a pardon in 1971 but Touvier's past eventually caught up to him. Former members of the resistance filed charges against him for crimes against humanity. He went on the lam once more, aided by certain networks of fundamentalists in the Catholic church. In 1988, investigating judge Claude Grellier put the gendarmerie on the case. One of my predecessors, Colonel Jean-Louis Recordon, and lead investigator Philippe Mathy showed great perseverance in chasing Touvier. They tapped the phones of the leaders of the Knights of Notre-Dame, notably Jean-Pierre Lefebvre, a former member of the collaborationist Charlemagne division and a fervent Christian. Enough information was gathered to arrange a sting. At the end of May 1989, gendarmes surround the monastery at Wisques. They came up empty.

Next, investigators followed a trail of money from Notre-Dame de la Merci, a Catholic order, *Notre Dame de la Merci*, to Geneviève Penou, the director of a special education chaplaincy linked to the assembly of bishops and housed by the charity Secours Catholique. A second raid was planned.

Roughly forty gendarmes surround a monastery in Saint-Michel-en-Brenne and found pieces of Touvier's luggage. Confronted with this evidence, the abbey's chaplain confessed and handed over Touvier. He was placed under arrest May 24, 1989, at Saint-Joseph Priory in Nice.

Touvier was tried and sentenced to life in prison in 1994, the first French citizen to be convicted of crimes against humanity.

In the course of the investigation, a network was established between Colonel Recordon, Phillipep Mathy, the Nazi-hunting lawyer Serge Klarsfeld, and the Simon-Wiesenthal Center. Their cooperation led to the authorization of new warrants, most notably one for John Demjanjuk.

Demjanjuk was known as Ivan the Terrible to prisoners of the Treblinka extermination camp. He was accused of having directed the installation of the gas chambers and having assassinated over one hundred thousand Jews. He lived in the United States.

Extradited in 1986, Demjanjuk's was sentenced to death in Jerusalem in 1988. This ruling was overturned in 1993 by the Israeli Superior Court of Justice on the grounds of insufficient evidence to prove that Demjanjuk was indeed Ivan the Terrible. The court concluded that the suspect had undoubtedly served as a guard in the extermination camp, but that serious doubts existed as to whether he was Ivan, although he was identified by eighteen witnesses.

Another important case coming out of Paris investigations unit involved Alois Brunner, an Austrian member of the Nazi Party and an SS Officer notorious for having committed war crimes against the Jews in several European countries. He helped organize the Final Solution alongside Adolf Eichmann. At the end of the war, he managed to escape allied forces and change his identity, but still found himself interned at an American prison camp near Vienna. After his release, he lived a quiet life in Essen, Germany despite being at the top of the list of war criminals established by the International Military Tribunal in Nuremberg. Finally, out of fear of being arrested, he made his way to Syria in 1954, actively assisted by the Grand Mufti of Jerusalem.

Simon Wiesenthal and other investigators tracked Brunner relentlessly. He was sentenced to death in abstentia in 1954 (and again in 2001). In Syria, he went by the name of Dr. Georg Fischer. He lived in a safe place until spotted in 1961 by Mossad, which sent him a parcel bomb. Two Damascus postal agents were killed. Brunner, reported dead by Syrian police, actually survived, although his face was burned and he lost his left eye.

During the 1970s, Brunner served as an advisor to Syrian president Hafez al-Assad.[6] Another mail bomb in 1980 deprived him of several of his fingers. In the meantime, he is said to have trained all the heads of Syria's intelligence agencies, aiding in the establishment of systems of repression and torture in their prisons (work currently being investigated in OCLCH's Syrian files).

Brunner is presumed to have died in a Syrian dungeon in 2001. Philippe Mathy confided to me that his presence in Syria was confirmed through his ear print in a photograph. The analysis was performed by a German expert at the criminal bureau in Wiesbaden at the request of the investigators and Serge Klarsfeld.

In the 2000s, the Paris investigations unit began to tackle cases dealing with the Rwandan genocide where, between April and June 1994, more than eight hundred thousand Tutsi men, women, and children were massacred by the Hutu population. Many of the genocide's authors were pushed into exile in August 1994 by a counteroffensive and the Tutsi's Rwanda Patriotic Front. Some of them were in France under false identities. They were later identified by survivors and judicial proceedings were set in motion. The arrival of the OCLCH in 2013 provided highly specialized investigators and allowed for greater concentration on the Rwandan file.

The OCLCH has around twenty investigators who come from either the gendarmerie or the national police. It is divided into two divisions: one in charge of investigations; the other, known as the strategy division, is tasked with upholding international procedures and maintaining international relations.

While Rwanda was a major focus of our investigations, many other countries are now included: Liberia, Central African Republic, Syria, Iraq, Libya, Chechnya, Sri Lanka, to name a few. We currently have more than 150 cases open and under investigation. It is a big load for the twenty people under my command, all of whom must become expert in international law, complicated financial transactions, and the subtleties of the Internet, while taking into account the diplomatic, political, ethnic, religious, and nationalist dimensions of each case. Fortunately, I am surrounded by men and women who are creative, adaptable, curious, and committed to bringing criminals to justice.

It's no walk in the park. We're reminded of that with every investigation. Each brings new challenges because this type of investigation is unique, especially in comparison to what I experienced running routine criminal investigations. In the case of homicides, we would usually start with a crime scene which might reveal clues about the perpetrator. With other organized crime activities, there were usually multiple offenses that would reveal operational styles and patterns and lead to quick arrests. In OCLCH cases, the starting point for investigators is far removed from the crime scene in time and distance. Generally, the investigators have either identified a perpetrator but not the victims, or they have identified the victims but not the perpetrator. This leads to an enormous amount of work, searching for clues and collecting testimony, sometimes with generous international cooperation, sometimes not.

Fortunately, we're seldom alone. In the fight against war crimes, cooperation is essential. We are supported by an evolving galaxy or national and international governmental organizations and NGOs. My starting point is typically to reach out to contacts to see how we can work together. Police investigations work best when men and women know and appreciate one another.

At the national level, we cooperation with French intelligence services, including the International Cooperation Directorate (DCI) of the ministry of the interior and its network of security attaches, with whom I'm quite familiar. Also, the ministry of Europe and foreign affairs and its crisis and support center, as well as the national police service and the gendarmerie.

At the international level, we have valuable partners in Interpol and such UN agencies as the Office of the High Commission on Human Rights (OHCHR). This agency was able to identify witnesses that the International and Independent Commission of Inquiry on the Syrian Arab Republic, known as the "Pinheiro Commission," had interviewed anonymously for its reports.[7]

Since March 2011, the International, Impartial, and Independent Mechanism (I3M) has facilitated the most serious investigations into international rights violations in the Syrian Arab Republic; it partners with UN members, including France.

The UN has also launched an important team of special investigators, UNITAD, charged with holding Iraq and neighboring Islamic states accountable for their crimes.[8]

Also among our partners are international or internationalized criminal jurisdictions, such as the International Criminal Court and its prosecutorial office, the so-called Mechanism which performs the residual functions of the international criminal tribunals for Rwanda and Yugoslavia (both bodies of the UN) and its task force on fugitives, as well as the special chambers for Kosovo and the Central African Republic.

Since May 1, 2017, we have worked with a variety of European agencies, including Europol, which provides criminal intelligence and support to the police services of member states in their investigations of genocide, crimes against humanity, and war crimes. It has created the Analysis Project on Core International Crimes (AP CIC), which gathers, processes, and shares information on terrorism and organized crime among seventeen participating countries.[9]

And since November 14, 2018, our partners have included Eurojust—the European Union Agency for Criminal Justice Cooperation, which supports investigations by financing and maintaining a network of contact points of persons suspected of genocide, crimes against humanity and war crimes.[10] Eurojust and our national office have the ability to jointly create and coordinate investigative teams.

Having worked extensively in police investigative units, a world that is, to say the least, highly compartmentalized, I was surprised to find that non-governmental organizations (NGOs) are a valuable source of information. Their contributions, always verified through our usual procedures, have been particularly useful in tracing and identifying criminals on French soil. They tend to have strong knowledge of foreign territories where crimes occur and are good at collecting evidence.

Several NGOs, including Amnesty International, Human Rights Watch, and the International Federation of Human Rights Leagues (FIDH), regularly publish reports containing valuable information on both domestic and international armed conflict. Others, such as the International Commission for Justice and Accountability (CIJA) specialize in collecting testimony and evidence related to atrocities committed in Syria. Similarly helpful are the Syrian Center for Media and Freedom of Expression (SCM) and the Independent Commission for Human Rights (ICHR). The Association for the Study of War Crimes (ASWC) specializes in crowdsourcing—publishing calls for witnesses through Facebook and producing reports on the basis of its research. With respect to open-source research, I should also mention the Netherlands-based investigative journalism group Bellingcat, the photo and video aggregation site Eyewitness, and Open Facto, a French-language non-profit that facilitates open-source investigations.

Still other NGOs specialize in victim assistance, including the FIDH, which has branches in a number of countries, and others that collect evidence of particular types of international crimes. For instance, in the area of sexual crimes constituting crimes against humanity or crimes of war, there is We Are Not Weapons of War and the Dr. Denis Mukwege Foundation, whose founder was awarded the Nobel Peace Prize for his work on behalf of women raped and mutilated in armed conflict. Similarly, Physicians for Human Rights (PHR) documents attacks on medical personnel in times of war.

The more precise and ethical their approach to collecting evidence and testimony, the more useful these NGOs are to our investigations. Contributions of this kind are assessed by magistrates in the crimes against humanity division of our national anti-terrorist prosecutor's office.

The objective of all this activity is to bring perpetrators of major international crimes before French courts or the courts of nations that request their extradition, as was the case with Bosnian Serb war criminal Radomir Šušnjar, arrested near Paris, or the three Rwandans—Pascal Simbikangwa, Octavien Ngenzi, and Tito Barahira—who were all flushed out of hiding in France and sentenced to life imprisonment for their crimes.

In March 2018, we saw the first definitive conviction in France of a Rwandan for "complicity in genocide and crimes against humanity." This was the first of its kind since the actions against Klaus Barbie, Paul Touvier, and Maurice Papon.

In 2008, Pascal Simbikangwa, an ex-Hutu dignitary who had been on the run since the summer of 1994, was arrested in the Comoros off East Africa. He had been calling himself Safari Senyamuhara David and was trafficking in illegal documents. A former Rwandan army captain and head of military intelligence for the Hutu government, he was unmasked during his pre-trial detention and indicted in April 2009; the investigation was entrusted to our Paris investigations unit.

All this was facilitated by the reestablishment of diplomatic relations between France and Rwanda in January 2010. They had been frozen since 2006, after the decision of French judge Jean-Louis Bruguière to prosecute Rwandan president Paul Kagame at the International Criminal Court for Rwanda. The judge had been in charge of the investigation into the death of two French pilots of Rwandan president Habyarimana's plane, which was shot down in April 1994. The attack claimed the lives of Habyarimana and his Burundian counterpart, Cyprien Ntaryamira. It served as a trigger for the Tutsi genocide. Judge Bruguière suspected that people close to Habyarimana's successor were involved in this terrorist act.

The abandonment of this line of inquiry by Judge Marc Trévidic, who took over the case from Jean-Louis Bruguière, revived judicial cooperation between France and Rwanda. Investigators and investigating judges could now meet with witnesses and victims implicating Pascal Simbikangwa, also known as The Tormentor. According to the investigation, he played a prominent role in the organization of roadblocks set up in the capital, Kigali, just after the assassination of April 6. The purpose of the roadblocks was to flush out Tutsi and eliminate them. Two days later, he was in Karago, his native village, while Hutu militiamen supported by elements of the army stormed a hill where Tutsi had taken refuge. The death toll was 1,697.

Charged in the Paris Assize Court in March 2013 for complicity in genocide and crimes against humanity, Pascal Simbikangwa was tried the following year and sentenced to twenty-five years in prison. He appealed, appearing in October 2016 before the assize court of Bobigny, which refused to alter his sentence. A further appeal was rejected in 2018.

Two other Hutu officials, Tito Barahira and Octavien Ngenzi, were arraigned before the Paris Assize Court in July 2016. Both were accused of having planned, coordinated, and facilitated meetings with military leaders to organize the massacre of the Tutsi population. The most significant event was a bloody attack at a church in Kabarondo on April 13, 1994. Tutsi who had taken refuge there were exterminated. The two men were sentenced to life imprisonment. The sentence was upheld on appeal two years later.

Three convictions for crimes against humanity. It's a small number compared to the multitude of victims. But for the NGOs engaged in the pursuit of war criminals, it sends a strong message.

It was in the context of these NGO contributions that I met a person I will call Bob, a fact finder who contacted us with vital information about a genocidal Rwandan who was hiding in France. After performing the usual due diligence on Bob, I decided to accept his proposal for a meeting.

6

THE INVESTIGATION
IN FRANCE

"It is therefore out of the question for France to remain a sanctuary for genocidaires"

—Bruno Sturlese, general prosecutor in
the trial of Pascal Simbikangwa

November 6, 2018—Paris, café Le Papillon

We arranged a meeting at a café near the OCLCH.

Michel, the police officer in charge of OCLCH intelligence, joins me. Meetings with sources are always covered by two people. That's the protocol. One observes and analyzes, the other asks the questions. In our line of work, we need to be on guard against manipulation.

Bob enters the café. Stooped. He has a heavy tread and looks tired. Wrapped in a thick parka, he might be six feet tall. His long gray hair is tied in a pony tail. He looks at me through piercing blue eyes and extends his hand.

"Sorry I'm late."

"No problem."

"Phew . . . the weather's much better in Rwanda."

"Have you just come from there?" Michel asks.

"Yes. That's why I wanted to meet. A very serious case. They called him the Lone Warrior of Gisenyi, in the west of Rwanda, near the border with the Democratic Republic of Congo. He was an army man, rank of captain.

He commanded the Gisenyi military company. We have attributed at least three thousand five hundred deaths directly to him. Another ten thousand taking into account the people under him."

"Good. Is the file with the magistrate?"

"No, not yet. My lawyer is finishing the steps necessary to file the complaint. You will receive it soon through the public prosecutor's office."

"Well, in any case, it's nice to meet you."

Bob takes a small blue pouch out of his bag and places it on the table. He opens it and shows us a photograph taken on a smartphone. I pick up the photo, look at it closely, and hand it to Michel. It shows a tall man in fatigues in an African setting.

"This man is living in France. Apparently, he's become a citizen."

"Did you take it?"

"No, one of our sources did, an insider . . . in the Democratic Republic of Congo.

"You mean to say this guy's a naturalized French citizen?"

"Yes, according to the insider."

"Does he suspect anything?"

"No, there's no danger."

"Can you tell me more? When we approach him, I need to know what I'm getting into."

"I need to check with the insider."

"I understand. How does that happen?"

"Kivu region, eastern."

"Ah, OK."

"This guy is a bastard."

"I don't doubt it, but we'll have to prove it. That's the job. You document your cases, but we have to confirm them forensically, make sure all of the evidence and testimony is solid.

"I trust you. The other guys have been handed correctly. It's up to you. But be careful. This guy is a smart one. He managed to con citizenship out of the French administration."

"Any political connections?"

"Not that I'm aware of, but who knows. His record is surprisingly clean."

"Well don't worry, as soon as you transmit the information, we'll start working on it."

Bob looks at me. "So I'll see you in Rwanda soon?"

"Maybe, I don't know."

"By the way," asks Michel, "what's your interest in this case?"

"Let's just say I represent the insider. This guy did not respect his commitments to the insider."

I get up to see him off. Bob shoots me a smile and turns toward the door. I order another coffee. A moment to think things through.

December 10, 2018—Annecy

It doesn't take long.

We receive the Lone Warrior's file quickly. After some coordinated research with OFPRA, we locate an individual corresponding to the description. He has been living as a priest at Tamié Abbey in Haute-Savoie.

Part of our African team is dispatched to Haute-Savoie to undertake an environmental scan of the target. That involves establishing contacts, tapping phones, and conducting surveillance. Cristopheh, a new recruit from the judicial police in Paris, goes on stakeout with Élodie, a warrant officer and Rwandan case veteran. They work out of a Peugeot 405. Well hidden.

We create a WhatsApp thread. Code name: Papa Pépère. I introduced this system to allow us to share information among our investigators in real time. We even integrated the public prosecutor, Brice Coutin, into the feed.

The point of the stakeout, in front of a group of several buildings at the Tamié Abbey, is to spot Father Jean Fourier, whose real name is Théogène Mukasago, the Lone Warrior, now sixty-five-years-old.

He is passing himself off as a Tutsi, one of those he massacred, a man named Justin Malbonaga. A resident of Gisenyi who died on April 22, 1994, Justin Malbonaga was among those who had taken refuge in the church. He and his family were among the 3,500 Tutsi who had taken refuge there.

We had been searching for the name Jean Fourier in all the police and administrative databases at our disposal and coming up empty. That's not unusual. War criminals tend not to make a lot of noise. They want to stay below the radar, which complicates our investigations but it's all part of the game.

Fortunately, the file sent from over to us by the prosecutor's office, which includes Bob's information, is more detailed. In May 1996, Théogène Mukasago, then living in the Congo, boarded a flight from Zaire to France. He took up residence in the Southwest, near Toulouse, then moved to a village in Ariège called Ax-les-Thermes. We pick up his trail again in 2001. He is in Lourdes where he must have made the miraculous conversion that led him to the priesthood.

He spent time in two different seminaries before landing in a parish in Cloyes, near Châteaudun, in the west of France in 2007. Nothing of note for nine years. Then, suddenly, a transfer, for no apparent reason. He retires in Haute-Savoie where we locate him by his vehicle's registration.

Certain facts still need verifying, so for the moment we don't move on him. We continue with our field work, surveillance and phone tapping. Our target does not suspect anything. In this respect, we are one step ahead.

"He's coming out!" Christophe cries.

The team takes photographs of a tall man walking out of the monastery alone, briefcase in hand. He gets into his vehicle, a khaki Range Rover, the latest model.

The team tails him, leaving a lot of space. The road is not busy. The Range Rover heads toward Annecy and a few minutes later turns toward Saint Jorioz. Fourier parks in a lot on Noisetiers Road. He gets out of the vehicle and walks over to a building.

A few minutes later, Élodie strolls past the mailboxes and finds a label with the name Father Fourier. The team goes back into hiding.

A WhatsApp message from Sophie: "Attention! He called someone named Marie. She'll be there any minute."

Sophie, a member of OCLCH's strategy division, has tapped Fourier's line from Paris.

Twenty-five minutes later, a mixed-race woman parks in a Peugeot 205.

We check the license plate. The vehicle belongs to Marie Comparie, age forty-five, from Annemasse. Two hours pass. Marie Comparie emerges from the building.

WhatsApp [Sophie]: "New call, a woman named Catherine is coming to join him to spend the night."

The team keeps out of sight. Another car, a Mercedes convertible, pulls up. It has a Swiss registration, canton of Geneva. A woman gets out of the car, blond, slender, fur coat, fifties, elegant.

We take photographs and run background checks on the woman.

WhatsApp [Christophe]: "Finally, he's going to make his confession."

WhatsApp [Me]: "Lone Warrior, not as lone as you think."

I give the team instructions to stay with Fourier for the week. "Take as many photos as possible. We'll show them to witnesses in Rwanda. Even if he has aged, they will recognize him. We'll feed you his communications and his geolocation in real time. I've informed GOSIF [the observation and surveillance group] in Lyon, and the investigators in Chambéry that we're working in their region. The public prosecutor has signed off on us asking the GOSIF to put a tracking beacon on Fourier's vehicle."

The GOSIF team performs its own evaluation. The beacon is installed five days later.

December 17, 2018—Paris, office of the prosecutor

Christophe, Élodie, and I enter Brice's office in the new *Palais de Justice*, the largest law court complex in Europe.

Glass, natural light, and an incredible view. Thirty-eight stories climbing more than 500 feet above the Batignolles district, right alongside Porte de Clichy. It is the second-tallest inhabited building in Paris behind the Tower of Montparnasse.

The magistrate's offices are on the same floor as those of the National Anti-Terrorist Prosecutors (PNAT), into which they'll be integrated in a month.

"Hey, Brice."

"Hello, Colonel."

I like Brice. Small beard, round glasses, brown hair, young father. His tall stature gives you the impression he's floating above the world. Not judgmentally, but with a shrewd smile. He always has something nice to say, for any occasion. He does it either for pleasure or to keep his mind sharp. It's like a form of exercise for him. As a prosecutor, he's always looking to heal, to give dignity back to the victim.

"So? Papa Pépère is quite clever, it seems.

"Yes! And very talkative."

I let the team download their week of observation. Elodie does the talking.

"Well, we found him in Saint-Jorioz. As agreed, we had his vehicle tracked. A rather quiet life, except for the antics with his mistresses. He seems to be retired. Up to now, we haven't questioned anyone so as not to arouse suspicion. He spends his days at the Tamié Abbey in Savoie. Nothing special. We're going to do some financial and banking checks. He received a visit from a woman named Catherine Boulaz, a resident of Geneva and a banker in Switzerland."

"Okay, we'll come back to her later. We'll do some interviews in Rwanda to see if she was involved in the genocide."

"It would be good to plug in the other woman, Marie Comparie, as well," suggests Christophe.

"OK, I'll write it up for you."

I jump in. "The next mission gets rolling in March. Before then, we'll make a list of witnesses with the help of the Rwandan authorities, in particular the department of witness and victim Protection."

"OK. The files and the list will then be sent to Rwanda's attorney general," says Brice. "Who is working on it?"

"Christophe and Élodie."

I glance over at the pair. Satisfied smiles. The police/warrant officer pairing works well. We take our leave, feeling positive. We need to maintain our positions until we can substantiate Bob's allegations. The next step is the key. Rwanda. But first, I'm going to ask Bob to pay another visit to his insider.

December 21, 2018—Paris, Porte de Bagnolet

WhatsApp [Bob]: "The insider agreed to share some information with you. When can we meet?"

WhatsApp [Me]: "Today? Same spot?"

WhatsApp [Bob]: "OK, 3 o'clock?"

At the appointed time, Bob enters café Le Papillon. Michel is with me.

"Hello, I have news," he says, taking off his scarf and winter jacket.

"OK, we're listening."

"It turns out Mukawago is playing a double game. He is financially sup-porting a political group called FDLR [Democratic Forces for the Liberation of Rwanda]. They're based in the Democratic Republic of Congo, in the east near Lake Kivu. The FDLR was formed in Congo in the 2000s out of the thousands of Hutu refugees who fled west after Paul Kagame took power in Rwanda in 1994. The Congo's president, Kabila, supported them at first but eventually broke ties. Locally, the DFLR are believed to be responsible for acts of violence against the civilian population, including looting, rape, kill-ings, and recruiting child soldiers. Their goal is to overthrow Kagame and install a new regime in Rwanda. Some of their leaders have left for Europe to sow the seeds of their movement. The ICC has issue arrest warrants for certain FDLR leaders. Currently, the FDLR has about 20,000 fighters just waiting to return to Rwanda and get their revenge."

Bob continues, quite proud of this information.

"Mukasago has political ambitions should the FDLR win. In the mean-time, he's laundering money through a Swiss Company in Geneva called Francoport. It resells precious metals in Kazakhstan, including coltan and gold."

That explains the link to Switzerland and our blond.

"Vital minerals from coltan are used in cellphones and the aeronautics industry. The East Congo is rich in minerals. So the objective of the rebel movements take advantage of local poverty, exploiting people who work in the mines. The mines are difficult to access. The rebels take advantage of the remoteness and lack of security to enrich themselves. They sell the raw material to certain European companies that are not too careful about the origins of the materials and who is profiting from them. They resell these metals, usually through intermediaries in exchange for false UN export certificates. Mukasago uses his proceeds to finance arms purchases on behalf of the FDLR. It's a circular system. Follow the money flows and the arms trafficking and you are never far from war crimes. Investigating the finances is critical because they fund a lot of criminal activity."[1]

"Why did the insider tell you all this?"

"Mukasago owes him a lot of money. He wants to take him down."

"But, if we take him down, the insider will never see his money,"

"It doesn't matter to him. The main thing, for him, is that Mukasago falls. Obviously, the rebels will also be suppressed. They'll likely abandon their reconquest project."

"That's all good. It's a bit far afield from our investigation into the genocide but it's important context."

7

THE INVESTIGATION
IN RWANDA

"Truth passes through fire, and does not burn."

Rwandan proverb.

March 2019 – Rwanda, Kigali

Having located and stalked Father Pépère in France, our investigation now moves to its second stage in Rwanda. Gathering evidence, interviewing witnesses, corroborating the information we receive. The details are important. We remind ourselves all the time that we work for the prosecution and not for the defense.

In typical cases, investigations proceed by way of an international letter rogatory; investigators employed by the recipient state carry out the work. In this case, the rules of international criminal assistance apply. Subject to prior authorization from Rwandan judicial authorities, we can collect testimony ourselves in the forms required by French criminal procedure.

On March 5, Brice forwards to me an invitation from the prosecutor general of Rwanda in response to his request. The OCLCH's investigators are authorized to proceed, and local investigators have decided to assist us.

To help move things along, in particular the subpoenaing of witnesses through local authorities, we dispatch a preliminary team to work upstream of us, coordinating agendas.

I leave France to join our team on the ground.

After a nine-hour flight and a good night's sleep, I get to work. First on my list is a visit with the GFTU [Genocide Fugitive Tracking Unit], an office of the Rwandan prosecutor that specializes in the genocide. Then the PVT, a unit in charge of protecting victims and witnesses.

But before all that, I want to take a look at the house of former President Habyarimana, assassinated on April 6, 1994, a day that lives in infamy.

Vincent, my driver, sends me a WhatsApp. He's in front of the hotel. We head out in a 4×4 toward the airport. Kigali's sea of hills still challenges my sense of direction. It's hard to get one's bearings. Traffic is dense. Vincent weaves in and out of the streams of cars and motorcycle cabs, their drivers wearing brightly colored helmets signifying the company they belong to. The air is filled with engine noise, honking horns, and the whistles of policemen, impeccable in their uniforms. Kigali has the reputation of being a very clean city. I can confirm this. I like the country as a whole.

Our car speakers blast African music: *Bye, Bye* by Naason, part of the latest generation of Rwandan singers. Our first time out, Vincent, wanting to please me, had unearthed a CD of old French hits from the 1960s. He played it for our whole five-hour trip from Kigali to Gisenyi. More than enough. On the way back, he figured out that African tribal music suited me better.

The airport passes on our right and eventually park in a small lot. The Habyarimana house appears ahead of us, majestic, draped in foliage, with magnificent trees, diverse perfumes, African birds. The gardeners are busy at work, maintaining what has become a museum, housing works of artists mainly commemorating the genocide. I suggest to Vincent that he accompany me for the visit.

Catherine, our guide, small and nonchalant in her candy pink blouse, invites us inside. We take off our shoes. Photography is not allowed.

When we're up on the second floor, Vincent points to a room and says, "There was a place reserved there for Agathe, the president's wife, to practice magic. Obviously, they've removed it."

We stroll around toward the back of the villa and come up against a brick perimeter wall. Catherine guides us to a door that opens to a vast field, upon which rests the remnants of the president's plane, the Falcon, shot down on that evening of April 6 as it was about to land.

We walk in silence around the grass field. I let it sink in that the plane crashed into the president's own home. Hard to believe. Catherine's watching me out of the corner of her eye.

"What do you think?"

"Let's say, I'm just processing the fact that we're standing at a point of impact that triggered one of the worst genocides of the 20th century, a million dead in just a few weeks."

Neither Vincent nor Catherine say a word.

The painting "Black" by Pierre Soulages comes to mind. I'm reminded of what he said: "That light comes from what, by definition, is the greatest absence of light, provokes a disturbance in me."

In the blackness of genocide, I have difficulty perceiving the slightest ray of light. Maybe later? For the moment, I feel I'm following a deep black gash in the earth that runs from country to country and reverberates with the apocalyptic noises of war crimes, crimes against humanity, genocide, forced disappearance, and torture.

While the practice has been around forever, it was not until the Second World War that the term "genocide" became part of our spoken language. In August 1941, in a radio speech, Churchill said of the barbarity of the Nazis: "We are in the presence of a crime without a name." He was right. There are no words that adequately describe the horror. Genocide will have to do.

It was Raphael Lemkin, a Jewish legal expert, Polish and later American, who constructed the term and the concept of genocide in 1943. It was first asserted at the Nuremberg Trials and then again at the UN in October 1948. Lemkin drew on two ancient languages: the Greek *genos*, meaning lineage, family, clan, group, race; and the Latin suffix *cide*, from the root *caedere*, meaning to kill. This neologism would find its way into law on December 9, 1948, with the adoption in Paris of the Convention for the Prevention and Repression of the Crime of Genocide. Lemkin was the principal drafter.

"Would you like to stay a bit longer?" Catherine asks.

I take another look at the engine embedded in the earth, a symbol of one of human history's deadliest events. Rwanda's history, but the international community's as well.

"No, that's good. Let's go."

It's time to visit the genocide investigators in the GFTU.

Thirty minutes later, I cross the barrier that leads to a peaceful Kigali neighborhood with quaint individual houses. These small buildings are home to the magistrates.

Over the course of a single year, mountains had been moved to normalize French relations with Rwanda and its leader. I watched it happen: the handshake between President Macron and President Kagame at the UN in September 2017. Macron's speech in the Ivory Coast in November 2017 declaring a new chapter in French-African relations. A year later, Louise Mushikiwabo, a loyal follower of the Rwandan president, was chosen as secretary general of the *Organization Internationale de la Francophonie*. For this country, which aspires to be the Switzerland of Africa, a hinge between its English- and French-speaking populations, it was a propitious time.

And last but not least, on October 10, 2018, France dropped its case against President Kagame at the International Criminal Court over the French crew members that died on President Habyarimana's plane.

Relations between Rwanda and France are at an all-time high and I notice on this trip that some of my contacts who spoke English during my last visit have rediscovered the charms of the French language. The friendliness is also evident in the radiant smile of Immaculée Mukarwego, the prosecutor who welcomes me to the GFTU. She is wearing a splendid multicolored green dress, African style, with a matching scarf on her head. She holds out her hand to me. I can feel her strength in her eyes, at once gentle, firm, and stubborn.

"How are you, Eric?"

"Very well, and you?"

"Wonderful. Tell me about our cases. We were pleased with the judgments in the recent trials of Octavien Ngenzi and Tito Barahira. Life sentences confirmed for both, and they survived their appeals."

"We brought many witnesses from Rwanda for those trials. It wasn't always easy but it was worth it. Even at the cost of a million euros."

"You can extradite suspects to us as other countries do," retorts Immaculée.

"Yes, other countries, but you know that the jurisprudence of our Court of Cassation won't let Rwandans be extradited because genocide was not in your penal code in 1994 when all this happened."

"So it's your choice."

"Certainly. But what about you? How many genocidaires are you looking for?"

"Three hundred in Uganda, three hundred in the Democratic Republic of Congo, and three hundred scattered around the planet."

"This time, we are here mainly to work on a certain soldier, a captain. It is estimated that he is responsible for at least three thousand five hundred deaths directly, and more, considering the extent of his command."

"Yes! I saw his file come through. Keep me posted, and good luck."

8

HEADS AND TAILS

"On a voyage, you never know where the falling night will find you."
—Rwandan proverb.

Before leaving Kigali, I grab breakfast with Brice to brief him on our progress with Théogène Mukasago case.

"So, Papa Pépère? The Lone Warrior? Who are we dealing with here," Brice asks while sipping a ginger tea.

"It's going well. Today Élodie and Christophe are interviewing a key witness from Gisenyi prison. I'm headed out there for a few days to listen in. After that, I'll let you know."

"Have a good trip, Colonel. I have a meeting with the attorney general at 11 o'clock. I'm planning on asking him for the details from the *Gacaca* [pronounced *gatchatcha*] trials."

I make a note to go back through those myself. In 1998, Rwanda's government declared that it would take at least a hundred years for justice to be done. In the meantime, no justice, no reconciliation. So it decided to create a sort of hierarchy in its judicial processing: the big fish are sent to the International Criminal Court; intermediate suspects who carried out orders would be dealt with in the local courts; and the mass of suspects, those accused of killing neighbors and sometimes even their own family members, would be handled by the traditional *gacaca* system.

The principle of *gacaca* is as follows: a general assembly of persons above eighteen years of age living in the cell (an administrative entity comprising several communes) elects a body of nine judges whose mission is to gather evidence, hear testimony, and reconstruct facts for and against the accused.[1]

Since the majority of the accused were neighbors, Rwandans became deeply involved in these proceedings which were often held at the sites of the massacres in the presence of witnesses, survivors, and suspected killers. The proceedings began with a reading of the charge and supporting facts. Actors would re-enact the crime scenes. Sometimes people laughed; sometimes they cried. The *gacaca* is a unique and open form of justice in which people speak freely and the whole community is involved. It is well suited to such a broad-based genocide. Once these trials finished in 2012, the judgments were handed over to an English NGO which is digitizing them. We can request access to the judgments through Rwandan authorities. They will certainly be of use to us in prosecuting the Lone Warrior.

March 15, 2019—Rwanda, en route to Gisenyi

Three and a half hours on mountain roads. The land of a thousand hills lives up to its reputation. Summits as far as the eye can see, some of them almost five thousand feet high. Fortunately, the roads are good, better than in Bosnia-Herzegovina.

Vincent throws on an African playlist and the tribal rhythms seem to keep pace with the bends in the road. I keep one eye on the pavement and the other on the landscape. We drive through immense eucalyptus forests, the gray-green leaves flicker as we pass.

On the side of the road, every now and then, we pass children playing with makeshift balls fashioned from banana leaves. Cyclists go by, too, with large, full luggage racks protruding from each side of their delicate frames. They ride at full speed regardless. The slightest misstep and you've got an epic mess on your hands.

"Is there a *Tour du Rwanda*, like the *Tour de France*?" I asked Vincent.

"Yes, every year."

"That can't be easy, especially with the huge variations in altitude."

I look back out to see tea fields, bright green in the sun. Women working on the mountainsides. Rwanda is famous for both its tea and coffee. It's a magnificent country. What more can be said?

We pass many villages, clinging to hillsides. Houses with corrugated iron roofs. The wealthy have brick houses. Everyone else uses adobe. The homes are often surrounded by banana plantations, some of which are bare.

Every village has its own brightly colored shops, each more animated than the next. Rwanda is full of energy and life. Youth is everywhere, as in every African country—a real challenge for African leaders and European countries.

On each storefront is an artistic representation of the goods and services available within. I see ironmongers, carpenters, hairdressers, grocery stores, shoemakers. Often, huge speakers play African music. The center of a village typically features a market where traders present their wares on clothes laid out on the ground: peaches, bananas, sweet potatoes, beans.

Children wearing school colors run in noisy packs on their way to class. Some are tasked with carrying water in yellow tins.

Motorcycle taxis pass the time nonchalantly at strategic intersections.

We pass another town and reality intrudes. A genocide memorial speaks to the duty to remember. This commitment to never forgetting what occurred is a significant departure from Bosnia-Herzegovina, where the tendency is rather toward revising and forgetting.

We head north toward Volcano National Park, a sanctuary for gorillas and the one who protected them. Dian Fossey, more than thirty years ago. It's been thirty years now. She was known as *Nyiramachabelli*, the woman who lives alone in the mountains. She was murdered in 1985, the day after Christmas, in the Virunga mountains of the Democratic Republic of Congo. According to her wishes, she is buried in the cemetery she had built for the gorillas in Karisoke.

Fossey had been in an open war with poachers, in particular a man named Protais Zigiranyirazo, the local prefect and suspected head of a ring that trafficked in baby gorillas. He himself directed the investigation into Fossey's murder which, it goes without saying, led nowhere. Small world, Protais Zigiranyirazo is also the brother of Agathe, the wife of President Habyarimana. He is said to have belonged to a secret cell called the "Akazu," or little house, that planned the genocide. Its members, who were all close to Habyarimana, held important ministerial and economic positions in the country and lined their pockets at the expense of the population, which was starving at the time.

Protais Zigiranyirazo was arrested at Brussels airport in 2001 for his alleged involvement in the genocide. He had been hiding with his false passport among African refugees in a reception center at the airport. Prosecuted for the crime of genocide before the International Criminal Tribunal for Rwanda (ICTR), he was initially found guilty, but was acquitted on appeal in 2009. The five judges of the appeals court concluded that their colleagues had "seriously misjudged the evidence" and that there was no choice but to acquit.

Vincent snaps me out of my thoughts.

"We are now driving through the Nyabihu district, Habyarimana's birthplace. The hill where the massacre you are investigating took place is not very far. But first we will go to Gisenyi to get a room at the nuns' house."

"OK. I have a bag with medicine and clothes for them."

It is a tradition at the OCLCH for investigators to take advantage of their trips to Rwanda to bring donations, usually for the mother superiors of the monasteries.

An hour later, we slow and park underneath a porch. I can make out an arc of blue letters reading *Ermitage Saint-André*. The convent sits slanted on the mountainside, giving it a magnificent view of Lake Kivu, one of the largest lakes in Africa (located between the Congo and Rwanda). The lake is beautiful but also known for having been a basin for cadavers during the genocide, much like the Drina River in Bosnia-Herzegovina. Water is said to purify, but who? The victims or the killers?

The reception area is soberly decorated with traditional Rwandan artwork—spirals, squares, and rectangles in black and white—on its light blue walls. A smiling hostess welcomes us and we are soon joined by Sister Indulgence, a little nervous woman dressed in sky blue. She thanks us for our consideration, takes the bag of clothes and medicine, and leaves us there.

2:00 p.m.—Gisenyi, Palais de justice

The courthouses has dark pink walls and is organized in an L shape. I pass through the entrance which is next to a magnificent purple bougainvillea.

About twenty people of all ages are resting inside. The heat is relentless, despite it being the rainy season. I'm the only white person. Everyone observes me attentively. Five soldiers and policemen stand armed with Kalashnikovs. On my way into the deposition room, I get a text from Brice.

"Permission to share the *gacaca* proceedings granted by the attorney general. This will be useful to us with Papa Pépère."

In the corridor, I run into Agnès from the victim and witness protection department (PVT).

"Hello Agnès, how are things?"

"Hello Éric. All our witnesses will be present today. Your preliminary team and our local people were able to make all the necessary arrangements. Everyone on your list has been summoned, and brought from prison the witness who was sentenced in *gacaca*."

As in any investigation, those involving the most serious international crimes require the collection of material evidence and depositions from witnesses who may reside in France or abroad. These witnesses can incriminate or exonerate the alleged perpetrator. They are recruited in different ways. They may have cooperated in various investigations already established in Rwanda, or they may be summoned by interested parties—the defense, for example.

In the absence of conclusive evidence, or to support evidence that dates back to the 1990s, witness testimony is crucial to investigations. Our investigators have been trained in a special method known as PROGREAI [general process of interviews, hearings, and interrogations] developed in Canada by criminologist Jacques Landry. It calls on an emphatic approach that requires the investigator to put his or her self in the place of the suspect or witness to better understand how events unfolded. The interview becomes a privileged means of establishing a constructive dialogue with the person, while at the same time absorbing previous investigative work into the character, intentions, motivations, and values of the individual to throw additional light on events and actions.

"Your investigators are in this room."

Agnès points to an office door flanked by two armed guards. I push it open.

"*Mwaramutse,* good morning to you all."

Élodie and Christophe stand. Handshakes. The room is ripe with body odor despite the wide open window. The office is rudimentary, everything made of wood. The walls are empty. The paint is dirty. A man in rose-colored prison clothing raises his eyes and looks at me. Graying hair, in his sixties. To his right, Matthieu, the regular Kinyarwanda interpreter. Translation slows the proceedings but is essential to their quality. The suspect was a chief warrant officer working under the Lone Warrior. His name is Jean-Marie Vianney Mukamazi.

"So?" I ask Christophe.

"The deposition started a minute ago. You just in time."

"OK, don't mind me."

Élodie proceeds.

"Monsieur Mukamazi, we're about finished with your resume and would now like to return to the facts at hand. First, have you ever testified before a court?"

"Yes. In 2000, I testified in the International Criminal Court for Rwanda on facts concerning the assassination of Karzenzi, a magistrate. Afterward, I was sentenced in *gacaca* for participating in the genocide and instigating others join in the massacres. I was sentenced to life in prison. I've been in prison since December 1996."

"What ethnicity are you?"

"Hutu, like my parents."

"Are you affiliated with any political parties?"

"No, but I was a supporter of the MRND [National Republican Movement for Democracy, the party of President Habyarimana]."

"OK. Please explain to us your role in the Gisenyi company."

"I was the deputy of Captain Théogène Mukasago. I was under his command. I was following his orders when I committed the acts I've been sentenced for."

"Silence, please. And continue."

"After April 6 and the assassination, the whole situation was a bit confusing. The captain called all of the sector chiefs of the region to a large meeting at the home of sub-prefect Faustin Katana."

"What day was this?"

"April 13, I think. Captain Mukasago had a bullhorn. He knew how to talk to people. He announced that the Tutsi had killed the president, and that we needed to exterminate them, pillage their belongings, and burn their houses. At the meeting, everyone agreed."

"How many were present at this meeting?"

"About a hundred."

"Who was there?"

"Some villagers had been summoned, the Interahamwe [a paramilitary group], some police, military personnel, the district's council and mayors. The captain explained that things needed to be done quickly, barriers needed to be placed on all major roads before they could Tutsi kill us. He said the barricades would be manned by villagers and Interahamwe. The police would ensure that the barriers were properly maintained. Every person reaching the barriers must be checked and, if it is a Tutsi, killed."

"How many barriers were set up?"

"About fifteen on the major intersections around the perimeter. Later, the captain said he had intelligence indicating that the cockroaches were gathering on the hill of Kabaya, where there was a parish and the Italian congregation of the Mission of the Sacred-Heart of Jesus. He said they had armed themselves and were planning maneuvers. The sector leaders and the Interahamwe began shouting slogans and making death chants. Then the crowd took them up."

"And you?"

"I did too. We had to end it once and for all. It had been announced that it was the season of the machete.[2] A final answer, as we used to say. The captain said that he would use 60 mm mortars if necessary to start the harvest, and that after, we'd finish the work by hand with grenades. According to the intelligence, there were three thousand five hundred Tutsi barricaded at the mission on the hill. Their numbers were growing. There was a risk that they would organize themselves effectively. The captain told the crowd to meet at the same spot the following morning, after the cows went out."

"What does that mean?"

"Around 9 a.m."

"Then what happened?"

"The next morning, the 14th, everyone showed up with machetes, farm tools.

"How many of you were there?"

"Around two thousand. The captain showed in a blue full-sized Toyota pickup. He had seven Tutsi chained in the back along with Mayor Didace Kayegi from the next village. The captain had the Tutsi brought down in front of the crowd. I knew the mayor well, we played cards together regularly. I also knew two of the Tutsi. Everyone started shouting death chants. The captain ordered us, the soldiers, to shoot the Tutsi. So we fired. Then he said to the crowd: 'See here, I've shown you the example.'"

"The Tutsi didn't say anything?"

"No. What could they do? The captain then brought out Mayor Kayegi. He pushed him to the front. The mayor asked how he should position himself. The captain said he didn't give a damn and shot him. Then we all headed out toward the hill to do the job. The captain asked me to flank the crowd with Interahamwe and police."

"Who else besides you witnessed the mayor's death? Could you provide us with names?"

Mukamazi lists around ten names of witnesses, police and civilian, whom we need to follow up with to confirm his version of events.

"How long did it take you to get to the hill?"

"About an hour, walking."

"How many of you were there?"

"The same number, two thousand. When we got there, the captain already had the 60 mm mortars and ammunition all set up. He was waiting for us with twenty other soldiers. He told us to surround the Hutu on the hill. Fifteen minutes later, everything was ready. He gave the order to fire about twenty mortar shells. Then he launched the assault. The shells had mowed down a number of the Tutsi but many were still standing. "How many?"

"I don't know. A hundred. Those who were outside the church."

"The church was not hit?"

"A little."

"Go on."

"When we got to the top, blood was everywhere. The Tutsi survivors tried to flee, but we had the hill surrounded. To go faster, we cut the tendons on their legs and came back later to finish them off. The police and the soldiers used firearms, the civilians used machetes and clubs with nails. We had to move quickly and take care of those who were in the church. The captain joined us in his 4×4. He drove over the bodies for fun, honking the horn and shouting. Then he parked in front of the church. He jumped on the hood of the car and congratulated everyone. Then he said: 'There's still a lot of work to do with those still in the church.'"

Silence.

"The door was barricaded. We pushed it open. It gave way quickly. So we went in screaming and singing. And we killed."

Silence.

"How many people?"

"I don't know. Three thousand, about."

"With what weapons?"

"All of them—guns, machetes, bats."

Silence.

"And after?"

"We brought the corpses to the pit."

"To the pit? What pit?"

"There was a pit that had been dug a long time before, quite deep. Fifty meters at least. Some of the Tutsi had been spared, the most valiant. They were made to undress. Each one had to bring a corpse. And when he had thrown the body into the pit, he was killed with a knife."

"This seems like it had been planned out in advance. Who came up with the idea for the pit?"

Silence.

"It was my idea. The captain congratulated me on the idea. I knew the priests of the parish well. Some were Italian, others were Rwandan."

"Where were the priests?"

"We warned them the day before that an attack was planned."

"So they left?"

"Yes. They said they needed to go shopping."

"Are they still alive, these priests?"

"No, I don't think so."

"One of the Italians returned after the genocide and he died in the village. At least, that's what I was told."

"Understood. And then?"

"We continued like that until 4 p.m. and then we went home. We had decided to finish the work the next day."

"And what did the Captain do the rest of the day? Did he stay there?"

"No. He returned around 4 p.m. to check on things and congratulate everyone. He pulled up in his 4×4 honking, music blasting. Then he got out and took bottles of beer out of the back and handed them out as a sort of reward. It was hot, and we were thirsty after so much work."

We looked at each other. He continued.

"It was evening. We'd left. The captain asked me to return the next day with fifty men to bury everyone. So that's what I did. We finished off any survivors. They joined the others in the pit."

Silence. The interpreter uses a moment to exhale. He must have heard a lot of these stories.

"Do you have anything else to declare regarding the facts on Kabaya Hill?"

"No."

"Can you give us any information about the massacre on the hill."

"I've heard talk about it in prison when they were gathering information for a *gacaca* trial Something about another five thousand dead Tutsi. The captain was behind that massacre as well. The police were called in by the mayor, who had himself guaranteed the Tutsi his protection."

"Do you know where the captain is now?"

"No, no idea. He escaped to Goma in Congo before the government forces arrived."

"We have several individuals photographed here. Can you indicate to us which one is Captain Mukasago?"

Christophe shows him a board with ten photos, ten numbers. The former chief warrant officer looks it over.

"He's number six."

I look at where the finger is positioned. On the face of Pap Pépère.

"Are you sure?"

"Yes, I'm sure."

Silence.

"Do you know Mukasago's nickname?"

"Yes, Lone Warrior."

"Why was he called that?"

"He always drove around alone in his four-wheel drive and would show up unexpectedly, even before the genocide. He was a bachelor, but he liked women, and as a captain, he did not hesitate to take them."

"Do you know of anyone who could provide additional information on the facts we have just mentioned?"

Mukamazi gave us the names of ten other individuals who, like himself, were in prison and who participated in the Kataya Hill massacre. They will be interviewed to check the veracity of Mukamazi's statements, which are nevertheless clear. These witnesses will then be later subpoenaed to France and flown in from Rwanda to testify before the Assize Court. It will be a culture shock, on both sides.

"Do you have anything else to declare?"

"Yes, I hope that you catch him so that he'll pay, as I am. I didn't do anything but obey orders. His orders. I'm in prison and he's out in the cold."

"Do you know where he is?"

"No. They tell me that he's somewhere in Europe."

"Anything else?"

"Yes. I regret what I did, and I ask the Tutsi for forgiveness."

Later, Christophe would tell me that this was the first time that he heard someone who committed genocide ask for forgiveness.

"We're done. You may return to prison. We'll see each other tomorrow at the prison to review the situation."

Élodie calls the guards. Mukamazi stands up.

"Goodbye, Mr. Mukamazi."

"Are you police officers? I was supposed to join the police before the genocide happened."

Silence. Do not judge, I tell myself. Do not judge.

He exits the room, crossing paths with a victim in the hallway. One of those he had overlooked to eliminate. Not a glance.

I follow behind our witness. As I watch him walk away, I'm thinking about theories of social psychology I've studied in the past, in particular the problem of obedience and conformity to the group. In an experiment carried out at the beginning of the 1960s, a psychologist by the name of Stanley Milgram wanted to evaluate the degree of submission of an individual to someone he considered a legitimate authority, particularly when the order received was immoral.[3] Participants were led to believe they were assisting in an unrelated experiment in which they had to administer electric shock to a "learner" to test the effectiveness of punishment on the memorization of data. Basically, they were applying shocks to test learning abilities. The electric shocks were gradually raised to what would have been fatal levels (they were fake).

The results, which Milgram found disturbing, were as follows: about twenty-five out of forty participants were shocked three times with 450 volts, the maximum. The psychologist was appalled at how docile ordinary people could be, and how willing to do serious harm to others if ordered to do so by a seemingly legitimate authority. For most people, belonging to a seemingly legitimate hierarchical structure seems to destroy moral judgment and any sense of responsibility. The individual, Milgram explains, abandons autonomy in favor of an "agentic" state in which he or she is simply an agent of authority.

The experiment has been repeated in very contrasting cultures, in other countries and on other continents, and in different periods of time.[4] The results are similar: obedience to authority is a universal act that does not go out of fashion.

Another experiment probing a different motive of obedience—conformity—was published in 1957 by Salomon Asch. The results are now known as the Asch effect.

Asch, who was Milgram's research director, invited groups of eight students to participate in a so-called vision test. All but one of the participants were actors. The focus of the experiment was to study how the non-actor would react to the actors' behavior.

The groups were presented with two images: one with a single line, and a second with three lines of different lengths. They had to choose which of the three lines was the same length as the line on the first card. The actors would choose first, always unanimously picking either the correct line or an incorrect line. The real participant always responded last.

At the beginning of the experiment, the actors gave the right answer, and the subjects of the experiment also gave the right answer in greater than 99 per cent of the cases. But when the actors unanimously gave the wrong answer, the real participant gave the correct response only 63 per cent of the time. And over multiple rounds of tests, only 25 per cent of the test subjects consistently stood up to majority opinion to insist on the right answer. Even in the absence of coercion, punishment, or rewards, people tended to disbelieve their own eyes and conform to the majority opinion, often attributing their errors to their own substandard vision.

The bottom line? When people with ill intentions rise to power or occupy high positions in a government, they can easily manipulate ordinary people into becoming ordinary killers by exploiting human frailties.

The genocide in Rwanda is one of the most striking examples.

9

BLOOD OF THE DEAD

"Pancrace: 'People aren't created by God in the same fashion. There are good-hearted killers who are willing to confession. There are cold-hearted killers who nourish their hatred in silence. These are particularly dangerous because faith does not soften their character. They never miss a religious service, throwing themselves into prayers and hymns with joy. They never fail to make the sign of the cross."

—Jean Hatzfeld, *Une saison de machettes*.

March 16—Parish Kabaya

We decide to re-enact the mass crime scene around the church and the parish. The victims and witnesses protection department organize the event at our request. Agnès welcomes us along with Jacques, a local representative of the department, and a police officer from the Rwanda Investigation Bureau (their FBI), who is helping with the re-enactment.

Eight original witnesses are present, including a new defendant. The search for witnesses is so vital to our work that we often rely on assistance from outsiders such as the Association for the Study of War Crimes (ASWC), an NGO specializing in tracking witnesses via Facebook and gathering and analyzing their testimony.

Captain Bertrand R., the head of OCLCH's African Division, and Stéphanie, a chief warrant officer, have joined us on site.

The parish church has been partially reconstructed with the aid of bricks manufactured locally in special kilns. It is adjacent to the genocide memorial. In front of the building is a large esplanade of packed clay. It welcomes those, young and old, who have come to observe. Everyone is still. It's difficult to know what is going on in their heads.

We pass through the iron gate of the parish, now surrounded by a red brick wall. It did not exist at the time of the massacre. Inside the enclosure, in addition to the church, are several buildings, including offices, housing for the community of priests, a garage, gardens, a chicken coop, a stable for goats, and huge water tanks. In the center is a sign that reads "Mission of the Sacred Heart of Jesus" with a faded blood-red heart topped by a cross.

It's an overwhelmingly peaceful and silent atmosphere. A man approaches. Rwandan, over six-feet tall, stout, about thirty-years old, simply dressed. He welcomes us with a big smile.

"Hello everyone. I'm Father Innocent. Welcome."

We ask him if we can borrow two offices to run the depositions. He proposes the priests' lounge. A few armchairs, a little table in the center, and a pot of bright yellow plastic flowers. A buffet runs along the entire length of one wall, with shelves displaying photos of European and African priests, clearly bygone, along with several nuns and an engraving: "Les Martyrs of Otranto. Roma 1924." In the corner, a three-foot statue of Christ watches us, one hand on the chest, the other extending to the sky.

Captain R. will hear the first victim. To ensure a clean record of testimony, interpreters have been carefully chosen for quality and probity. Witnesses, too, have been vetted for credibility. We lean on them to speak precisely and are constantly pressing for clarifications and watching out for those who are too eager to please and merely state things they think investigators want to hear. Precision is important because memories can fail over time; especially where trauma is involved, a witness's recollection can be influenced by collective memory.

Due to threats and intimidation, we sometimes request that a witness be permitted anonymity. On occasion security is necessary to give physical protection to witnesses and their families. This can be granted by the National Commission for Protection and Reintegration and carried out by SAIT (the Interministerial Technical Assistance Service).

Captain R. summons a woman seated on a bench in the corridor.

Upon hearing her name, Désirée stands up, struggling a bit, holding her back. She is one of the few who escaped the massacre and is still alive today. Quite tall, she is wearing a brown dress and glasses. The right arm of her eyewear crosses the beginning of a scar, the rest of which is artfully concealed by a wig. She has a thousand-yard stare.

As with each deposition, I take a seat at the back so as not to disturb those doing the work.

"Welcome, Madame Désirée Sebaka, I'm Stéphanie. This is Captain R. and that is Colonel Emeraux. We're here to listen to what you have to say regarding the facts of what took place on Kataya Hill on April 9, 1994."

Désirée sits silently.

"Let me introduce you to our interpreter, Matthieu. Here is a bottle of water to refresh you."

Désirée takes the bottle without saying a word.

Stéphanie is beginning carefully. Désirée, as a survivor, will have told her story before but not to a room full of foreigners.

After verifying Désirée's identity, Stéphanie opens with a few straight-forward questions and gradually allows Désirée the floor. Her voice is deep and she speaks slowly. It is obviously a trying moment for her.

"I am Tutsi like all my family and my parents. We have always lived in Kanama. I live alone in this village. I am fifty-five years old. I was born in 1964. My father was a librarian. I had three sisters. We were a beautiful family. My father was very loving. I was the youngest."

"My older sister died during the 1959 massacres. In spite of everything, my father always had faith in human beings. We were surrounded by Hutu and Tutsi friends. My father and mother died of illness in 1990. It is fortunate that they did not witness the disaster to come."

"I married Alphonse, a good man, a teacher like me. He was very intelligent and cultured. He was a good father. We had two children, Anne and Jean."

"I became a teacher because opportunities for educated Tutsi were either to become a sister, a priest, or a teacher. I worked in the school in Kanama."

"On April 6, 1994, when the death of the president was announced, and in the days that followed, there were rumors that we were going to be killed because of this. We didn't know what to think about it. The radio told us not to leave our homes. But we heard the mayor and the gendarmes say, 'Kill them all. Take their plots, their cows. You won't be punished.'"

"Alphonse went to see his former colleagues, those with whom we shared kebabs and Primus, the local beer, on weekends. But he found the door closed. The moderate Hutus were afraid. He asked our best friend, Jean, our son's godfather, for protection but he turned his back on him.

"On the morning of April 13, my husband came home, scared and sweaty, and told me we had to leave, and quickly. I refused. The children were small, seven and ten years old. I was also looking after my sister's two children, a boy and a girl the same age as mine. My sister had gone to Uganda for work."

"Alphonse took me by the arms, shook me, and ordered me to prepare. I decided to follow him. When we left the house, a crowd of Hutus was starting to form. They were screaming their heads off, wielding machetes and clubs. We decided to flee to the back of the village. They did not see us."

We ran through the corn fields for an hour. My husband told me that we'd go to the parish, like they'd done in the previous massacres. In 1959, that's what saved us, except for my sister, whom my father was forced to abandon. We met other Tutsi who were fleeing as well. Everyone was going to the hill of Kataya where there was a church and a parish. We thought we'd be protected by . . ."

Désirée did not finish her sentence.

"We ran together for several more hours, just until nightfall. The children were crying. We did everything we could to keep them quiet. We finally arrived at the parish. Two priests were there, a Rwandan and an Italian. My husband organized the defense of the site. He had a machete, as did others. Finally, a lot of us were there, at least 3,500. In the evening, the priests told us they were going to look for food. They never came back."

"In the morning, around 10 o'clock, we heard screaming from below. And chants of Hutu power: 'You don't drink the water of the power without having worked for them.' Then we saw them encircling the hill, they were unleashed. The men had organized a defense around the entire hill. The elderly, the women, and the children were inside the church. Then there was silence, no more shouting, nothing. That lasted five minutes. We were beginning to feel reassured when a whistling broke the silence. The first shell landed on the parish esplanade. Then, immediately after, others. A rain of shells. Perhaps a dozen. When I looked up, a shell had hit the church and a section of the wall collapsed on people."

Silence. Désirée goes on, eyes staring into space. Still the same deep voice.

"After that, we heard screams of terror. The Hutu were storming the hill, along with the army. Some had grenades, rifles. Others had machetes. My husband came back to me, in the church, to defend the children and me. He told me to run out the side door. He followed after. We went and hid behind the rectory, my husband and my children, Anne and Jean. I had left my nephews, Claude and Yvonne, in the church."

"That's when I saw the man in his 4×4 blasting music, honking the horn and riling the troops. He was in the military. A high-ranking officer. It was around noon. He shouted that the work needed to continue. He made the people inside the church come out and ordered them to sing a psalm in chorus for the salvation of their souls. The Tutsi walked out, calm and singing. Then the Interahamwe and the villagers rushed in and cut, slashed, beat, and killed everyone. Then some rushed to the back of the church for the women. They raped them, knocked them unconscious, impaled them with spikes before hacking them apart. I watched them from our hiding spot. They cut off their breasts, broke bottles and shoved them in their vaginas, cut out their intestines. The women were screaming. Then Anne and Jean started to cry out. About a dozen Interahamwe found us. Alphonse tried to defend us, but they hit him in the head."

Silence.

"They took huge machete swings at the children, cutting off their limbs, their heads. Me . . . I was knocked in the head, I screamed, and I lost consciousness."

Silence.

"When I awoke, I was in my husband's arms. He made a sign to keep quiet. He was marching with the other Tutsi, nude, who were carrying bodies. Some of the villagers were dragging bodies along the ground by their feet. Then the Interahamwe shouted to throw the bodies into a huge pit. My husband refused. He took a knife through the back and we fell in together."

Silence.

"It was a long fall. A lot of bodies were already in the pit. Some were still alive. My husband had broken my fall. He didn't die immediately. Another Tutsi, at the bottom of the pit, saw me and we clung to the edge of the pit as the bodies rained down. Each time, we had to climb on the bodies. And then, after a long while, it all stopped. No more sounds. Night fell. Blackness. Everything was silent except the groaning. The only thing we could see was the top of the pit and a few stars. We were standing on thousands of dead bodies. We were alive, but dead inside. My husband was in pain and I tried to keep him alive. He died in the morning. He'd lost too much blood."

"How long did you stay inside the pit?"

"Five days."

"How do you survive?"

"A little water fell down from time to time, because it was the rainy season."

Silence.

Désirée starts again in a low voice.

"And we drank the blood of the dead."

I swear I see Christ, at an angle across the room, widen his eyes. But no, he remained impassive.

We take a moment, letting all this sink in.

"But, how did you get out of the pit?"

"It was a Hutu family that came to save us. Three of them. A man threw down a rope. Those that were alive, about a dozen people, clung to the rope and he pulled us out.

Later, I learned that this Hutu family was killed because someone had denounced them.

"After making it out of the pit, I fainted from exhaustion. When I woke up, I didn't move. I thought I was dead, in heaven. But I felt pain. My head was splitting. I thought about my children and my husband. He was so good, you know. A very tender man, very sweet. He did everything he could

81

to protect us. I wanted to die, but the heavens decided otherwise. I waited until nightfall and then I ran."

Silence.

"I live alone now. It's how God wanted it."

Désirée adjusts her glasses.

"I wandered. I stayed hidden during the day, in the banana groves, in abandoned houses. I was thirsty, very thirsty, but I couldn't ask for water. I went towards Zaire. Along the way, I found other Tutsi who were running away, too. We helped each other. We were filthy, humiliated, weak. It was so hard to find food and water. But the hardest part was the fear. The fear of dying.

"I had wrapped a piece of cloth over my wound. It took a long time to heal. When I arrived in Zaire, French military doctors tended to it."

I looked at her scar, mostly hidden by the wig. I show Désirée several photos and ask if she recognizes the captain in charge of the attack. Désirée looks them over. She points at number six: Lone Warrior.

"That's him. Before everything, he would drive through the village, showing off in his 4×4. He'd flex his muscle. He was very cruel. He liked Tutsi women. You could see it in his eyes."

"Is there anything else you'd like to add to your testimony?"

"Yes. Why are you asking these questions, you're *muzungu*."[1]

"We're investigating this man."

"The French are?"

"Yes. Why? Is that surprising?"

"Yes."

Silence.

"I didn't think you'd come back here. Seeing that you and all the others chose not to intervene. This genocide, you could have stopped it from happening, right?"

Silence.

"Where are you working now?"

"I studied humanities, which, after all this, I'm now teaching to the inhumane people who made me lose everything. I've never understood why the Hutu hated us so much, telling themselves that we were thinner, taller.

Politicians are responsible for all this, just like in the rest of the world. And it will never stop."

Silence.

"I should go on living for Alphonse. He told me before dying: 'Don't die for me. Live for me.' I promised. We grew up practically on the same hillside. We knew each other since childhood and fell in love immediately. Right away, we decided to work in the same profession. Teaching. Raising souls was our vocation. His family all lived nearby. I was happy. When night falls, I turn around and I can see them. They are all there. I see Jean, Anne and Alphonse, and myself, playing, laughing, shouting. I see Alphonse hold me gently in his arms. Until sleep takes me away.

"But, very quickly, the dead come back and dance the death dance, cut up, into pieces, the women completely dismembered, disembowelled, raped, this captain driving over the bodies in his 4×4, blasting music, the Hutu shouting, laughing. Then, the day returns. Each step, each movement resounds in the void."

Silence.

"Then I return to the pit and I talk to Alphonse. Then I go to the church and I pray, every day. I'm no longer afraid to meet those who hurt us. I have been able to forgive, and to forgive myself for being alive. You know, forgiveness has two sides. It's the only way to overcome. And I sing. Singing makes me feel good. Prayer as well. I thought God had abandoned us, but I found him again and he accepted me with open arms."

Silence.

The victims are the real heroes, I think. A hymn to life.

"Thank you, Désirée. If you wouldn't mind, could you show us to the pit?"

Désirée raises herself up, again with noticeable pain, and walks out of the room in silence. A sort of wraith, a life on hold. We all look at each other.

"Follow me."

Désirée leads us towards the memorial. We ask for her to help us with photographs to make the facts visible. We also take footage of the ground with a laser rangefinder and a GPS beacon. We will come back later with a drone in order to get a better view of the terrain and to allow future jurors a precise view of the situation.

When we arrive at the memorial, a guard opens the door at the entrance. In the center of the enclosed space is a white canopy about four meters high. Désirée goes to the canopy, opens the door, and shows us the gaping open pit.

I lean over the guard rail and look down. The blackness swallows me. I don't know what to think at this point. It doesn't seem real, but it's there.

The guard pulls me out.

"The pit is fifty meters deep," he says. "We were looking for water. When we reached forty meters deep, we came across a stone that we blew up with dynamite. There are three thousand people at the bottom of this pit."

Around us are two enormous tombstones, twenty meters by five.

"And there?"

"Almost five thousand in total. All those who were killed nearby."

No one speaks a word. No one dares. Désirée prays.

It's the guard, in the end, who breaks the solemnity of the moment. Back at the parish, I thank Désirée for her valuable help and ask her to forgive us for having made her relive this scene. Her testimony is vital to establishing the facts of the case.

"Désirée, we might ask you to come to Paris to testify at Théogène Mukasago's trial. That is how our criminal procedure works. He will be tried in the Paris Assize Court and you will be summoned to testify."

Because France refuses extradition to Rwanda, we have no choice but to ask witnesses to travel. This brings the cost of a trial to around a million Euros. A price of justice.

"When?"

"That's difficult to say right now. It depends on how the trial plays out. Appeals. It takes time. In about five years, roughly."

"Hah! That's more than a few minutes . . . I hope I'm still alive."

Silence.

"I hope so too, Désirée. We'd really like to see you again. *Murakoze.*"[2]

Désirée leaves. Slowly, stooped, holding her back.

It's hard to comprehend how a human being can overcome such an ordeal. We can only listen, transcribe, act. That is our role. To take a picture of the situation as accurately as possible and to transmit it to the magistrates for the rest of the process.

We wave goodbye to Désirée one last time.

I call Brice. Leave a voicemail.

"Things are processing. The case against Papa Pépère is coming together. We'll fax you the transcripts and the details from Kigali."

Before I leave, I take a look around the church. It is vast and silent. Light pours out of the multi-colored stained-glass windows to illuminate its center. It has seen the worst. There are large images devoted to the Martyrs of Otranto, Roma 1924. A chapel is dedicated to them. But not a word for the Rwandans, brutally murdered. A guilty silence? On the walls of the church, the Calvary of Christ—all the stations of the cross. But no stations for the Tutsi.

I hear footsteps. Father Innocent approaches.

"So, Colonel, are we praying?"

"No, I am thinking. I have a question. Why speak of the martyrs of Otranto who are far away, and not of those who were martyred here?"

Father Innocent is silent. Then evasive.

"Ah, you know, I do what I'm told, that's how it is here. We are obedient."

It's the old totalitarian principle: what is not forbidden is obligatory.

I cut things short.

"Thank you for making your premises available."

A few minutes later, a downpour sweeps through the region. It breaks the serenity of the lake, doing violence to its mirror-like surface. But it seems to cleanse and refresh the atmosphere.

The evening is devoted to a good meal at the edge of the lake in the company of the team. A Congolese band performs, crazy and inebriated. We'll drink *urwagwa,* a banana wine, and *ikigaga amasaka,* sorghum beer. The lead singer has a rich deep voice, like Rag'n'Bone Man:

Some people got the real problems.
Some people out of luck.
Some people think I can solve them.
Lord heavens above.
I'm only human after all.

I'm only human after all.
Don't put the blame on me.
Don't put the blame on me.

The night that follows is complicated. An earthquake awakens me with a start. I don't know where I am. Everything is confused. Dreams, nightmares, cadavers, pits, black holes, Kiwu lake raging outside. Cold sweat.

I think it will pass. But it does not pass. I'm wide awake. Waiting for the rest of the world to wake up.

In the morning, I meet Vincent to head back across the country. I salute Captain Bertrand R. and his team, Élodie and Christophe. They will spend the rest of the week deposing new witnesses, either offenders or people who can corroborate facts pertaining to Captain Théogène Muskago's role in the Rwandan genocide.

As for me, I find it impossible to leave Rwanda without first making a stop at the Kigali Genocide Memorial.

10

THE MACHINE

"The Bahutu are generally small and stocky, and have large heads, jovial figures, lightly smashed noses, and enormous lips. They're unreserved, noisy, cheerful, and simple. The Mututsi of good lineage having nothing, apart from colour, in common with the blacks. These traits, during youth, are of great purity: straight aquiline foreheads, fine lips that open to bright teeth."

—Minister of the Colonies, Belgian Administration
Rwanda-Urundi Report, 1925.

March 18—Kigali Genocide Memorial

Voiceover: *"In July 2016, Netanyahu, during a visit to this memorial, declared, 'My people also know the pain of genocide. It is a unique bond, albeit one that neither of our people would wish to have.'"*

Dieudonné, the director of Victim and Witness Protection, walks beside me through the hallways of the memorial. Rwanda's history of genocide after genocide, each splattering a dark stain across the surface of the planet, unfolds.

"Everything begins at the turn of the nineteenth century with the arrival of colonization," he says. "The Germans arrive first. At the time, they discovered a society centered around a king, Mwawi Musinga, and three ethnic groups, the Tutsi, the Hutu, and the Twa, who are the Pygmies and less numerous. The wars that shook Rwanda were mostly the result of groups fighting over territory. At that time, the word 'race' did not exist in the vocabulary of Rwandans, nor in their hearts. It was the settlers, first the

Germans and then the Belgians, who, from 1916 onwards imported the concept of a superior Tutsi race, an idea according to which these 'white negroes' came from the Horn of Africa and were of superior stuff."

The Belgians gave this social cleavage a racial dimension that suited them because they relied on the Tutsi to control the country. In the 1950s, the decolonization process began. And when the Tutsi began to seek to emancipate themselves, the Belgians counterbalanced their movement by promoting the Hutus. In 1959, the Hutus used their majority to overthrow the monarchy. The racist and hateful virus had been lodged in their minds.

The first ethnic clashes broke out in 1959. Many Tutsi went into exile in neighboring countries, Burundi, Tanzania, Zaire, and Uganda. Although they never stop wanting to return to Rwanda. In 1962, the country became independent and in 1973, in July, Juvénal Habyarimana, a Hutu, took power and led the country with an iron fist. But the country was not doing well and in the 1980s it suffered a serious economic crisis. In 1990, there were an estimated 340,000 refugees in Burundi and Uganda. The Tutsi, especially those exiled in Uganda, decided to take up arms to return to their country. Thus, in October 1990, the Rwandan Patriotic Front [RPF] entered the country. But, at Habyarimana's request, it was blocked by the Belgian, French, and Zairean armies. The real race war had only just begun.

Tutsi living in Rwanda were designated as the enemy. But at the same time, Habyarimana faced political opposition within the country, which forced him to adopt a multi-party system. In 1992, negotiations opened in Arusha, Tanzania, between President Habyarimana and Paul Kagame's RPF at the urging of the international community, particularly France.

The resulting agreement was far from unanimous and created a rift between those who supported cohabitation and those that fervently oppose the RPF. President Habyarimana presented himself as a defender of the Hutu race and played a double game. He organized a civilian militia, particularly in the north, and trained it to handle weapons. The name of this militia, the Interahamwe, is now tragically notorious. It literally means "those who work together."

They formed brigades, recruiting increasing numbers of young people into death squads that terrorized the Tutsi. At the same time, the Hutu

Power movement, a radical faction of the Hutus, emerged. In 1992, the first massacres began, particularly in Bugesera, with military and police support. No one was convicted for these acts. A culture of impunity developed, setting the stage for the genocide in 1994. A trial run of sorts.

I'm looking at images of battered corpses on the walls. We continue down the hallway, entering a section dedicated to the rhetoric leading up to the genocide.

Dieudonné continues:

"Hutu propaganda was a crucial mechanism in the process. The authorities spread information claiming that the Tutsi were planning a genocide against the Hutu and that the people should be prepared. This is galvanized in 1993 after a Tutsi coup in neighboring Burundi. Hutu President Melchior Ndadayeso was assassinated by the Tutsi. This was a blessing for Hutu Power, whose slogan was 'kill to avoid being killed.' In Rwanda, Hutu moderates are sidelined. The Hutu Power message was broadcast through media, especially radio. Later, at the beginning of 1994, they broadcast lists of Tutsi and their whereabouts, notably on the infamous Radio Télévision Libre des Mille Collines (RTLM)."

"Newspapers and radio conditioned the masses for the worst. The designers of this well-oiled propaganda machine, the politicians, explained to people that the enemy was present, that it had infiltrated the walls built to protect them. It was living among them, right next door. They embellish this ideology with historical perspectives manipulated to produce the desired effect. These notions become embedded in the language itself. The Nazis said that the Jews were no longer to be considered as human beings. It was the same in Rwanda. The Tutsi were dehumanized. They became *Inyenzi*, meaning pest or cockroach, inciting disgust. They went so far as to say that it was necessary to 'rip out the roots' meaning kill the babies. The use of these simple agricultural metaphors conveyed to people exactly what was expected of them. *Umuganda*, a term for community work, came to mean go out and massacre the Tutsi. To 'clear' meant to go out and hack the Tutsi to pieces. And so on. This vocabulary was intended to normalize genocide and make it everyone's duty. In a largely illiterate country, this language, coming over the radio—for many, the only means of communication—was considered legitimate and authoritative. It had impact, like the word of God."

"The propoganda worked so well that President Habyarimana found he'd created a sort of Frankenstein with the Hutu Power movement. It began to turn against him. He received direct threats. One of his relatives, Colonel Bagosora, infiltrated the armed forces and political circles and organized the importation and distribution of mass quantities of machetes. On the order of 500,000 pieces. One can say that 1993 was the year of preparation. A critical turning point."

"The UN deployed a peacekeeping force, UNAMIR, commanded by General Romeo Dallaire, who quickly understood the problem and alerted the UN that a powder keg was ready to explode in Rwanda. The UN didn't take seriously the reports of impending catastrophe. Worse, according to some testimony, the UN forces were prohibited from doing their job and preventing what was being prepared."

I interrupt Dieudonné.

"I saw the same situation in Bosnia-Herzegovina. Remember Srebrenica: 'You shoot back but don't shoot first.'"

He continues.

"By April 1994, the mechanism was in place. On April 3, Radio Télévision Libre des Mille Collines broadcast an alarming message. 'Something is going to happen in the next few days, and it will continue for a few days more.'"

"And as if by design, on April 6, two SAM-16 missiles shot down President Habyarimana's plane just before it was about to touch down on its return trip from Tanzania. That same evening, Bagosora seized power and eliminated potential obstacles, Hutu moderates, including the Prime Minister as well as Belgian soldiers who were providing security. A puppet government was appointed, by which point Bagosora could count on the army, the administration, the Interahamwe, and RTLM to execute his sinister design."

"Barriers were raised throughout the country. ID checks were systematically imposed. The Belgian administration had chosen to include ethnicity on IDs. This facilitated the elimination of the Tutsi. Their bodies were thrown into ditches. All of this happened under the watchful eye of the international community, which, according to the great principle of non-interference, ended up doing nothing and evacuating its own people. Death was everywhere, by the thousands. In three months, a million."

Silence. A simple administrative decision to include ethnicity on ID cards facilitates thousands of deaths.

We continue slowly through the memorial. I see Dieudonné's face pop-up on one of the screens. He's crying in the video, explaining how he saw his parents murdered in Kigali.

I remain silent. Dieudonné is watching me. I better appreciate his role in the victims and witnesses program.

We are standing in front of photographs of the UN peacekeepers tearing off their blue berets.

"On April 21, the UN Security Council voted to extract 90 per cent of its UNAMIR forces. The number two in command, Colonel Marchal, bids farewell with a 'Good luck Let's get out of here and let these savages save themselves.' The French also abandoned the Tutsi. The Americans had backing the English-speaking RPF against the French-speaking Hutus, countering the Europeans. The RPF decided to invade Rwanda and met little resistance. The Hutu armies were focused on the genocide."

"In New York, the UN chooses its words carefully. It speaks of a humanitarian crisis. Civil war. Inter-ethnic massacres. The word genocide is used sparingly. Meanwhile, people are dying."

We stop in front of a photograph of François Mitterrand and Rwandan President Juvénal Habyarimana shaking hands. I look it over without speaking. I remember Marie-Christine, daughter of a liberal parliamentarian and a fervent socialist, who once confessed to me that she had cried in front of this photograph.

Dieudonné continues.

"France bet on the wrong horse, supported a racist regime, and trained and equipped its army. It could have simply stayed away, or supported the English-speaking RPF. It chose Habyarimana and his genocide. Moreover, when Paris requested in July 1994 that a humanitarian mission be launched from the East Congo, in Goma and Cyangugu, on the border of Lake Kivu, Rwandans largely perceive it as an effort to block the RPF. Paris used the mission to evacuate the genocidaires. Surprising, no, for the country of the rights of man? And what about Bisesero?"

I don't respond. That investigation is currently underway. Meanwhile, the shadow of France hangs over this memorial. As it does the memorial in Murambi in the south of the country near Butare.

In Murambi, the bodies have been laid out on wooden beds, preserved in lime as in Pompeii. The guide assigned to us there leveled serious allegations at France, although I was frankly not convinced that he could support them all.

As I returned to Kigali, I wondered why those bodies were not buried. A man named Charles, the only remaining Tutsi of his village, explained that the decision was made to prevent any revisionism in the future.[1]

A last room brings Dieudonné and I to a chronology of genocides throughout human history. I see again the images of Bosnia-Herzegovina, the Shoah, Armenia, Namibia, and the Herero.

We leave the building and walk along gravel paths, winding among rose beds and tombs. Silence and reflection are the orders of the day. Only birds presume the right to break the solemnity of the place. Clouds roll through the sunlight, casting shadows on the memorial.

Dieudonné continues.

"My parents, maybe, are here. Or there. Two hundred and fifty thousand people are buried in this memorial. The corpses were brought in from all over the capital, after they'd been discarded in the street or thrown into the river."

It's time to return.

11

FLIGHT

"In face of danger, the spineless flees, the coward hides, and the brave meets it head on."

—Louis-Philippe de Ségur *La Lâcheté* (1816)

April 8, 2019—Paris, OCLCH Headquarters

It is the twenty-fifth anniversary of the genocide. An opportunity for France to reconsider its role in the horror. The Élysée released a statement on April 6: "In the context of the twenty-fifth commemoration of the genocide against the Tutsi in Rwanda, the president of the republic today received survivors of the genocide and members of the Ibuka ['Remember'] association. He expressed his deep solidarity with them in this moment of mourning and reflection in memory of the victims of one of the worst atrocities of the 20th century. He paid tribute to the strength of their testimony and their efforts to pass on the memory of the Tutsi genocide to younger generations."

Consistent with the commitments he made during President Kagame's May 24, 2018, visit to Paris, President Macron announced that a historical commission has been established to research all National Archive materials pertaining to Rwanda between the years 1990 and 1994. Eight historians and analysts under the direction of Professor Vincent Duclert will analyze France's involvement in Rwanda, contribute to a better understanding of the Tutsi genocide, and create materials for teaching about the genocide in France. The commission is scheduled to submit its final report in two years.

To be continued. The fact is that light is needed on some shady areas and on the roles of individual actors. Painful or not. It's time to put an end to decades of doubt and suspicion.

I turn off the "Geopolitics" podcast on *Radio France* and climb the four floors of Bastion XIV. Our offices are located at the top of this austere building. It is built from remnants of the fortification known as *l'encientei de Thiers,* dating from between 1841 and 1844. The stairwell is decrepit.

A coordination meeting has been scheduled for Théogène Mukasago's arrest. Throughout the corridors of the top floor are large posters of the perpetrators and victims of barbarity, past and present. Men armed with machetes and barbed wire, women lying on their children, bruised faces— images that remind us of the purpose of what we do.

Like every morning, the scent of coffee permeates the investigators' offices. It is an atmosphere common to police forces. Personnel from Lyon's surveillance group are present, along with investigators from Chambéry. The strong turnout reflects the importance attached to the arrest of this particular genocidaire. It's more than enough to convince them to put their usual narcotics work on hold. As our case load has grown to more than a hundred files, spread out over the entire country, I've proposed to our leadership that we need crimes-against-humanity contact in each of the investigative sections in France.

"Good morning, everyone. Thank you for all your help. Our plan is to proceed with the apprehension of Father Jean Fourier, whose real name is Théogène Mukasago, next Tuesday at 6 a.m. He'll be kept under tight surveillance for the next week. I remind you that, in this context, the special investigative measures pertaining to cases of crimes against humanity may be employed.[1] In particular, an initial custody period of up to ninety-six hours. With judicial authorization, we can search premises apart from the suspect's residence and outside the usual hours of 6 a.m. to 9 p.m. We are permitted to intercept electronic communications and access stored electronic communications by means of a digital identifier, and we can use the IMSI-Catcher device if necessary."[2]

The head of the surveillance group briefs us on recent observations.

"According to the GPS beacon, he's leading a rather quiet life, no movements of note. The roads he's using are not too busy so we are considering using other devices just to make sure he doesn't get off the hook. We have kept an eye on Marie Comparie's home in Annemasse and we are considering requesting a cross-border observation from the Swiss authorities for Catherine Boulaz, the sales representative of the Francoport company. Our Swiss colleagues seem very interested in the information gathered by the OCLCH on this company. You should receive a phone call from their investigators."

"Excellent," I respond. "We need to search Marie Comparie's house. I'll make a call over to the *Institut de recherche criminelle* to mobilize their radar equipment so we can scan for hidden compartments. We'll also be bringing in the dogs to sniff for guns and cash. What have we got from the wiretap on her phone?"

Christophe answers:

"A bit turbulent. Her behavior has changed. She must know something. She's become very aggressive with Papa Pépère. Seems like she's driving him crazy over the phone. Otherwise, nothing out of the ordinary. We've been monitoring her contacts, seems like she works in the fashion business. We imported her cellphone billing activity. Nothing unusual there either. Papa Pépère, though, is keeping up with a lot of contacts in Switzerland."

Élodie takes over.

"We contacted Open Source Intelligence concerning both of them. The strategy division is running with it. Nothing on Mukasago, which is normal given his age. However, Marie Comparie is all over Instagram, Facebook, Twitter. Mostly selfies and showing off her new clothes. She is an only child, daughter of a Congolese father. We did some digging on him: he wrote several articles opposing the regime in Kinshasa. He was a professor of law."

"Well, Marie and her current attitude are lucky for us. What about money?

"A lot of Western Union activity. He's been wiring money to the Democratic Republic of Congo. The individual amounts are large enough, around €4,000. It adds up. His bank accounts seem normal, but it's a good bet that he's got some funds stashed in Switzerland. Other than that, we found a lot of round trips to Dubai, some paid by credit card.

"We sent a separate request through Europol to our Swiss colleagues, in the context of Core International Crimes, and are expecting a response via Siena."[3]

I take the floor. "If trouble starts, we have to make sure our priest is blocked before he can cross over to Switzerland. Is he registered with the RPF?"[4]

"Yes, ever since we returned from our trip to from Rwanda."

"Anything else we should know? Everyone's mission files will be handed out next Monday at the final meeting before we proceed. Chambéry's investigators will take the lead in interviewing the other priests at the parish. In the meantime, everyone stay on the WhatsApp feed and be ready to react if the situation changes. See you in Chambéry next week."

The Swiss authorities approve our cross-border surveillance request approved by the Swiss authorities, opening the door to a look at Francoport and another company, Quai Wilson, in Geneva.

April 15—Paris, OCLCH Headquarters

Around 9:30 am, Élodie lands in my office, hair disheveled, visibly worried.

"Boss, the shit has hit the fan. Mukasago is spooked. He just used a different phone line to contact Marie to verify a meeting at her place. Looks like he's ditched his original cell phone. There's more. This also happens to be the day that the surveillance group dropped him to focus on the Swiss commercial angle."

"How did he get tipped off? Did surveillance lose him?"

"No, they're still in play."

"OK, what does the beacon say?"

"He's on the highway headed for Annemasse. Right now, he's in the mountains near Cruseilles."

"OK, I'll call the highway patrol. They might have people in the area. They can at least set up a speed-trap to intercept him."

On a hunch, I send a WhatsApp to Bob: "Hey Bob, did your insider make contact with our target?"

Two minutes later, my colleague from the Haute-Savoie highway patrol confirms they're set up a speed-trap on our target's route.

I decide to head toward Chambéry to be closer to the action. Thirty minutes later, we're speeding southward down the A6. Three cars, three teams:

Élodie and Christophe; Captain Bertrand B and Stéphanie; Daniel, from the strategy division, and myself. My deputy, Lieutenant Colonel Maxime L. C., stays behind to manage the other cases and communicate with the magistrates. Captain Jean V. and his Chambéry investigators are hurrying up highway A41 toward the Swiss border.

No word yet from our colleagues in highway patrol. Maximum tension in the cars. Then, finally, a phone call.

"Colonel, everything's taken care of. We picked him up at Saint-Julien-en-Genevoix doing 120 mph. No pretext necessary. We gave him a high-speed ticket, took his license, and impounded the vehicle. The investigators will be here in fifteen minutes."

Relief fills our car. I send a WhatsApp message to everyone: "Target intercepted."

A few minutes later, we learn through WhatsApp that the investigators are on the scene. The target has been notified of his rights and placed in custody. He can't believe what's happening.

We arrange to meet at Mukasago's apartment in Saint-Jorioz for our authorized search, putting the cash-and-guns dog to work.

Two hours later, around 1:00 p.m., we meet up at Mukasago's apartment. It is roughly 900-square-feet, relatively new, well maintained, white walls, African masks, plain IKEA furniture, one bedroom, an open kitchen. Not a single piece of clothing in the closets. The German Shepherd scours the apartment under the watchful eye of his master. He is noticeably disappointed not to find anything.

I get my first look at Théogène Muskago. He is tall, square shoulders, graying hair, almost no wrinkles. His face is a little round, as is his waist. He is wearing clerical clothing and is very attentive to the activity around him.

A snake, this Lone Warrior.

He seems quite sure of himself but isn't saying a word. We make eye contact when one of the investigators comes out to greet me by rank. He stares and me. I hold his gaze and look through him.

"You've made a mistake," he says.

"Is that so?"

"I don't know who you're looking for. Arresting me for crimes against humanity? I'm a Tutsi. That's crazy!"

"You're Tutsi?"

"Yes, check my ID. French now, though now, by naturalization," he says proudly.

"Well, we'll see about that when we're finished looking around. By the way, what do they call you? Father? Captain? Sir?"

"You can call me 'My Father', my son," he says, smiling.

"And you can call me 'My Colonel.'"

Captain V. informs me that the search is complete. Nothing much to note because the apartment is empty. We head toward Chambéry to process Mukasago into custody.

On the way, I receive a WhatsApp from Bob: "The insider confirmed that he put pressure on the target in order to obtain payment. He told the target that French authorities had been alerted to the situation. Sorry."

"Not a very smart insider."

"What now?"

"It would be nice if he could just keep a low profile for the moment."

"I'll tell him. Did he compromise your work?"

"No, not as yet. The target is not going anywhere now."

"OK."

12

LORD ABOVE

"You have the devil for a father, and you want to carry out your father's desires. He was a murderer from the beginning, and he did not stand for truth because he has no truth in him."

—John, VIII

Same day, April 15—Chambéry Headquarters

The office I walk into obviously belongs to investigators who love film. Each wall is decorated with posters of great crime films. Alain Delon in *Borsalino*, Jean Reno in *Léon*, *Les Ripoux*, *Pulp Fiction*. All these interspersed with children's drawings and postcards of white sandy beaches and turquoise seas, worlds far away from the daily routine of a gendarme or police officer.

Élodie and Christophe are in charge of collecting Mukasago's statement. They'll probe for an understanding of what went through his mind before, during, and after the events in question while paying close attention to behaviors, attitudes, and mannerisms that might otherwise pass unnoticed. The idea is to engage empathetically with the target to construct a personal connection and encourage him to speak openly. Above all, avoid confrontation.

For my part, I take a corner and listen. They run the interview. I only intervene if I have something useful.

Mukasago enters the room with his lawyer, Frédéric Clounier, after the thirty-minute meeting time guaranteed by law between lawyer and client. Of course, he's been advised to remain silent but Mukasago has apparently decided otherwise.

That's good. Élodie and Christophe use the target's assumed name.

"Monsieur Fournier, we're here to hear your version of the facts pertaining to certain charges being considered, namely concerning crimes against humanity and genocide committed in Rwanda between April 6, 1994, and June 30, 1994."

"My lawyer has advised me not to answer any questions and to remain silent for my own protection. But this is so ridiculous. I have absolutely nothing to reproach myself for. I told you already, I'm a Tutsi, like my entire family. I escaped death myself during the war. I was the only survivor. My entire family was decimated by the Hutu in Ruhengeri."

Élodie takes notes.

"Very well, could you please elaborate on the circumstances surrounding those events? And let me remind you, your testimony is being recorded on video. To start off, could you tell us about your childhood, the region you grew up in, and your family?"

"My name is Justin Malbonaga. I was born on December 20, 1954 in Nyakinama, a village located right next to Ruhengeri in the northeast of Rwanda. I'm sixty-five-years old. I'm the first-born of a family of five children. My father was a farmer, and my mother raised us. I had three sisters and a brother. My mother had given birth to a child every year. I lived in our family's house and attended grammar school in Ruhengeri, until the European priests arrived and created a religious school specializing in agriculture. That's where my vocation came from, if I may say so. For the church, I mean, not agriculture. So I worked in the school as a supervisor for at least ten years. I became the treasurer after that, but I had always wanted to become a priest. That's why I never married. I was supposed to be in the seminary when the killings started."

"OK. Tell us about what happened in April 1994."

"By April 7, we knew that something serious had happened with the attack. In Ruhengeri, in the days that followed, the Interahamwe had raised barriers and organized controls under orders from the political authorities. We stayed at home and didn't go out. Those were the orders. But I decided to visit the school anyways to discuss matters with the white priests. I stayed with them an entire day analyzing the situation. When I returned to see my parents and reassure them, our house was burning. My parents had been killed, they were laid out near the front door. That was April 11, 1994. I fled across the banana groves to meet a Hutu friend who hid me in his car. In the night, he drove several miles to drop me off at the Zaire border. I crossed over early in the morning. I was saved. Later, I learned that my whole family had been massacred, my brother, my sisters, and their children, including those that were married to Hutus. It was horrible."

Silence.

"What was the name of the man that helped you?"

"I only remember his first name. Théodore."

"But he was your friend?"

"Yes. Well, in a manner of speaking. He worked at the school, and was a recent hire."

"And you aren't able to recall his last name?"

"No, he was hired just before the war. But I remember he came from Butare."

"He owned a car though?"

"It belonged to the school."

"Afterward, in Zaire, what did you do?"

"I decided to do everything I could to make it to France. That had always been my dream. One of the priests at the school was French, but unfortunately he was killed during the war. He had promised to take care of the formalities for me to live here. He had a brother in the military. That's who ended up taking care of everything for me. I can never thank him enough . . ."

I noticed that he had three times choses to use the word war instead of genocide. Something more characteristic of the Hutu. I decide to point this out. "Well, that's unusual!"

Mukasago looks at me.

"What?"

"You prefer the term war instead of genocide."

"Well, I can certainly say genocide, if you like, but basically it was a war. The Hutu against the Tutsi."

Élodie continues.

"Can you give us the names of these two French brothers?"

"Father Jean, he was the white priest. And his brother went by a code name because he was in the special forces. We called him Nick."

"Do you know where Father Jean died?"

"No. I received word of his death, but I wouldn't be able to tell you when it happened, nor who told me."

"And the brother in the special forces, do you know what unit he was in?"

"I told you, the French special forces stationed in Zaire, in Goma."

Mukasago has obviously done a lot of work on this story.

"We'll have to verify all this, of course," Christophe says.

"Please. That's the point. Proving my innocence."

His lawyer gives a sigh of approbation.

"Very well, please continue."

"I arrived here in May 1996, on a commercial airline through Paris, then Toulouse, and finally stopped in Ariège. That's in Ax-les-Thermes. I worked odd jobs. As a Tutsi, a survivor of the genocide, people were very welcoming, and I put in an application for asylum and was accepted. Then, one day, grace shined upon me. I was in Lourdes at the time. So I decided to become a priest in order to bring my life into line with my spirituality."

Struck by grace? Like hell. I'm sure the Lourdes thing is a fiction.

"So, in 2001, I attended the magnificent seminary in Orléans. Afterward, I left to pursue my ministry in a parish in Western France, in Cloyes, near Châteaudun. That was 2007. Finally, in 2016, I decided to join the Abbey of Tamié. And here I am in front of you, having to explain myself."

Elodie glances at her watch.

"OK, it's getting a bit late, lets take a break. Counselor, we're pausing the interrogation and we'll pick things up tomorrow. Your client will get something to eat and he can rest in our cells downstairs."

My phone vibrates. Captain R. let's me know that Marie Comparie has arrived in our building. I leave the two investigators to join them. Marie's testimony is crucial.

I head toward the door. "Sleep on it, Father . . . See you tomorrow."

He gives me a cold look.

Five minutes later, I'm in an office full of female investigators. These are mountain women. There's a poster showing the high mountain police platoon in Mont-Blanc, the Aiguille du Midi peak, a characteristic blue helicopter winching a rescue worker. It brings back good memories of a past life.

In front of a desk sits a mixed-race woman. I recognize her from the photographs. Marie Comparie. Navy blue coat, jeans, high boots. She removes her hat and gloves and folds her hands on the table. She doesn't look forty-five. Right away, she fixes her green eyes on me, attempting to get a read.

After the usual formalities, Captain R. begins the interrogation.

"Would you explain to us how you met Father Fournier?"

"We met each other at a family reunion. My father, who's Congolese, invited him to our house in Annemasse about two years ago. He was attractive and I fell for him pretty quickly. But wouldn't you know it, a priest, unavailable. But I quickly learned that he was not insensitive to my presence."

She pauses, then continues.

"We saw each other soon after that, and that's when our relationship started. Everything went well, even though we had to avoid being seen together. Then, one day, I discovered that he was hiding things, certain activities, outside of the church, of course."

"OK, what activities?"

"He was using my father, and his relations to the RDC, to political ends."

"What does your father do?"

"He's a law professor. But ever since he exiled himself to France, he's no longer been involved in politics. He doesn't get mixed up in anything anymore. He's a pacifist."

"How was he used then?"

"Father Fournier, it turns out, is financing a political group stationed in the East Congo, near Lake Kivu. The FDLR. He used my father's local political networks. They're getting rich in the process. He owns them. He has future political ambitions, should the FDLR be victorious. Right now, he launders the money."

"How do you know all this?"

Pause.

"I spied on him."

"Why?"

"He cheated on me."

And there's our witness' motivation.

"With who?"

"A saleswoman, a blond woman from Geneva."

"Are you sure about all this?"

Marie looks through her pockets, pulls out a USB drive and hands it to me.

"Everything's there. I placed a hidden camera a friend had given me inside his house. I hid it in one of the African masks. I took out the sex scenes, assuming that you won't have need of those for your investigations . . . The rest of it is his conversations. I was also able to get photos of some of the WhatsApp messages between him and his followers. I stole the password off his telephone. I'm giving you that, and the USB, because I don't want my father to pay for the ambitions of this individual."

"When were these photos taken? And the screenshots?"

"The first, about a month ago. The others, last week."

"Has he talked to you about his past?"

"Yes, he told me that he is Tutsi and a victim of the genocide, along with the rest of his family, and that he was the only survivor. But I'm not an idiot. When I saw that he was doing business with the FDLR, I knew something was up. You can't be Tutsi and support the FDLR."

"Do you have any other information for us?"

"No, I've given you everything. But I am at your disposal."

Captain R. is wrapping up the interview. I interrupt.

"You mentioned his house?"

"Yes. He bought a house. That's where we would meet."

"And where is this love nest?"

"In Cons."

I wonder why we haven't found it already with the GPS beacon on his car.

"What car did you take to get there?"

"He never wanted to drive his car to Cons. I would rent him one, or borrow one from a friend, so there weren't any issues."

"Thank you for the information you've provided, it will be very useful."

Bertrand takes Marie home. I join the investigators at the coordination meeting to bring everyone up to speed.

Chambéry's investigators interviewed three monks at the monastery, along with the father superior. Nothing of interest. The priests were shocked to learn of the charges against their Father Fournier and the double life he's been leading. Captain R. gives the team a rundown of Marie's testimony and puts some of the videos and screenshots on the projector. Élodie returns from the interrogation with Papa Pépère who is sticking to his story. But we still have time with which to seek his confession.

"Alright everyone, goodnight! We'll pick up tomorrow. Let's try putting two or three pieces of evidence under his nose to see if he can move him off his story."

13

CUSTODY: THE LAST ROUND

"You have to love the truth, find joy in it, spread it, whatever the cost."
—Paul Brulat, *Le Reporteur* (1898)

April 16, 8:30 a.m.—Chambéry Headquarters

The Chambéry investigators are out taking statements from Marie's father.

We focus on the next round of interrogation. An extension of the custody hold has been authorized. Brice spoke by video to Father Fournier. The lawyer, Maître Clounier, arrives a few minutes late, out of breath.

Élodie and Christophe restart the interrogation with the same setup as before, except this time Élodie positions herself physically closer to Father Fournier, seeing as he's not insensitive to women. She offers him a coffee, which he gladly accepts.

"Doesn't compare to the coffee in Rwanda," she says, "especially Butare, but it's not bad."

"Yes, Butare produces excellent coffee."

"Don't you miss it?"

"What?"

"Rwanda?"

"Yes, of course. But my life is here in France now. This is my country. And I have prayer, the parish, meditation."

Still sticking to his story.

Élodie, in her customary style, goes for broke.

"Father, what does the Bible tell us about lying?"

"There's a lot of text written on the subject."

"I came across one passage, John 8:44. 'You have the devil for a father and you want to carry out your father's desires. He was a murderer from the beginning, and he did not stand for truth because he has no truth in him.'"

Well played, Élodie.

"Yes, quite right. I love the Gospel of Saint John. It's my favorite, especially Revelation."

"Does that mean that you have a devil as your father?"

Maitre Clounier takes offense. But he has no right to intervene. I learn later that he e-mailed Brice directly during the hearing to complain about the behavior of the investigators.

Fournier, too, takes offense.

"Why do you ask that? Especially of a man of God," he says indignantly.

"Because, Father, we have good reason to believe that you are lying to us and that you are not Justin Malbonaga. In reality, you are Captain Théogène Mukasago, commander of the Gisenyi company at the time of the genocide, that is to say from April 6, 1994 to June 30, 1994."

"Oh, well, my daughter, you'll have to prove it."

Elodie smiles. She stands up, walks behind Fournier, puts her hand on his shoulder.

"Consider it done."

Fournier is shaken but maintains his dignity.

I break the silence.

"I suggest that we go for a little walk, just to get some fresh air."

Mukasago gets in the back of my Volkswagen with Captain R. and Élodie on either side of him.

He doesn't say a word. He's probably wondering where we're headed.

The red and white gate lifts up and we exit the compound.

"You're not curious as to where we're going?"

"I imagine the monastery. To shame me."

Silence.

Mountainous countryside passes under the spring sun. The summit of Croix du Nivollet where I used to hang out in my former life towers over us.

We pass through Albertville, then Ugine, and at the exit to Marlens I glance in the rear-view mirror. Mukasago stirs in his seat. I think he understands that we know.

Turning off toward Cons, we find the chalet, built in the local style around the turn of the century, tastefully renovated, nestled among the trees. The sun is doing its work. The fruit trees are in bloom. The air is filled with fragrance and birds fluttering off in all directions.

Two vehicles are already parked at the site. The dog handler with his German Shepherd, and our colleague from the IRCGN (*Institut de recherche criminelle de la gendarmerie nationale*) whom I've invited to make use of his radar equipment. It can detect hiding places in the ground and the walls.

I ask: "Are you familiar with this house?"

"Yes."

"Do you have the keys?"

"No."

"Not a problem. We've got it covered."

We walk up the steps to the front door. A locksmith gets busy. Suddenly, the door swings open to a large room in the Savoyard style. Toward the right, I open a door leading in the basement and work our way up. The German Shepherd rushes down.

The basement room is large with exposed stones and a dirt floor. The IRCGN technician deploys the radar. He watches a screen while his assistant uses a sort of robot on wheels to scan the floor.

Soon everyone is standing in front of the screen, watching the machine at work.

Five minutes later, the technician raises his hand. A dark streaked area has appeared on the screen.

"Very likely something's there."

He points to a spot in the corner.

The German Shepherd is brought over. It almost instantly darts to the designated area and starts clawing away at the dirt floor.

Mukasago is watching this unfold.

After a few seconds, the dog is scratching on a wooden plank, roughly one square foot with a ring handle. Captain R. walks over, pulls the ring and discovers a large cavity underneath containing a bag. The Shepherd barks its satisfaction. The captain opens the bag and pulls out bundles of currency. The dog gets a treat. The investigators, too, are pleased.

I watch Mukasago. He is visibly less at ease. He's lost some of his superiority, but is already working up a defense, I am sure.

"Well, if there's one hiding spot, there may be another. Can you have a look at the walls?"

"Yes, no problem."

"Do you have anything to say about this discovery, Mr. Théogène Mukasago?"

"I'm Justin Malbonaga, not Théogène Mukasago. And who is this Mukasago. I have nothing to do with that bag. I don't understand what it's doing here. Nor myself, for that matter."

"This is your chalet though?"

"Yes. I purchased it not too long ago with an inheritance from Rwanda. I was going to end my apartment lease in Saint Jorioz and settle permanently here. You'll have to ask the former owners. They might know where all this money came from."

"We'll be sure to do that."

But if your DNA is on the sack or the bills, you're finished, my friend.

As our IRCGN colleagues continue along the east wall, one of them suddenly waves me over. Another anomaly. A dark zone on the screen indicating a cavity. One of the investigators picks up a hammer and chisel and starts dislodging some of the stones. A few minutes later, he reaches a metal box. Inside are a couple of Glocks and about fifty rounds of ammunition.

"Do you know how the handguns got here?"

"No. I suppose they belong to the former owners."

"OK. We'll take note of that."

Good pickings, as they say. Money and weapons. We continue the search upstairs, finding nothing except a small video camera hidden behind the grimacing features of an African mask. It has a direct view of the sofa, obviously intentional.

The IRCGN officers seal the money and weapons into evidence. The labs will check for DNA and have promised I'll see the results before our custody period expires.

Chambéry Headquarters

An hour later, we meet the lawyer again. Our custody of the target is now on firmer ground.

Élodie resumes the interrogation:

"Do you know a person by the name of Marie Comparie?"

"Can you repeat the name?"

"Marie Comparie."

"Is she a member of the parish?"

Mukasago pretends to think for a moment before answering.

"Yes, she's the daughter of a dear friend, a brilliant professor emeritus and law professor. Professor Marcel Comparie. He's originally from the DRC and now lives in Annemasse. He was an opponent of Joseph Kabila. But since then, he's left politics."

"Is that all?"

"Yes."

"Marie Comparie gave us her statement yesterday evening. She told us about your liaisons."

A gut punch.

Silence. Mukasago lowers his head. His counsel as well.

"Do you have anything to tell us about your relationship?"

Silence.

"Nothing special, why?"

"Nothing special at all?"

"No, she would visit me from time to time to speak about God."

"Was there any hands-on work?"

"What do you mean hands-on work? On the catechism? No, not particularly."

"Well, we've got a sense of humor but you're pushing it. We just told you that she confessed to the liaisons."

"Nothing happened. She tried to seduce me, and yes, I can't deny it that the woman made my head spin. It was the devil tempting me, but I never succumbed."

"Never?"

110

"Never! That's why she holds such a grudge against me. Which is the reason why, as you've seen, I was preparing to leave for Switzerland to escape this vileness. I was going to tell her to stop harassing me."

"So why did you bring her to your house in Cons, when your apartment in Saint Jorioz would have been perfectly acceptable?"

"I didn't want people to get the wrong idea!"

"Yes, we know. Incidentally, what's become of your cell phone?"

Silence and a pensive look.

"I misplaced it."

"Oh. Would it please you to know we've located it?"

Pause.

"Yes, of course."

"Then I should also tell you that we've also recovered the messages it contained."

Another heavy blow lands.

He tightens up. Almost ready to spill.

Mukasago looks at his lawyer who huffs and puffs and tells him to shut up.

"So?"

"I have nothing to tell you."

"Very well. Would you like to take a break? Coffee?"

"Yes. Thank you."

Christophe leaves to find coffee.

I step in, place my hand on his elbow and look him directly in the eyes. Without blinking:

"I think it's time, Théogène."

"Time for what?"

I notice he did not react to my using his real name.

"To confess everything and ask for forgiveness. We have a lot more information. If you keep this up, you'll only digging yourself deeper."

"You're bluffing!"

"We don't bluff. We know you were a captain in the military. We have many testimonies about you. We have just returned from Rwanda. We went to the parish of Kabaya where we heard from victims and witnesses, and even some of your subordinates. . . . How do you expect to live the rest of your life with something like that on your conscience? I don't doubt the depth of your conversion or your faith, that's not my role. But if there's a time for you to confess your faults, this is it."

Mukasago lowers his eyes. Reflects. A long silence. The trap has closed.

His counsel clears his throat to get his client's attention and, above all, to prevent him from speaking. But it's too late. His client lets loose.

"You think that it was easy?"

Christophe returns with his coffee. Mukasago quiets down, takes a long first sip.

"What's not that easy?"

"To refuse to take part in the war!"

"The war?"

"Yes. It was a war. It was the Tutsi or us, that simple. They were there, everywhere. They had to be eliminated. The government sent down orders. I followed orders, that's all. You would have done the same."

"So, you're not Justin Malbonaga?"

"No."

Silence. Mukasago continues.

"Sometime around April 7, Prefect Misuhano called me in and ordered me to do the work, to organize the meetings with the Interahamwe, to raise the barriers in the communities where my company was stationed, and to kill all the Tutsi. So I did what I'd been ordered to do. Nothing more, nothing less."

"You were a captain in the military, then?"

"Yes."

"We're not here to judge you. Our mission is to try to understand what happened on April 13 on the hill and in the parish of Kabaya, where approximately three thousand five hundred people died."

His lawyer's eyes widen at the number of victims.

"Before the parish episode, seven Tutsi and Burgomaster Didace Kayegi had also been murdered."

"I've told you what I have to say. Orders are orders. You know that good and well, Colonel."

I hold back, not wanting to get into a debate.

"Do you admit that you are Captain Théogène Mukasago, commander of the Gisenyi company?"

Pause. "Yes."

"Were you present at the parish of Kabaya on April 13, 1994? Were you in charge of that operation?"

"Yes, I was there. But I was not the leader. It was anarchy. The devil was in charge."

"The devil?"

"Yes, he took control of Rwanda. The Hutu massacred the Tutsi and the Tutsi massacred the Hutu in return. And we took our burden of defeat with us to Zaire. We became cursed."

"Well, while we're on the subject of Zaire, I have some more bad news. L'Agence France-Presse just announced this morning that Ignace Murwanashyaka has died. Code name Mihigo. Does that mean anything to you?"

Théogène fixes his eyes on me, wondering if I'm bluffing or not, visibly affected. I show him the article on my phone. His world seems to be collapsing on itself.

"You seem touched by this news. The leader of the FDLR in Europe, dead . . . Who will be his successor, do you think? What are your relations with the FDLR?"

"I'm moved because the death of any man affects me personally."

It does? News to us.

"I don't have any contact with the FDLR."

"How about we take a look at the video."

Élodie shows a clip from Marie's hidden camera. His counsel protests, but it's no use. Evidence of this sort is fine in France. Recordings, collected by civilians and turned over to the police, are perfectly admissible.

Mukasago doesn't bat an eye. We watch him in the middle of a long conversation with the woman from Francoport, among other things.

Élodie continues.

"Let's return to the facts surrounding April 13, 1994."

"I told you. I was obeying orders."

"OK, what were the orders?"

"To kill everyone, eliminate the enemy. That was it."

My cell vibrates. The director of the IRCGN sends me a text to confirm that Mukasago's DNA is present on the guns and the bag of money. That clinches it.

I propose a break and improvise a coordination meeting with all the investigators. At the same moment, Brice calls for an update. Élodie, who's directing the investigation, brings him up to speed. Brice thanks her and schedules another meeting over the phone to arrange Mukasago's transfer and deferment.

Élodie gets back to work.

"Looking at your recent activity with the FDLR, it seems that you've done much more than obey orders. The FDLR has a very publicly known objective. They're set on reclaiming power in Rwanda. It was founded by Hutu genocidaires. Do you have anything to say about that?"

"No. I have nothing more to tell you."

"In that case, you'll explain yourself in front of the judge. Oh, and on that point, there's some bad news. Your DNA was found on the bag of money and on the two Glocks. Do you have anything to say regarding these findings?"

"Nothing. I have nothing more to add."

His counsel gives a sigh of relief.

I step in.

"In any case, this is all very good Captain."

"What?"

"Letting it out. Getting the weight off your chest."

"Will I be extradited to Rwanda?"

"No. France doesn't extradite Rwandans. You will be judged here."

"Really?"

"But don't worry, you will be given the opportunity to meet some of your victims. They'll be flown in from Rwanda to testify."

Mukasago lowers his head. He remains still several moments, staring into a void, silent. I hear what seem to be muffled sobs. But no tears.

"It's not the justice of men that I fear."

Silence.

"I wouldn't know much about that. You're the expert. Although I'd prefer not to be in your shoes."

I think about Désirée, so far away yet close to justice at last. Will it be enough for her to move on in her life?

It crosses my mind that the Lone Warrior will atone alone, like the humanimal he is. I remind myself not to judge.

I take a call from the Chambéry investigators. They spoke to Marie's father. No new information. He confirmed his daughter's statements and his relationship with Théogène Mukasago. He says he is ignorant of her activity with the FDLR.

We drive back to Paris in a relaxing silence. I watch the scenery go by and listen to a podcast.

Mukasago. Done.

The French media is already reporting his arrest.

I get a WhatsApp from Bob: "*Merci.*"

A few hours later, a new client is delivered to the majestic glass palace of the *Tribunal de Paris* as authorized by the universal jurisdiction under which OCLCH investigates acts committed on foreign soil by individuals now in France.

Mukasago meets with the public prosecutor and then the investigating judge, Margorie B., who will take charge of the ongoing investigation, and finally to the judge who will decide the terms of his custody.

Swiss authorities accept our rogatory request to interview Catherine Boulaz, the saleswoman from Francoport, as well as its director, Étienne Hedin, whose company in Rwanda is quickly liquidated. Both confirm the facts of the case.

Later, we will learn that Father Fournier's sudden departure from his parish in Orléans followed inappropriate behavior with one of his parishioners, who will also confirm the facts of the case in a deposition. The circle is closed.

It will take a few years for Théogène Mukasago to be tried and for his appeals to be exhausted but justice will be done. Désirée and the other victims will obtain reparations.

The next day, Brice congratulates us on our results and asks me to come and see him. We have an agreement with Liberian authorities to continue an investigation started a little more than a year earlier, on February 15.

Our target: BFM, Big Fat Man, a "warlord." Another humanimal.

14
GAME OF THRONES IN AFRICA

"The only thing necessary for evil to triumph is that good men do nothing. It suffices to say, evil triumphs everywhere."

—attributed to Edmund Burke

February 15, 2018—Paris, Palais de justice

As I wander the hallways of the new palace, I see "corridor rabbits" everywhere, people who are usually afraid of their own shadow but perfectly confident in an office environment. I pass one just as I'm about to enter Brice's office, an individual in a tight tailored suit, rocker-bottom shoes. He gives me a suspicious look. Another toxic type who see the world through the narrow lens of the Paris ring road.

"Good day Colonel, how are you? Thanks for meeting on such short notice."

"Hello Brice. Not a problem. How about that guy?"

"A suppository."

"Suppository?"

"That's what we call them. A guy so smooth he'll slide right up the hierarchy. Not a big believer in the usefulness of universal jurisdiction, either, especially for the victims of war crimes."

"I get the picture. We have a saying for that, under tall trees fat mushrooms grow. They seem to thrive in Paris's climate."

Smiles.

"Coffee?"

"With pleasure."

Brice gets up and prepares two espressos.

"Let's get to it. It's about a Liberian warlord . . . James Blayde, known as BFM, or Big Fat Man."

Brice turns his computer screen toward me to display BFM's photo.

"Appropriate."

The individual sits on a large black chair decorated with palm trees, a kind of throne. He's wearing military fatigues and a red wig tied up in a red bandana. Chiseled face, disproportionately tall, large shoulders, enormous body, bulging eyes and two vertical markings on each cheek. Scars, obviously. His neck is draped gold chains with amulets of pieces of bone. There are about ten black leather rectangles sewn onto his beige vest. They hold Kalashnikov cartridges, more pieces of bone, and scalps crusted with dried blood.

He is surrounded by a court of women in fatigues and children armed with AK-47s. On the ground in front of him is a decapitated corpse, the torso split wide open. He has placed his right boot on it.

"What do you think?"

"Hell of a customer. Where did you get this photograph?"

"It in his case file. It was taken in the 1990s in Lofa County in northern Liberia, when Charles Taylor's troops were taking over the area."

"And he's our problem now? Apparently he practices JuJu?"

"JuJu?"

"It's traditional religious practices of West African. VooDoo, in short."

"I don't know but, yes, it seems he's hiding out in France."

"Do we have an idea of where?"

"Swiss Universal Jurisdiction is working with a Liberian NGO that specializes in the fight against impunity in Liberia and Sierra Leone. The NGO has obtained information that this guy may be in Rosny at the home of a member of our Liberian community. Both are affiliated with Charles Taylor's NPFL [National Patriotic Front of Liberia]. They are very close, apparently."

"How long is he supposed to have been living in France?"

"Two or three years. We don't really know. We've also received a judicial assistance request from Denmark. They want him in the context of a separate case involving an individual named Michael Paynes who is in prison in Denmark for war crimes. On top of that, we just received another complaint filed through a Swiss NGO called SUJ."

"What's the story in Denmark?"

"It seems that he fled Denmark after receiving a summons from authorities in connection with the Paynes case. He'd obtained Danish citizenship after leaving Liberia in 1999 through the Ivory Coast."

"What was the summons for?"

"Michael Paynes, also known as Colonel Black Mamba, was under BFM's command. They all have war nicknames. Colonel One-Foot Devil, General Mosquito, and his arch-enemy, General Bug Spray."

"We've got enough General Mosquitos in our own ranks."

Brice smiles.

"Yes, us too."

So, are we doing the whole thing?"

"Yes, track him down and let me know. Meanwhile we'll decide on whether our complaint or the Danish request has highest priority."

I get up.

"Wait. Before you leave, go and see Sarah. She's prepared some background on Liberia, the civil wars, the NPFL, and its opposition, ULIMO, and so on."

A minute later, I walk into an office occupied by three specialists in international humanitarian law. With experience in one or more international jurisdictions, they have been recruited to support the investigative magistrates in the public prosecutor's office. When they receive a case file, they analyze it from the perspective of jurisdictional eligibility, and provide notes on relevant political, historical, and diplomatic contexts. The notes are useful in framing the context of our mission.

Sarah's wearing purple and scarlet and, as usual, an abundance of jewelry around her neck. She's been waiting for me. She hands me a sixty-page dossier with a smile.

"Hello Colonel, here it is. You will find it fascinating. The county is unique, to say the least."

"Thanks Sarah. A little light reading. I've been missing that."

I head out with the file under my arm, wondering how we're going to go about finding BFM.

I spend the following day pouring over Sarah's report.[1]

Liberia occupies a roughly 40,000-square-mile region of West Africa, bordered by Sierra Leone on the west, Guinea on the north, the Ivory Coast on the east, and the Atlantic Ocean on the south. It figures among the ten least developed countries in the world, and has a population of four million, divided into thirteen counties. Religiously, roughly 10 per cent of Liberians are Christian (mostly Protestant), 30 per cent Muslim (especially in the country's interior), and majority Animist.

In 1822, an American philanthropic company, the National Colonization Society of America, launched a colonization enterprise with the goal of giving land to freed slaves and spreading Christianity. Despite disease, heavy rains, and attacks from Indigenous tribes, nearly 13,000 settlers arrived between 1821 and 1867 and succeeded in taking the territory by force, starting at the coast and moving to the inland region, rich in natural resources.

The Liberian population was thereafter divided into two broad categories. There were those who called themselves Freemen—freed slaves formerly from America, strongly Christianized by Methodist missionaries. And there were those whom they exploited, namely the Indigenous population that they called bushmen or natives. The latter were not a monolithic block but were comprised of sixteen tribes, each with its own language and identity. Convinced of their superiority, the American-Liberians, also called the Congos (it was supposed that the freed slaves originated from the Congo Basin), established a republic in 1847 with a constitution modeled on that of the United States. Their flag, red and white stripes and a single star, emulates the American flag.

The republic was uniquely tailored to the Freemen, but it bore the seeds of conflict that would erupt one hundred and forty years later as a consequence of segregation. The right to vote was reserved for land owners, but the indigenous population was not allowed to own property, at least not without having first been declared "civilized" and Christian. In 1931,

Liberia was condemned by the League of Nations for subjecting Indigenous populations to forced labor on behalf of multinational rubber companies.

Indigenous Liberians remained second-class citizens until 1945. The elite American-Liberians controlled state power through a system of patronage, corporatism, and a single party, the True Whig Party. They pitted Indigenous groups against one another, in some cases widening divisions that had existed in pre-colonial times. The Krahn and Lorma, considered excellent warriors, were recruited into the armed forces. The Mandingo, seen as brilliant traders, were invited into commerce with the Congo, controlling trade routes between the north and the coastal zone.

Toward the end of the Second World War, a period of appeasement and relative prosperity set in with the presidency of William Tubman (1944–71), an American-Liberian considered "the father of modern Liberia." He was consistently re-elected by large margins until his death, by which time his administration had devolved into a dictatorial regime. Increasingly paranoid, he brutally repressed any hints of resistance to his policies, creating a climate of terror throughout the country.

William Tolbert, another American-Liberian, took power from 1971 to 1980. By then, the social inequalities between African-American descendants and Indigenous populations had boiled over. Tolbert's decision to raise the price of rice provoked a demonstration in Monrovia on April 14, 1979. It resulted in dozens of deaths. The government attempted to restore order and arrested many of its opponents but the situation continued to deteriorate.

On the morning of April 12, 1980, soldiers led by Staff Sergeant Samuel Doe, a native Krahn, stormed the presidential palace. President Tobert was disemboweled and defenestrated. Samuel Doe became Liberia's twenty-first president and the first Indigenous Liberian to hold power.

Following the coup, Samuel Doe publicly executed former government officials and much of the former president's family on a beach in full view of press and video cameras. It was the revenge of the Indigenous on the Freemen. The national assembly was dissolved. Doe set up a Council for the Redemption of the People, which he led. It consisted of a dozen military men, most of them Krahn.

The regime was strongly contested, especially since Doe repeated many of the mistakes of his predecessors. He favored the Krahn and Mandingo. The country sank into a disastrous economic crisis, leading to more revolts, which were severely repressed.

Doe's politics forced many opponents to seek refuge abroad, notably Côte d'Ivoire. It was there that Charles Taylor created a new force, the National Patriotic Front of Liberia (NPFL).

Charles Taylor was born in 1948 to an American father and an American-Liberian mother who were among the country's elite. At the age of twenty-four, Taylor moved to the United States to study economics. On becoming president, Doe put Taylor in charge of general government services. After embezzling $900,000 in three years, Taylor lost his job and fled to the United States where he was arrested and imprisoned. He managed to escape and find his way to Libya in 1985. There he trained in guerrilla warfare before moving to Côte d'Ivoire to found the NPFL and plan his insurrection against the Doe regime.

On December 24, 1989, Taylor set out from Côte d'Ivoire with 160 men who had been trained and equipped by Libya and Burkina Faso. He was supported within Liberia from the Gio and Mano ethnic groups. The NPLF made rapid progress and by the summer of 1990 controlled almost the entire country except for the capital, Monrovia, where Samuel Doe based his resistance.

To prevent the NPFL from taking Monrovia, the Economic Community of West African States (ECOWAS) sent an intervention force of 4,000 men known as ECOMOG.

At the same time, Prince Johnson, a founding member of the NPFL, fell out with Charles Taylor and created the Independent National Patriotic Front of Liberia (INPLF). Johnson and his INPLF men captured Samuel Doe in the ECOMOG offices on September 9, 1990, and tortured him to death. The filmed scene shocked the international community. Johnson's men displayed Doe's mutilated body on the streets of Monrovia for several days.

Prince Johnson is currently a Liberian senator for Nimba County.

Partisans of Samuel Doe's regime, the majority being Krahn and Mandingo, regrouped in the ULIMO (United Liberation Movement of

Liberia for Democracy) and launched attacks against the NPFL. At the end of 1992, the NPFL and ULIMO are engaged in guerrilla warfare, with multiple dissident warlords from each camp fighting each other, none achieving significant victories. Our target, BFM, served as a general in the NPFL during this period.

Several rounds of peace talks attempted to obtain a ceasefire. The Abuja II Accord, signed on August 17 under the aegis of ECOWAS, finally put an end to the war. By March 1997, all factions have been disarmed. Charles Taylor was elected president with 75.3 per cent of the vote.

In 1999, a second civil war broke out.

One rebel group, LURD (Liberians United for Reconciliation and Democracy), attacked from the Guinean border. A second, MODEL (the Movement for Democracy in Liberia), emerged in the South. By June 2003, Charles Taylor controlled less than a third of the country. LURD bombarded Monrovia and laid siege to the city. On July 29, after rounds of negotiations, a ceasefire was accepted. Charles Taylor resigned on August 11, 2003. A political transition was arranged and supervised by the UN. On November 23, 2005, Ellen Johnson Sirleaf was elected president of Liberia.

In 2006, Charles Taylor was arrested and sentenced to fifty years in prison for crimes against humanity with respect to Sierra Leone by the Special Court for Sierra Leone. He is currently serving his sentence in a high-security penitentiary in Northeast England.

Don Blayde is a former member of NPFL and associate of Charles Taylor. He and Taylor were trained together by Libyan intelligence at a time when Libyan leader Muammar Kadhafi had his sights on West Africa as a counter to U.S. influence. Part of Taylor's first guard, Blayde was responsible for control of Lofa County in northwestern Liberia, where he allegedly committed atrocities.

James Blayde, or BFM, was born in Sanniquellie, Liberia, on August 23, 1969, to Don Blayde and Rose Suah. He rose rapidly to the rank of general and also found his way into the hierarchy of the NPFL, reportedly due to his ruthlessness.

The Truth and Reconciliation Commission (Liberia) was established in 2006. After three years of work, including hundreds of public hearings and thousands of written statements, it delivered its final report to parliament on June 30, 2009. The purpose of the TRC, modeledl on the famous South African commission, was to investigate war crimes and violations of human rights in Liberia between 1979 and 2003. Its conclusions recommended public sanctions against fifty persons associated with armed groups. The commission sought to bar these individuals from public office for a period of thirty years.

Among those named was President Ellen Johnson Sirleaf. The Liberian political class therefore buried the TRC's conclusions on the grounds that the stability of the country demanded that a line be drawn under its past. It was a strange outcome, to say the least. Liberia's inter-ethnic strife and two civil wars resulted in more than 150,000 deaths, according to the United Nations. To this day, Liberia refuses to punish its warlords for the crimes they committed.

Now it is France's turn to try under the auspices of universal jurisdiction.

15
NEW DIGITAL WORLD

"There has never been a time of greater promise or potential peril . . . We must have a comprehensive and globally shared view of how technology is changing our lives and those of future generations, and how it is reshaping the economic, social, cultural and human context in which we live."

—Klaus Schwab, World Economic Forum

February 20, 2018—Paris, OCLCH

I enter the strategy division. White hallways, posters of crimes against humanity. The division head, Major Philippe L., a commissioned officer, Arabist, and criminal analysis specialist, is in the middle of a discussion of the Syrian file with his deputy, Daniel M., a police major.

"The prosecutor has given us a new case," I interrupt. "We have to locate him and size-up his physical environment quickly.[1] He has a fire under his ass. He's already skipped out of Denmark and found refuge here. A Liberian. The Swiss Universal Jurisdiction NGO places him somewhere in the area of Rosny."

Daniel follows. "OK. I'll handle the requisitions and verification with the judiciary, check the administrative databases, and the rest of it. What's his name?"

"If he's not using an alias, it will be James Blayde, born in Sanniquellie, Liberia on August 23, 1969. Son of Don Blayde, former member of the NPFL, Charles Taylor's party. Belongs to the Mano ethnic group."

Philippe's turn: "I'll ask Jonathan to check with Europol and Eurojust,

Interpol, and the UN, M3I,[2] and the Office of the High Commissioner for Human Rights."

I suggest that we also start researching right away in OSINT, or open-source intelligence. The old adage that "every individual leaves a trace" is especially true on the Internet. Useful evidence can be turned up on Facebook, Instagram, and Twitter. Photographs, perhaps, showing him at the scene of alleged crimes, or in the company of people of interest to the investigation. YouTube often contains useful videos providing clues about people, locations, and dates.

"Are you putting Sylvie on the case?" I ask.

"She already has her hands full, but . . ."

"Don't forget your five C's, Daniel."

"Five C's?"

"*C'est Con mais C'est Comme Cela.*" [It's stupid, but there you have it.] Smiles.

An hour later, Daniel informs me that the judiciary databases turned up nothing on James Blayde.

"And we're off. So he's not using his real name in France. Let's lean harder on the open sources."

After forty-eight hours of OSINT research, Sylvie arrives in my office with her laptop.

"You look happy about something, Sylvie."

"Yes. I think we have a nice lead. I've been working with the NGO Open Facto. They specialize in open-source investigation."

She shows me the screen of her laptop. I'm looking at what appears to be a giant moving spider web with a rainbow of color coding. Each thread is linked to a name. The image is in 3D, rotating.

"I started out thinking there might be a gathering of the Liberian community in Paris. I searched through Facebook group pages linked to Liberia, then those with specific relations to Nimba County: the soccer team, music, etc. Three associations caught my attention: The Association of Liberians in France; the NED Association [Nimba Education Development] which has branches in France, America, and Liberia; and the Mandigon of France. We put the Mandigon of France to the side as they're aligned more with the

ULIMO, so in opposition to the NPFL. The other two associations have their own pages, which I downloaded and data-merged. This is what it looks like. Then, on Open Facto's advice, I looked for recommended Liberian or West African restaurants, as well as pages for soccer teams. We merged this data, too. Bottom line, I've found some decent restaurants."

Wink. Sylvie is an epicure.

"OK, so you shook the data around, what came out?"

Sylvie rotates the graphic with her mouse and zooms in on a node where a large volume of colored links converge. Each color represents a subgroup linked by strong friend relations. We can distinguish five large sub-communities in this network of friends. All relate to soccer.

"The merged data shows a convergence point around a Liberian named Tanguy Banto, who's the president of NED, and he lives . . ."

Sylvie pauses briefly.

"In Rosny?"

"That's it!"

"His list of friends is private. However, by analyzing the names of people who have liked his public photographs, especially those related to soccer, we've constructed a list of 267 names linked through 1,451 relationships. But Banto also has a second Facebook account, which happens to share the same banner as the first. It is very Rasta."

Sylvie minimizes the first graphic and brings up a second, equally intricate.

"Here we mapped out the relations to concentrate more on family, friends, and the environment of the target. We've found someone named Annie Livingstone, who appears to be his girlfriend, and other friends who also showed up on the previous graphic. A certain number of them are in Libya . . ."

"Ah, interesting. Not bad considering the NPFL's major players were trained by Kadhafi. But nothing further on our target?"

"No. The next step is to go through all of the accounts of Banto's Facebook friends, analyze the photos, and so on. Apparently, Banton lives in Bois-Perrier, a housing estate in Rosny."

"OK, go ahead. We'll proceed along the lines of the NGO data. Run the photos. We'll start looking into Banto."

"I've already created a data archive. I'll check in with Daniel on the rest."

Our own database analysis tells us that Tanguy Banto is indeed Liberian, born on July 15, 1969, in Ganta, Nimba County. He has a ten-year residency card that's been renewed. He is indeed the president of Nimba Education Development, affiliated with the NPFL. He owns a blue Ford and works for Wolf Sécurité in Magny-le-Hongre. Most importantly, we get a phone number to tap.

Two hours later, Sophie comes back with her laptop.

"After importing the photographs from Banto's accounts and pages, we ran them through RecoFace[3] software and compared them to the photos you provided from Liberia in the nineties. Check this out."

Sylvie shows me photos taken during soccer matches near Paris. We see two individuals, arm in arm. On the right in Banto. On the left is our giant, BFM.

"I sent the picture to Hervé at Open Faҫto so that he could locate the stadium for us. He used Google reverse image. You see there, in the background—the huge tower? In front of it, you can make out a sign on the roof of a smaller building. It's a Carrefour store. Hervé says the stadium is Déjerine Stadium, near Montreuil. On a hunch, I also sifted through the Annie Livingstone's Facebook page. Banto's girlfriend. She's much more forthcoming. Not shy with her comments."

Sylvie brings up Annie's account.

"One photo was particularly interesting. A birthday party. Hers, apparently. And look here, in the back of the room. Not hard to spot our man."

"Is there a date? Location?"

"Yes, she celebrated her fortieth this year on January 10 in a West African restaurant called Kumba, in East Paris. We see her later at Mask, a Caribbean-style club, also in Paris."

"Well done, Sylvie."

She opens up Google.

"This is what we found on the stadium photo. Check out the same location six months earlier. The sign isn't there. That's must be about the beginning of September."

"Great. So our guy is probably still there. Lost a bit of weight but still beefy enough. Thank Open Facto and Hervé for their help. As always, very efficient . . ."

With his presence confirmed on French soil, it's now time to find out whose identity BFM is using. I have to assign a new director for this file. It will be Captain Bertrand R. Brice authorizes a wiretap on Banto, access to his phone records, and GPS tracking, a tag on his vehicle if we need it. Now we just have to wait, see how things evolve, and hope that Banto leads us to BFM.

March 9, 2018—OCLCH

More than ten days go by and no activity on Banto's wiretap. Zilch. Nothing. The investigators start to worry. Is it the right number? It did seem a bit too good to be true. We consider contacting his employer but it's too risky. We need to set up a stake out to physically track our target.

We make the most of the personnel we have. A three-person team: Captain Bertrand R. and Daniel, with Stéphanie on a scooter.

A decision is made to gear our efforts toward the security company. It's less risky than tracking the target in town. Wolf Sécurité is located in an industrial zone in Magny-le-Hongre. Luckily for us, the facility is surrounded with medium-high buildings that give us an unobstructed view of the company's entrance. In the parking lot, there are about twenty vehicles, all with the company logo.

We search on Google for an address that we can work out of with a good view of the building. We find an apartment in the name of Madame Katz.

March 9—Magny-le-Hongre

Bertrand R. rings the bell. A woman comes to the door. A small woman, maybe five feet tall with short gray hair, about seventy-five-years-old, in great shape. Bertrand shows his badge and introduces himself as a representative of OCLCH. Ginette Katz's face freezes. Images from her past—the war, the Nazis, the camps, the hatred, Nuremberg—flash through her mind.

But she opens the door and gives the team permission to set up in her apartment. It's a disruption of her peaceful daily routine but she seems excited to play a small part in a police exercise.

The hallways of her home are strewn with photographs of smiling, joyful people. This is a woman who has lived a full life. A menorah sits on the sideboard along with a splendid painting with a Star of David.

We set up our video and photo surveillance in Ginette's guest room. Flowered wallpaper, a bit dated. At least in this room we won't be interrupting Ginette's gameshows. Bertrand R and Stéphanie are stationed at the apartment for a day and a half, and stuffed with sweets, cakes, and especially doughnuts—Ginette's famous doughnuts.

It took thirty-six hours to get our first look at Banto, dressed in the company's black uniform with its black logo representing a wolf with red eyes. He's of average height, shaved head, in good physical shape. He takes a muzzled Rottweiler out of the back of his Ford. At least we know we've got the right vehicle.

Banto enters the company garage. Five minutes go by. Probably getting his next assignment. We use the time to get Daniel into his undercover Volkswagen and Stéphanie onto her scooter. Both vehicles were seized in police actions and reassigned to OCLCH. The state feeding off the beast of organized crime. That's how it goes. We say goodbye to Mother Ginette and thank her for the doughnuts. She offers a bag for the road.

The Rottweiller hops into the back of a Kangoo station wagon. Banto takes a bag out of the Ford, throws it in beside the dog and drives off. Our tracking device locks into the Kango. The scooter follows at a safe distance, with the Volkswagen bringing up the rear.

A few kilometres down the road, the team follows the Kangoo toward Val d'Europe mall. Banto parks on a side street, Hymne-à-la-Joie—Hymn to Joy, you can't make this up. He's there to start his shift.

We replace the Volkswagen with our Mercedes submarine and prepare for a long night.

A thermos of coffee, sandwiches. It's tight in there, watching surveillance video of the mall exterior. The Rottweiler takes Banto for a walk around the parking lot three times during the night.

Around 7 a.m., he returns the dog to the station wagon and heads back toward Rosny. Not terribly productive but the team at least has the opportunity to follow Banto to his home.

March 11—Val d'Europe Mall

Our plans will take us back outside Wolf Sécurité, but this time with an interceptor to grab Banto's cell number. A team of specialists will join us for this part of the operation once he shows up for work. In the meantime, we head up to Ginette's. She hugs us and flies into the kitchen. Several doughnuts later, the team catches site of Banto who is ready for his shift. It's 6:30 p.m.

Bertrand and Daniel, mouths still full, tail him to the mall. They take their positions in the same place, with a direct view of the vehicle parked *on Hymne-à-la-Joie.*

Night falls. Around 10 p.m., the interceptor team knocks on the back door of the submarine. They set up their gear. Before long, two numbers are triangulated. They repeat the procedure several times for confirmation. At 1 a.m., the interceptor team is getting ready to head out when Banto emerges, probably to make his rounds.

But, unlike the previous night, he positions himself at one of the exits of the larger parking lot and waits. Ten minutes later, a succession of motorcycles and scooters starts arriving. Once every fifteen minutes. Impossible to get a visual ID on account of the helmets and the speed of the bikes. Each driver gets a package from Banto as they pass. About a dozen in total. Enough time, however, to catch cell numbers.

It seems Banto is running a narcotics racket, or at least he is seriously implicated in one. The parade continues until 1:30 a.m. when an Audi A4 speeds into the parking lot. A big fellow gets out. Our infrared cameras film the scene. Daniel zooms in. Banto and the guy say hello and slap hands. The big guy helpfully takes off his hat and the camera can get a glimpse of its face. BFM.

Who was it that said, help yourself and the heavens will help you? The interceptor spits out BFM's cell number.

2:30a.m.

I receive a WhatsApp: "We're in. We got it." Meaning BFM's cellphone.

The infrared camera keeps a bead on BFM, who is wearing fatigues and still holding his cap.

Five minutes monitoring the screens, the target returns to the Audi and drives off. Stéphanie follows on the scooter, keeping her distance. The submarine takes off behind but we don't have the numbers to safely follow him. The Audi is moving fast. Captain Bertrand R. decides against risking it and everyone backs off.

Still, a good harvest. Our license-plate check finds that the Audi belongs to a person going by Samuel Tuah, address in Noisy-le-Sec.

Tuah is a good Liberian name. Probably BFM's latest alias. We return home.

March 12—OCLCH

After a short night's rest, we reassemble and take stock. We didn't expect the drugs. In any case, we pass the details along to the narcotics detectives in Rosny. It'll be a nice feather in their caps.

Our focus will be BFM, or Samuel Tuah. We've tapped the cell numbers picked off during the night.

Digging into the cellphone records, we learn that BFM is using yet another name: Bakayoko Doou, and claiming to be from the Côte d'Ivoire. He's registered with the unemployment agency and receives $1,500 a month based on falsified paperwork and employment histories. He uses one of the wireless numbers we captured during surveillance to receive his benefits. He also gave an address: 67 Michelet Boulevard in Noisy-le-Sec. Samuel Tuah's house.

We gain access to BFM's banking records. We can get his withdrawals and seize video footage from ATM machines. Little by little, the image of our client is coming into view.

We have yet to verify that BFM actually lives at 67 Michelet Boulevard before we can arrest him. It shouldn't take long, except . . .

March 14—OCLCH

A crisis meeting. The cell lines registered to Banto and BFM have crashed for no apparent reason. Were we discovered?

Daniel, our police major and former narcotics agent, has a hunch. A quick check with his contacts confirms his fears. Narcotics agents immediately moved on Banto's drug network. Low-level distributors. We ask them to back off for a while so that we can work in peace.

It's not the end of the world. We didn't mess up. But we did lose our taps on the targets' phones. We need to start again from scratch.

Further research into BFM reveals that he works as a security guard at Mask, the club that showed up on the Facebook of Banto's girlfriend, Annie Livingstone. The ties that bind these people are becoming clearer.

We bring back the intercept team, this time on Michelet Boulevard. Fortunately, the team is able to isolate BFM's number but he's now using a small-time service provider that only pings his GPS once every third minute, which complicates our work a great deal.

The following day, Bertrand R. comes rushing into my office.

"BFM is spooked. He called a Guinean associate in Italy. We got a break. We found a Mano interpreter. According to the translation, BFM asked him to prepare a Guinean passport. He wants to leave France. Asked why, he replies that he is involved in drug trafficking and has been arrested. His contact asks him to go to the Guinean embassy in Paris in the 16th arrondissement. He's to look up a guy who will provide him with forms. He has to send his photo by Internet and transfer €1500 to Italy via Western Union. BFM's GPS placed him around the Guinean Embassy all day yesterday. We need to get a move on."

"OK, I'll call GIGN."[4]

"We need to get on his home, as well. The paperwork won't be finished until tomorrow. We still have some time."

After a telephone briefing with GIGN, the duty officer mobilizes La Force d'Observation et de Recherches (FOR), a unit I'm well acquainted with. I often worked with them before leaving for Bosnia, especially while I was running investigations in Montpellier. The men and women on the team are specialists in counter-terrorism and organized crime with particular expertise in undetectable surveillance and investigations. They live between the light and the shadows.

March 16—Noisy-le-Sec

FOR is in position on Michelet Boulevard: four gendarmes and their chief waiting for BFM to arrive home. GPS indicates that he's left West Paris and is heading towards Noisy-le-Sec.

4:34 p.m. His last stop. The Guinean Embassy. We presume he's picked up his documents. If all goes well, he'll swim right into our net.

5:05 p.m. Our target is spotted coming down the RER-E commuter route. Shouldn't take him more than eleven minutes to get here. The plan is to apprehend him onsite.

5:20 p.m. No sign of BFM. Either he's not coming to the apartment, or he's taking precautions and avoiding Michelet Boulevard. We're dealing with an experienced warlord, after all.

The other problem is we don't know his legal address, even if everything points to this apartment.

We confer with FOR's unit leader, Antoine, and decide to bring in the interceptor to check if BFM is in the building. Five minutes later, it's confirmed. Stéphanie, in civilian clothes, looking like a preppy social worker, adjusts her Hermès scarf, and proposes to go look at the mailboxes.

"I found him. Fourth floor, apartment 452."

We tear up the four flights of stairs. CIGN gendarmes take either side of the door. Stéphanie rings, holding a blue binder, all smiles.

The light through the peephole vanishes. The lock clicks and the door opens.

In less than three seconds, the four gendarmes are in the apartment, shouting "Gendarmerie nationale!" Notwithstanding his size, BFM decides not to put up a fight. A few seconds more and his hands are cuffed behind his back.

There's a dog in the apartment. It lightly bites one of CIGN's gendarmes until ordered by his master to release his prey.

With the situation under control, CIGN give us the signal to enter the apartment and read BFM his rights. He thinks he is being arrested for drug trafficking. In broken French, he says he is surprised, that he doesn't understand, that it must be a set up . . . He's even more surprised when he learns that he's being taken into custody for crimes against humanity for his alleged role as NPFL colonel in Lofa County during the first civil war in Liberia.

Dressed in a black leather jacket that reaches halfway down his thigh and jeans with holes in them, BFM stands straight and silent, watching us without flinching. He flexes his muscles. Arrogant. He smiles at the sight of the blood on the pants of the gendarme.

Our search of the apartment finds little except his Eurolines bus ticket for Italy. His departure was set for the next morning. We picked him up just on time.

We explain to BFM that he'll be summoned to give a deposition later on. In the meantime, he'll be travelling with restraints on his ankles and a motorcycle helmet on his head, the visor opaque—precautions due to his size.

We can't hold him long. His lawyer has advised him not to say anything. Each question we asked solicits the same response: "I don't want to answer this question." He's lost his use of French, but his cell phone still has things to say. We manage to pry out several photographs of African soldiers. Nothing that implicates him directly, however, nor anything from the time of events. The other witnesses we approach are a dead end. Either they did not know or did not understand.

Following standard procedure, the case is opened in one of the three offices of investigating judges who oversee cases of crimes against humanity.

As with Rwanda, we need to travel to depose witnesses and collect material evidence. In the meantime, we interview journalists and special envoys to Liberia and Sierra Leone who during the 1990s were the only people with images of armed conflicts and war crimes.

In contrast, the millions of images and videos now available on the internet and social media, largely due to the pervasiveness of smartphones, casts a spotlight on a significant evolution, both in investigative methods and the intensification of propaganda by this bias. Further digitalization, via the Cloud and AI, also holds great promise for investigative work.

Today, we can access no end of video and photographic evidence from the Internet, thanks to the widespread use of smartphones. In the future, the storage of all this material in the cloud and the development of artificial intelligence will open whole new avenues of investigation.

But for the moment, we're dealing with 1990s Liberia. We need to book flights.

16

WELCOME BACK
TO LIBERIA

Serpent spirit
I sense the vibrations of your body,
O mortal who begins to hope,
Who frees himself from death's embrace
As it squeezes closer.
I see you lifting this tombstone
That weighs on your crushed thoughts,
Your voice no longer this death rattles
Words ablaze now only ashes

Jean-Pierre Chemaly, *Le Bestiaire des Âmes*

April 23, 2019—Liberia, Monrovia Airport

We touch down at night, but the heat and humidity still hit hard. A shuttle bus is waiting for our delegation. Stéphanie H. and Valentin M., members of our African group, accompany me. We're escorted to a VIP room where Emmanuel Marry, chargé d'affaires of the French embassy, is waiting for us. Over the past ten days, we've been talking over secure lines, arranging operational logistics: cars, drivers, guest houses, relations with local authorities, justice departments, police . . . Five years in an embassy has given me some insight into how things work behind the scenes.

The ambassador was indispensable in getting our visit sanctioned by the country's political authorities. This is the first time Liberia has given a

European country the green-light to proceed with such a case. However, in contrast to Rwanda, where we were able to depose witnesses directly, here we are obliged to collaborate with a team of Liberian police investigators.

The air conditioning is at full blast in the VIP lounge. Its beige walls are sweating. Some of them feature colorful African paintings. A hostess graciously offers us seats on large, faded brown arm chairs, and brings us fresh drinks. After a twelve-hour flight, I prefer to stand.

Above the door frame, sixteen masks representing each of Liberia's native tribes. Their eyes seem to follow us warily. They frame an engraving of the country's motto, "The love of Liberty brought us here." It's hard to square the motto with my dossier on the country's history. I look closely at the Mano mask, our target's tribe of origin.

A few minutes later, we board the bus taking us to Monrovia. It heads out into the humid night. I'm sitting at the very front and can't see much. The windshield is foggy and cracked. Not sure I'd have time to get into a crash position if we had a problem. Our driver, at least, seems to know the road well. He slows down to dodge the potholes. We have no choice but to trust him.

The heat is broiling. My jeans are plastered to my legs. No one says a word. Faces staring blankly out the windows. Exhaustion, no doubt.

The route from the airport to the city isn't well lit. It's been like that for at least ten years, since the first time I visited Liberia. That time it was a narcotics mission. The day after I landed, wearing a suit in 90° heat and 98 per cent humidity, I was plunged into Monrovia's central prison with a French prosecutor. People serving life sentences. Hardened criminals. Fifty people crammed into small cells. Not something you forget.

From what little I can see, not much appears to have changed. I catch fleeting glimpses of pedestrians at the side of the road in the weak glow of our headlights. Reflective paint on the road. At one corner, huge speakers crash out wild tribal rhythms. Young people dancing, singing, beers in hand. Boys watching the girls dance.

The closer we get to the city, the more the night seems to come alive. Open markets where everything seems to be for sale. Even at night. Especially at night.

An hour later, thanks to several bottlenecks—the traffic at the entrances to Monrovia never stops—we finally arrive at the hotel. A Lebanese manager welcomes us with a big smile. There are about ten thousand Lebanese living in Liberia, giving a boost to the country's economy.

A good night's sleep will set us right.

April 25, 2019—Monrovia

6 a.m. The sun rises on Monrovia in a halo of humidity. We depart for our mission in the country's northeast. Idou, our Kissi, English, Liberian, and French-language interpreter, will be joining us for the entirety. A soccer fanatic, he is dressed in a track suit in the colors of the Paris-Saint-Germain team. He clearly doesn't play anymore. He drinks non-alcoholic beer instead, and it shows. Lively and sharp, Idou doesn't miss anything. Ethnically Mandigon, he speaks perfect French that he picked up in Guinea. Familiar with all of Monrovia, he assumes the role of our wise man, which is actually helpful in decoding local customs, the history of the country, and whatever else lies beneath the surface.

The Monrovian police force assigns two investigators to accompany us, David and Paul, along with an escort of five soldiers armed with Kalashnikovs. David, the leader, is a rather large man, forty-five years old, poised, calm, watchful. Mindful of his appearance, he moves nonchalantly under an inexpensive Borsalino. A four-inch scar crosses his face, left to right, terminating at the upper lip, under which he holds a half-consumed cigarillo. A war wound?

Paul, on the other hand, is short, loud, and rather nervous. He has small, deep black, shrewd eyes, and an American football cap glued to his head.

Our SUV is loaded with satellite phone, GPS beacons, computers, printers, spare batteries, evidence gear for crime scenes. Also, Doxycycline and Malarone to counter malaria, and eight gallons of water. It's a fourteen-hour trip, ten of which will be spent winding through various villages before we reach Voinjnama on the Gbarnga-Zorzor road.

Our convoy drives head-on into Monrovia's rush-hour traffic, which gets denser by the minute. Cars, trucks, and motorcycles separate themselves into three makeshift lanes, so close together that even our police escort has trouble advancing. Total anarchy. It seems like we'll never make it out of the city.

Our SUV sticks as close as possible to the police escort. I look out at the evident poverty on the city's outskirts. Shantytowns, makeshift shacks. Women, children, and men struggling to survive.

For a country rich in natural resources, it certainly has its share of poverty. A billboard catches my attention: "Love God more than Money." When you have a choice, at least.

I turn my thoughts to the mission ahead of us. We will attempt to reconstruct three different crime scenes in which BFM and his men were allegedly involved. We have a dozen witnesses to depose, including some who were close to our target.

We expect to be doing this in wet weather. We're on the verge of the African monsoon season, which can release staggering volumes of water. When it pours, we'll be stranded for days on end. There's also the question of the reception that we"ll get from Northern Liberians, how things will play out with the local police, and whether or not witnesses will be willing to testify in front of the entire nation.

In short, I'm eager to get started, to get some clarity.

An hour out of Monrovia, sunlight alternates with layers of mist that immerse the smaller valleys. Only the tips of banana trees, palms, and coconut trees can be seen.

Daddison, our driver, decides to entertain us with loud African music. For fear of offending him, Stéphanie, Valentin, and I hold our tongues.

We pass through a forest of neatly planted rubber trees. Each tree is bled to deliver its precious liquid into a gray pot. This region is exploited by the infamous Firestone factory, which came to Liberia in the mid-1920s.

At the time, European colonial powers, notably the Netherlands and England, had monopolized rubber production. Considering rubber of strategic importance, President Herbert Hoover delegated Samuel Firestone to locate a source of rubber controlled by American interests. Firestone sent experts to Liberia in December 1923 to perform soil studies. That resulted in one of the world's most important sources of rubber production, at least until the 1980s.

That success story was permanently stained in 2006 when factory workers accused Firestone's management of slavery. The United Nations Mission in Liberia (UNMIL) investigated and published a report on the state of human rights in Liberian rubber plantations. According to UNMIL, Firestone did not adequately monitor its work force in accord with the ban on child labour. Firestone's president told CNN that "each operator taps about 650 trees a day, spending maybe two minutes on each tree." In other words, a twenty-one-hour work day. This country is definitely struggling to emerge from slavery.

We leave Bong County and cross over to Nimba, home to Senator Prince Johnson who filmed the torture and murder of Samuel Doe. The Nimba mountains, rich in ferrous minerals, interlaced with winding tarred roads, rise up in the distance, some culminating at more than 5,000 feet.

A giant billboard declares "The President Meter Project." It keeps track of President George Weah's unfulfilled election promises. Seems as though Weah, a former Paris Saint-Germain soccer star, has a complicated political future ahead of him.

The road quickly deteriorates. Red dirt kicks up around the 4×4 and sticks to the windshield. Potholes large enough to lie down in. A Chinese crew is laying down more tar as best it can. As with so much else in the country, it's a game of catch-up game.

The closer we get to the county of Loga, the more majestic the trees. The richness of the vegetation is extraordinary. Hills are covered in layers of morning glory, palm trees, coconut trees, mango trees, and coffee trees. Certain sections are burned out, leaving only two-foot mounds in the shape of mushrooms, built by termites.

We pass through villages, roughly a dozen adobe houses each. Some have bullet holes, souvenirs of the civil wars. At the centers of most villages is an immense violet bougainvillea, under which are benches and chairs, occupied by old folks chatting in the shade.

A large group of children wave hello, shouting "Pumui." Some of the women are busy around kettles mounted over wood fires; many have a child on their back. Others are stationed behind stalls, selling either the produce of their harvest or tiny bags of pasta or rice, dried fish, or pieces of chicken. The stands are swarming with flies. Empty plastic water bottles litter the ground.

As the sun sinks over the wooded hills, we cross the bridge over the Saint-Paul river, lulled by the motion of the pickup. The river divides Bong County from Lofa County. We are finally in BFM's old territory.

Night falls, a couple more hours go by, and a hellish storm breaks out. The route has become slippery as a skating rink. Daddison cuts the music and focuses intensely on the road, counter-steering in all directions, plunging in and out of water-filled basins.

The storm dissipates as suddenly as it began. The airfield in Voinjnama, the capital of Lofa county, appears on the right, marking our arrival at the city's outskirts. The airport served as an important hub for transporting medical personnel and supplies during the Ebola epidemics which ravaged the country. Lofa in particular.

We have a meeting scheduled with French doctors and an Italian priest from the Saint-Jean-de-Vianney congregation. Emmanuel Marry, the chargé d'affaires, has asked them to organize a welcome for us and guide us to our accommodations at the King Guest House. Permanently guarded and surrounded by highwalls crowned with shards of glass, the guest house is composed of several buildings. The rooms are modest. The bar has a good atmosphere. In the parking lot are two huge mango trees loaded with fruit and yet another magnificent bougainvillea. This will be our base camp for roughly eight days. No running water and no electricity during the day (like the rest of the county). We're going to have to be diligent about recharging our cell phones. That said, we have a perfect Internet connection with France.

After a meal of omelets, rice, and plantain bananas, and patata leaf—all bathed in palm oil—we organize a Franco-Liberian working group to assign responsibilities, especially with regard to convening witnesses to participate in our reconstructions. The first site is scheduled in the village of Chowe for 9 a.m.

Looking up from the guest house, I notice the stars appearing and disappearing beyond the fronds of the palm trees, blowing in the night breeze. It is hot and wet here, too. I listen to the sounds of the tropical forest around us. Birds, locusts, insects of all kinds, like competing choirs.

I think about how long it has taken us to reach the north of Lofa County. Thirty years. I wonder what it was like back then, invaded and at the mercy of hordes of savages, with no help from the outside. Wolves and sheep on the same pasture.

Tomorrow will be another day. I WhatsApp Marjorie: "Made it to the site just fine. Real work begins tomorrow morning with the witnesses."

17

SCENES

April 26, 2019—Chowe, Lofa County

"Where were you, precisely?"

I'm questioning the witness, who just arrived.

It's 9 a.m. and the sky is profoundly dark, meaning the day is likely to be complicated. The wind is blowing gently, but in gusts. Our guards have exited their 4×4 and are now positioning themselves around the site for security. Guns. Helmets. Vigilant.

"There."

Steve Bardon points to the location he was at when events unfolded. Tall, slender, sleek face, shaved head, solemn, elegantly dressed. He's conscious of the weight that his testimony carries and, above all, of the hundreds of eyes watching him. Following BFM's arrest, which resonated internationally through the press, Steve voluntarily presented himself to a Liberian NGO and offered to testify. The NGO, directed by a former journalist, himself tortured by a series of regimes, is dedicated to fighting against impunity in Liberia. It put us in touch.

At the time of the events, Steve, now forty-nine, was a twenty-year-old teacher who had just finished his studies in Monrovia. He was planning to return to Lofa County to teach and help the children, whose futures were limited in this part of the country. And in the rest of Liberia, for that matter.

Attached to his land, Steve was eager to give his time to help others but the civil wars and their trail of atrocities shattered his dreams. And not only his dreams. Before the war he married Rose Tryber, a fellow schoolteacher. They had met at university in Monrovia. They were going to move to Lofa County. She was expecting. BFM interrupted their plans.

Steve stands under an immense mango tree, the fruit, still green in this season, bows the ends of the branches. A crowd of women and men of all ages has gathered around us. It's difficult to imagine what they're thinking.

White people coming to stir up our painful past?

Or, white people coming to finally right the injustice we've lived with for thirty years?

"Are you sure?"

Steve looks directly at Paul, the Liberian investigator now questioning him curtly in a high-pitched voice.

Steve looks right back at him: "I remember it like it was yesterday."

Stéphanie looks at her watch.

"It's 9:30 a.m. We're officially starting the reconstruction."

She marks the time and location in her notebook, which will complement the report written by Liberian investigators as required by their minister of justice.

I hand Steve a four-inch yellow cone labeled with a number "1" in black and ask him to place it at his feet.

"Where was Howard?"

"There. He was walking down the road."

I take a yellow cone with the letter "A" on it and use a tape measure to determine the distance between the two points.

"Fifteen meters."

"Where was he going?"

"Toward Foya."

"OK. Can you please point in that direction so we can take a photograph?"

Valentin and the Liberian investigator position themselves behind Steve who points firmly toward Foya.

"Perfect. Thank you. Explain what happened next."

Steve launches into a long, difficult narrative.

"It was June 1990. Howard was returning from the Danish Medical Care[1] clinic, which had been looted and totally destroyed by BFM's men three days before the event. In December 1989, Charles Taylor and his men had crossed the border into Nimba County, armed by Côte d'Ivoire with its Gio and Mano soldiers. They opposed the Liberian armed forces, composed mainly of the Krahn and Mandingo ethnic groups. Taylor wanted to gain territory quickly and control the inflow and outflow of diamonds from Sierra Leone and Guinea, especially along the Makona River, Liberia's northern border."

"For this, Lofa County is strategic. The soldiers were instructed to pay themselves with whatever they could find locally. To pay themselves, soldiers terrorized local populations in these civil wars. At the same time, the ULIMO was formed in Sierra Leone with Krahn and Mandingo ethnic groups whose objective was to reconquer Liberia. So the NPFL eliminated from the civilian population any individual considered Krahn or Mandingo; ULIMO did the opposite, or similar, with the Gio and the Mano. We were caught in a vice, easy prey to an arbitrary fate. Every morning they would take a man or a woman and do whatever they wanted with them. They said: 'Six feet!' Which meant: 'Stand at six feet and look ahead, or else . . .' One wrong look and you could be six feet under.

"Howard was a good man, honest, great character, hard worker. He was a husband and a father. We were from the same village. We played, ran, hunted, fished, and swam together. He was my best friend."

Steve chokes up. It's obvious that images are flooding in. I mentally follow the thread of his thoughts: two boys, friends since childhood, growing up, having fun, laughter, adolescence, first loves.

Steve brings himself together and proceeds.

"We lived next door to one another. His father was a farmer like mine. They worked in the palm forests and produced oil that they sold at the market or in Guinea."

"We helped each other out. When I left to study in Monrovia, Howard studied medicine as best he could, assimilating traditional techniques with modern ones he learned from white people at the NGOs. This clinic was his whole life. He didn't care about how much time or energy he was putting in."

146

"The NGO had paid a fortune for an electric generator which was desperately needed to improve living conditions."

"When we learned that Taylor's troops were on their way, everyone went into the forests to protect themselves. We abandoned the village. We could have fled the country, to Guinea, for example, and joined the refugees in the camps. But we didn't want to abandon our older family members. They wouldn't have been able to make the trip."

"When BFM's troops found the villages empty, they combed the forests looking for us. They shouted out that they'd slit our throats if we didn't return to the villages. So, to allow everyone's parents, grandparents, aunts, and uncles to return to their houses, we went back."

I interrupt.

"How many soldiers were there?"

"BFM had a good fifty men, organized in a kind of battalion. He had five or six lieutenants, each with a group of armed men. BFM was in charge and he obeyed a general who, I think, was in Gbarnga, close to Taylor's headquarters."

"BFM was easily recognizable, because he always wore a beige sleeveless vest to show off his bulging muscles. A bunch of amulets were sewn into the front of it, behind black leather squares. Some on the back of it as well. They were pieces of his enemies, I think. Teeth, skin. I remember seeing a dried finger. AK-47 bullets. He also wore a lot of charms around his neck. Pieces of scalp, hair, long fingernails."

"I read that Taylor's soldiers sometimes wore robes that were supposed to protect them from bullets. Ours were dressed in a mixture of fatigues and jeans. Some of them also had warrior masks that they usually wore at the roadblocks they had set up everywhere to control the exits from the villages and to extort money from the local people. I remember of the lieutenants called himself One Foot Devil. He was particularly cruel. He wore a black commando suit. He was BFM's favorite, the one who did his dirty work."

"When we got back to the village, we climbed to the top of the hill to see the clinic. Howard discovered that it had been pillaged, and that its equipment had been stripped and was about to be transported. He was furious. BFM's men were there and had assembled all the able-bodied men from the village and the surrounding areas. That's why they wanted us to return to the village. To work us like slaves and to take our women. They forced us to carry the medical equipment. There were about twenty of us there."

Stéphanie asks him: "Are there any other people besides you who can testify to this?"

"No. I didn't know them."

A strange silence. I take a look at the spectators surrounding us.

David, the Liberian policeman, steps in:

"They won't testify, anyways. They're afraid."

"After all these years?"

"Yes. You never know what will happen tomorrow . . ."

Steve continues:

"BFM was there that night. He was watching over the operation. The medical equipment was worth a fortune. He and his lieutenants had hit the jackpot. They locked us in the clinic and placed guards at the entrance. Early in the morning, we were woken up with a rifle butt. BFM told us that today our mission was to transport the medical equipment to the Makona River at the Guinean border. It was called Operation Till Go. It was forced labor. Anyone who flinched was eliminated. His men circled us like wolves. We had no choice. So we carried all this material for two days and two nights, non-stop for fifty kilometers. Five men, exhausted, didn't make it. They were shot like monkeys, a bullet to the head. It was Lieutenant One Foot Devil who eliminated them. When we arrived at the river, some Guineans were waiting for us to put the equipment on a boat that would take it to the other side."

"Was BFM there?"

"Yes, he was coordinating the operations and, above all, the delivery of the funds. He was strutting around with his lieutenants, shooting in the air, drinking beer. They gave us authorization to eat and sleep a little, under guard. The following morning, it was the same scenario all over again. The same wakeup call with a rifle butt. We had to make the same journey back but this time with ammunition, rockets, rice, and other food. We'd become their slaves. When we passed through the northern gate of the village, we saw the bodies of the men that had been shot on the way. They had been cut open. Their intestines were nailed in the trees that lined the route to the village. Their heads had been cut off and planted on spikes. The mouths had been stretched to the maximum to form a hideous grimace from beyond the grave."

Idou continues to translate Steve's account, but is obviously affected.

"Their objective was to create maximum terror in the population, and to forestall opposition. They would cut up the corpses and scatter them around the villages to make an impression. The more they killed, the more they were feared. These wars didn't produce any glory like sometimes in your countries where battles have names and become famous. Nothing like that here. Only predation by warlords who had the power of life and death over everyone."

Just like that, I feel I'm back in that fucking black gash in the earth, the apocalyptic noises of war crimes filling the air.

Steve goes on:

"Howard and I were exhausted, but the sight of those acted like a whip. A couple of days later, the Danish NGO tried to return to the village to establish a presence. They told us they'd negotiated with the general who ran the sector and with Taylor. When they saw the state of the clinic, they naturally questioned Howard, who explained the situation. He had signed his death warrant. When BFM found out, he chased the NGO away at gunpoint. Howard was arrested there."

Steve points to cone "A."

"What happened afterward?" Valentin asks, taking both video and snapshots.

"BFM's men got out of their vehicle and hit him hard. Howard lost consciousness. Then they used a cable to tie him to their jeep and dragged him down there.

"Steve points to a distant patch of red dirt, visible between palm and mango trees.

We follow Steve along the trail, arriving at a spot roughly 400 yards away. Part of the crowd follows, children running, screaming. The patch is surrounded by adobe houses. Women are working around wood fires, preparing the day's meal. At the center, a sort of bar: men conversing over beer. They watch us.

Steve pauses.

"BFM was sitting there."

He points at the foundations of a house surrounded by mango trees. Valentin hands him a yellow cone marked "B." Steve places it at the center of what remains of BFM's house.

"Me, I hid behind this wall."

Steve walks about twenty meters away and places cone "2." More photos and video. I measure the distance. Twenty-one yards. We take a shot of the GPS beacon to mark the spot.

"Lieutenant One Foot Devil untied Howard. He was skinned up bad and unconscious. One Foot Devil then started performed the Tabay torture.[2] He tied Howard's elbows tight behind his back. The pain woke Howard up and he started screaming. The soldiers hit him with their boots and weapons. His shoulders were dislocated. BFM then ordered 'practice.'"

"Practice?"

"He shouted a religious word that signals a ritual. It consists of eating the heart of his enemy. It is a ritual practice of the Poro sect, or some perverse derivative of that secret society. Certain organs, including the heart, are eaten with the conviction that its flesh will give courage to soldiers. It is about seizing the vital force of your adversary. Sometimes it includes drinking blood with a mixture of ginger, gunpowder, and honey. This sect still exists today and even has members among the highest officials of the state. In Liberia, some people combine Freemasonry and the Poro sect. For women, it is the Sande secret society. They are involved in mutilations. Revealing the secrets of these societies is punishable by death.

"Their leaders are called *zoe*. BFM claimed he was a *zoe*, which frightened people even more. He would perform these rituals sometimes to sow terror."

The skies rumble. The light breeze is giving way to violent gusts. A few minutes later, it's a downpour, rain pounding on the sheet metal roofs as we run underneath for cover. The rain lifts up the red soil, and torrents of red water flow through Chowe's courtyard.

While we gather under the awning, I wonder about the rest of the day. I watch Steve, lost in thought. No one speaks. No point. The roar of the rain on the roof drowns everything out. Finally, after fifteen minutes, the rain subsides. We can resume the hearing.

Steve continues:

"Howard was then lifted by his shoulders. One Foot Devil took a knife and split his chest open. Howard let out a final scream. His heart was ripped out by the lieutenant, who gave it to BFM. Holding it in both hands, BFM carried it over his head. The soldiers screamed, shouted, danced.

"One Foot Devil took the heart and cut it into several pieces.

"BFM stood in the middle of his soldiers, took a piece of Howard's heart, and ate it.

"The lieutenant threw the other parts on the ground and the soldiers scrambled after them, like hungry dogs."

Steve mimics the throwing of the parts and cried.

"There was nothing I could do. I had to save myself."

Steve's testimony is consistent with other findings in the report of the Truth and Reconciliation Commission of Liberia.

Everyone is silent for a minute. I ask a question.

"Is this One Foot Devil still alive in your opinion?"

"No, in my opinion he is dead."

I have no evidence to the contrary, but I'm surprised by his certainty.

Steve places some more cones. Another round of photos and video. I thank him for his courageous testimony.

"Are you still a teacher?"

"Yes, I am. At a school near here."

"And your wife?"

It was a mistake to ask.

"My wife is dead. And my child, too."

This surreal reconstruction ends around noon. When I turn to leave, I see an old man approach Steve. He extends his hand and thanks him for what he's done, on behalf of himself and the community. Steve lowers his eyes in thanks before returning to his school.

My mind then goes back to a story that our French doctors had shared with us the previous day. A few months earlier, they had attended a play organized by a Swiss NGO. The themes were freedom of speech and the fight against impunity. When it came time to ask the audience to speak, everyone left the room.

Later, Paul, who had spoken to the old man, would tell me that Rose had become a sex slave of One Foot Devil, like other women in the county. Pay yourself. She was a gift from BFM to his lieutenant, a reward for loyalty. Rose was a piece of flesh to be abused, at the mercy of this perverse, sadistic man. She could not bear it and ended her life the only way she knew how. She provoked him.

She was beaten to death.

Afterward, Rose, like other women, was dismembered, her body parts carried around in a wheelbarrow. One Foot Devil's men made the locals buy them.

Steve discovered this after returning from a forced march through the forest with about twenty other young men. They were transporting supplies and equipment to the Sierra Leone border.

I feel I have a better understanding of Steve's certainty about the disappearance of One Foot Devil.

I also have a better understanding of the attitude of Liberian women of all faiths, and notably Leymah Gbowee, the president of the pacifist organization Women of Liberia Mass Action for Peace, who denied themselves to men so long as hostilities persisted. The sex strike during the second civil war was successful. It forced President Charles Taylor back to the negotiating table. Leymah Gbowee received the 2011 Nobel Peace Prize for "mobilizing and organizing women across ethnic and religious lines to end Liberia's long war and ensure women's participation in elections."

We return to the guest house. I message Marjorie, the investigating judge, on WhatsApp: "Hello Marjorie. We're getting what we came for. Good testimony."

An hour after we return, David, our Liberian police officer, visits us and proudly announces that his team and local colleagues have found other witnesses to BFM's crimes. He also found a newspaper article that summarizes facts surrounding the cannibalism Steve described.

I glance at the news article, which indeed briefly describes acts of cannibalism. Surprising all the same. This trip is beyond comprehension. We've landed in some unspeakable dimension, far beyond what we anticipated.

Aspects of my criminology training come back to me. In particular, the work of Pierre Thys[3] who studied the criminal activities of armed individuals and groups. Most of the time, the behavior of these criminal actors is learned through contact with others, either their speech or more commonly their examples. Both the means of killing and the justifications for killing are learned, with most cases stemming from greed.

Thys developed three theories of criminal development. The first is contextual, focusing on environmental conditions in which individuals find themselves. It highlights the susceptibility of any person placed in similar conditions to resort to criminality.

(Christopher Browning elaborates on this point, noting that war itself is a principal instigator of brutality and atrocity. Bombardments, spilled blood, dismembered corpses, and related trauma serve to erase guideposts that would otherwise steer individuals away from committing war crimes.[4])

The second theory considers the disposition of the individual. It emphasizes personality and character traits, even while recognizing that deviance is immutable in human nature. It distinguishes between people who will commit a criminal act and those who will abstain. This is the bad apple theory, which presupposes that disobedient and deviant individuals are predisposed to criminal activity. In the context of a war, this disposition is unleashed.

Last is the situational theory, which focuses on the roles individuals take on, how submissiveness is instilled in them, obedience demanded of them. A desire to be recognized for their performance leads individuals to criminality in certain social situations.

In most war crime cases, the three approaches interact and men considered ordinary, without criminal pasts, wind up committing war crimes and crimes against humanity.

The My Laï massacre during the Vietnam War is a striking example: one of the largest massacres of civilians by the U.S. armed forces, and one of the darkest chapters in American military history.

On March 16, 1968, C Company of the 1st Battalion of the 20th Infantry Corps, was helicoptered to the outskirts of My Laï village. In less than four hours, Lieutenant Calley and the men of his platoon, anticipating strong resistance, wiped out the village, killing 400 civilians. The U.S. Army Criminal Investigation Command found that a process of moral and behavioral drift turned young conscripts from different states into reckless killers. The platoon underwent a gradual, brutalizing transformation, stemming in large part from Lieutenant Calley's lack of leadership and his encouragement of torture and massacres. He did not punish wrongs and did not respect or enforce wartime rules of conduct. Worse, several days before My Laï, he himself killed an old man in front of his men, effectively inviting subordinates to follow his example and kill with impunity.

In the end, Lieutenant Calley was the only one of the twenty-six men initially implicated in My Laï sentenced to life in prison, although he served only three and a half years under house arrest.

Along the same lines is Christopher Browning's study of the criminal proceedings against German reservists in the Second World War. These 400 mostly middle-aged men, workers, craftsmen, shopkeepers from the Hamburg region, showed a particularly zeal in eliminating Jews. In a few months, they shot and killed 38,000 people and transported another 45,000 to the Treblinka death camp.

Browning sought to demonstrate that in the right context, any human group can be led to commit crimes against humanity. Among the contributing factors to the right context: pressure to implement government policy, the dehumanization of the enemy, a culture of obedience to the law, conformity and peer pressure. Between 80 and 90 per cent of the men in his study participated in the killings, even though those who refused to participate in the killings were not punished. Ordinary men were transformed into murderers and after the war returned to their regular occupations.

I remember a certain grandfather whom I recently met in France. He confided to me, tears in his eyes, the story of what he'd lived through and never discussed with anyone. A small-time farmer, handed a rifle by the French government, he found himself taking the lives of men considered terrorists just nine days after arriving on foreign soil during French military operations in the 1950s and 1960s. He was following orders.

David pulls me out of these thoughts. I have no real answers, anyhow. It's time to pick up the new witness to hear about the murder and torture of two witches, so designated by BFM.

Our witness's name is Darius Bollow.

18

WITCH

"Witch, n. (1) An ugly and repulsive old woman, in a wicked league with the devil. (2) A beautiful and attractive young woman, in wickedness a league beyond the devil."

Ambrose Bierce, *The Devil's Dictionary*

After the busy morning, the afternoon looks to be a scorcher. The program: witness depositions.

I finish swallowing a spoonful of rice and sweet potatoes when I hear someone laying on the horn. The guard opens the large gate. A motorcycle enters the enclosure and bee lines toward me, David driving, another man behind him, quite old, about seventy, tall, lean, gnarled. The old man jumps off the back of the bike before it comes to a stop.

David cuts the engine and introduces me in Kissi.

"Mr. Darius Bollow, I present to you Colonel Emeraux and his team, Stéphanie and Valentin."

Darius, sharp-eyed and alert, shakes my hand with both of his, a sign of gratitude and respect in Kissi. He wears a long gray coat with synthetic fur lapels, a black velvet cap fixed on his head. He has a short salt-and-pepper beard and his teeth are in bad shape, otherwise age doesn't really seem to have caught up with him.

"I'm the leader of the village of Lalazu. When I heard the French had come all the way here to investigate BFM, I decided to stop by. I'm old. I will die soon. It is better that I speak now. Afterward, it will be too late."

"Very well, Darius. Thank you. We'll record your deposition."

David takes out several sheets of paper and a pen to write his report. We begin.

"I was born in Kolahun, but I wouldn't be able to give you the date. I'm a farmer. I always worked in palm oil. When I was young, I was the most agile boy in the village. I'd climb right up to the top of the palm trees and cut down fruits for the palm oil. My father worked in the palm grove, too. My mother used to go to market and sell produce."

In the palm grove surrounding the guest house, I've seen men climb the trees barefoot using a large strap for traction. They pick the fruit which is then cooked again in a large kettle and hot-pressed in a mill turned by hand.

"I came here to tell you what I saw. For several months, BFM had been terrorizing Lofa County with his men. We were trying to avoid them. When ULIMO[1] arrived, there were battles with BFM's troops. One day, BFM assembled the entire population of the village with his men. He said that several of their guns had jammed and that it could only have been the work of witches. The villagers lowered their eyes in fear. They had us standing in a semi-circle to control everyone. One of BFM's lieutenants then said that someone was missing. Indeed, two old women had remained in their houses, Édith and Mary, widows, both sick. BFM gave the order to pick them up. He said the women were Mandingo, which wasn't true. The soldiers returned with the two women, dragging them by their hair on the ground. Édith and Mary said nothing. They didn't resist. They were resigned."

"The soldiers threw them down in the center of where we were all assembled. The soldiers screamed 'Witch! Witch!' A lieutenant savagely ripped off their clothes. They were prostrate on the ground."

"Then BFM got up and said that these women had cast a spell on his men. They were responsible for the fact that they he was having trouble pushing back their enemy the past couple of days. He then walked around the villagers standing in the arc, pushing them around. His eyes were blood-shot, probably from drugs. Then he shouted: 'Who here thinks that these women aren't witches? Whoever thinks that, raise your hand.' And he aimed his AK-47 at us."

"He then looked at me and called out. I had to approach him. He asked me to boil some palm oil in a kettle, the kind used to cook fruit. I could not refuse. When the oil was boiling, I tried to spill it on the ground. But he caught me and hit me on the head with his rifle butt. I passed out. I came back to consciousness when I heard screaming. I saw him pouring the steaming oil down Edith's throat as she tried to scream and made foul gurgling sounds. BFM stood over her invoking the gods, reciting magic formulas. He was a *zoe*. It was horrible. No one could move, not even Edith and Mary's children. Mary got the same treatment.

Darius stops his story. A thousand-yard stare. He takes off his cap. He is sweating profusely. Valentin fetches a bottle of water and hands it to Darius. He drains it in one gulp.

David also stands up, visibly shaken. None of us move. The scene is bewildering.

Darius resumes his testimony.

"As Edith and Mary were about to take their last breath, BFM turned them over on their stomachs. He spread their legs and put their arms in a cross. Then he took his large black knife and carved the word witch into their backs. No one said a word. I was still on the ground and not moving. On his order, the soldiers took the two bodies away. They forbade us to touch them. When they left, I ran to the first palm tree to note their direction, toward the south. I could see where they had deposited Edith and Mary, next to the river, on a mound of earth. We waited several days and with a few able-bodied men and Edith and Mary's children, we found the bodies and gave them a proper burial.

Darius has nothing more to say but asks:

"Is it true that you have arrested BFM? In France?"

"Yes, it is true."

"That's unbelievable. Good though . . . With all the people who have suffered."

"Would you be willing to come testify in France during his trial?"

"If I'm still alive, I'll come. I want to see him, look him in the eyes. I want him to pay."

David asks if there's anything else that he'd like to add. Darius shakes his head. David then covers his index finger in blue ink from his pen and presses it into the bottom of his notes to certify his copy of the deposition.

I ask:

"Darius, are you willing to show us where all this happened in the village?"

"Yes, of course."

"Perfect, let's drive over there."

After an hour on the trail, we hit the outskirts of Darius's village. Our 4×4 skids on the still wet earth, crashing through pits full of water. We're on a sort of plain, without much vegetation. On the right, a sign identifies rice paddies established by Japanese humanitarian efforts. A bridge appears in the distance, spanning the river Darius spoke of. Far off to the left, I make out a little hill with groupings of stone blocks, reminiscent of dolmen. Édith and Mary's burial site, without doubt.

As we get closer, I realize the bridge is just two large longitudinal crosspieces. The wheels have to be exactly aligned. Davisson cuts the music, concentrates, and puts the truck in gear, hands glued to the wheel, ready to react.

I glance over the edge. Worst-case scenario, it wouldn't be a long fall. A meter or two.

We make it across, followed by the Liberian police's 4×4, and park near the center of the village. Houses have been built along both sides of the trail, surrounded by a wealth of vegetation: coffee and banana trees, bordered by immense palms. In the center is the palm oil mill, next to a shelter under which are stacked pallets of oil in plastic bottles. I get a look at the inscription on the label: "Pastis of France. Aniseed-flavored aperitif, 45 per cent."

Astonishing.

The heat is now stifling. My shirt is soaked. Following Darius's instructions, we form a circle with yellow tape that reads "Gendarmerie nationale/Crime Scene." Darius positions yellow cones to mark the locations of BFM and his men, for the purposes of our final report.

The reconstruction lasts about two hours. As before, we grab key video footage and photographs. Children watch us intently, not missing a movement. They keep part of the yellow tape as a souvenir, along with pieces of candy that we make sure to have on hand.

Before parting ways, Darius says goodbye in the Kissi fashion, too, shaking with two hands. He looks at me with small clever eyes:

"I'm still very surprised to see you here, but I thank you for the work you're doing. You've come a long way, you've left your families to come and meet us. You're doing the work of justice which we were unable to do. In our country, the criminals are in power again. It will never end. Thank you again."

Later in the evening, the guest house opens its outdoor bar. African hits resonating in the hallways, colored spotlights shine warmly throughout the room. Not a soul in sight.

I think back to the farewell scene with Darius, considering the meaning it gives to our actions, to France's role in the fight against impunity. Around me, the night is soft and rustling with insects of all kinds.

I also think of how this fight is, most of the time, fought against the odds in our own country. Stuck in logistical tangles. Obstructed by myopic people in suits. They make cold calculations, guard their prerogatives jealously, and hide in their offices. They have all the power and they are disinclined to share it. The fight against impunity is beyond them. It doesn't fit on a spreadsheet.

The following days bring other witnesses, depositions that confirm facts already gathered and grow the case. Then a return trip to Monrovia. A moment to touch base with the French ambassador. A warm farewell shared with our Liberian police comrades.

We leave without any question that we have what we need to make BFM more talkative in front of our judge, Marjorie B.

On the flight back to France, I still have a bitter feeling about leaving behind a country that is helplessly watching the return of political violence. A few weeks later, supporters of Liberian President George Weah, the former soccer star, will surround a building on the outskirts of Monrovia where Tellia Urey, an opposition candidate in a by-election, is holding a meeting. For more than an hour, they will hurl objects at the building, smash windows, and destroy her vehicle. One assailant will attempt to stab the candidate.

This sort of violence is like a stone in a shoe. Eventually a decision needs to be taken to remove it.

But back in France, we have other things to worry about, notably Syria, which now contributes a quarter of our files.

And in particular there is the case of Caesar, emblematic of the barbarism of the Syrian regime and its leader El Assad who told ABC News in an interview, December 7, 2011: "No government in the world kills its people unless it is led by a madman . . . There were no orders to kill or commit brutality."[2]

Cynical or blind?

19

#STANDWITHCAESAR

"I left Syria with pure and sincere intentions. There are many files on the crimes of the regime: chemical attacks, mass murder, detentions. All these files will be opened and used as evidence against Bashar al-Assad . . . The truth will lead to victory. There's a proverb that says: 'No right is lost as long as there is a person demanding it.'"

— Caesar, April 2015. Quoted in Le Caisne, Garance, *Operation Caesar*, Stock, 2015.

July 11, 2019—Paris, OCLCH

Heat wave. France is suffocating. I'm shut up in my office, windows closed. Not a ray of sunlight can penetrate. Maps of Syria line the walls, along with a diagram of its different intelligence agencies. It helps to visualize the maze of police and military bodies that make up this country. While waiting for our witness, I read a Human Rights Watch report published in New York on July 3, 2012: "The Archipelago of Torture."[1]

Testimony assembled by Human Rights Watch from former detainees reveals a state policy of inhumane treatment and torture. The methods employed by the Syrian intelligence agencies, and the locations where this work are carried out, are clearly identified. According to Human Rights Watch, the worst torture occurs in detention centers directed by Syria's four intelligence agencies, collectively known as the *moukhabarat*: the Military Intelligence Directorate, the Political Security Directorate, the General Security Directorate, and the Air Force Intelligence Directorate. Each directorate runs its own detention centers of various sizes in Damas, the capital, with regional and local branches distributed throughout the country. All of them have the same goal. To hurt, to break, to kill.

The rallying cry: "Our blood, our soul, for you, Bashar."

Branches of the directorates are commonly identified by numbers: 215 or 248. Number 225 is also called "Palestine" because it is in charge of monitoring Palestinians. Sometimes they are named after their location, such as the dreaded Bab Touma branch of the Air Force Intelligence Directorate. It's the worst. All rally to the cry: "Our blood, our soul, for you, Bashar."

Syrians are well aware of their existence and pray never to set foot inside them.

The population is under heavy surveillance. Tightly controlled. An open-aired prison. One word too many about the Assads, the President's clan, means an arrest. Captive in filthy basements, packed cells, where prisoners are nude, beaten, tortured.

I open the Caesar folder. Double click. Images appear on the screen. Emaciated corpses litter the floor of a filthy, piss-yellow hangar. Men in uniforms, said to be North Korean (again, you can't make this up), bustle around the bodies, masks covering their noses.

I scroll through the faces, the grimacing and emaciated death masks. Sometimes eyes are absent. Removed. Nothing more to see here, nothing more to say. No more challenges. Born on the wrong side, meaning not Alawite.

The corpses carry the stigmata of maltreatment. Dysentery and malnutrition, cause the bones to protrude, sometimes broken. The wounds are raw, full of pus, bloody. On the skin, brown traces, external signs of pain, testimony to burns. Cigarettes, stoves, electric heaters, electrodes. Evidence of repeated hits. The mouths are sometimes open in a dying breath. Voices gone.

It is the work of barbarians. Torture with an intent to kill. Punishing people who dared to stand for themselves.

The elimination of so-called domestic terrorists who are being aided by foreign agents—that is how the regime sees the mission of its intelligence services.

The skeletal bodies produce a dirty feeling of déjà vu. History stuttering. Impunity unchecked through Nazi death camps through Stalin and the Balkan war to this. The list is long. No difference, and the same indifference.

I continue with this morbid slideshow.

Zooming in, I notice that each cadaver wears on the chest or forehead a piece of tape with a number written in felt-tip pen. Three digits. The first for the detainee who lost his status as a human being; the second for the intelligence branch that imprisoned, tortured, and massacred him; the third for the medical examiner who completed the report.

The meticulousness work of a bureaucracy of butchers. For two reasons. First, to allow the issuance of a death certificate to families looking for a missing brother or father. The person is said to have died of a "respiratory problem" or a "heart attack." The coroner might also write: "while being forced to confess certain truths, the terrorist met his death." A message to assure the hierarchy that its work was being done. The deadly routine. Kill, record, report.

It is an administrative death machine, drawing on Alois Brunner and the Nazi heritage, honed for forty years by Hafez al-Assad who is thought to have trained Syria's intelligence agency directors in torture and maintained the regime's historic links to Eastern Europe and Russia.[2] Torture is taught in training schools. An array of methods: the German Chair that breaks your back in two; the Ghost technique of suspension by the hands for days on end; electric shock. Schools of crime.

Sometimes, for a large sum of money, families can obtain partial truths concerning the deaths of loved ones. More rarely, they are able to obtain the body. Most of the time, they won't receive any information at all. People simply disappear into the vast crushing machine.

The photos I'm looking through were taken by Caesar, a code name used to protect the photographer from fear of reprisals against his family which remains in Syria. In the beginning, Caesar took photos for the military police in Damascus. In France, we'd call him a criminal identification technician, specializing in forensic science.

Before the revolution in March 2011, his job had been to take pictures of crime scenes in which the military might be involved, either as victims or perpetrators. They might be suicides, murders, various types of accidents. Working with an investigator and a judge, he photographed crime scenes, weapons, and so on. His pictures were attached to the file prepared by the investigator or judge, which was then sent to military court. His services were in high demand and Caesar enjoyed his work. Until March 2011.[3]

In Deraa, demonstrators went out into the streets to take a few breaths of freedom. They were severely repressed. Some were beaten, others shot. Caesar's job changed. He was no longer photographing military cases but those of civilians. In particular, the bodies that arrived from the south of Syria, those of the "terrorists." He was no longer working at crime scenes but in the military hospital of Tichrine, north of Damascus, headquarters of the military police. The bodies had bullet wounds. They had been beaten. When they were unloaded from trucks, soldiers spit on them, calling them "son-of-a-bitch terrorists."

The bodies piled up faster and faster. Fewer bullet wounds, more signs of torture. The work of the intelligence services. Caesar's job was to photograph the corpses and keep quiet. No questions. He was closely supervised by the intelligence services.

When Tichrine could no longer handle all the bodies, Caesar was sent to photograph corpses at another military hospital in Messeh, branch 601, a stone's throw from the French high school and the presidential palace. The corpses were stored in sheds. Caesar was now working on an assembly line, photographing, labeling, filing. The coroner arrived in the morning to document the age, height/weight, and signs of injury on the dead. Never mentioned torture.

Eventually Caesar returned to his office to write his standardized reports. They were entitled "note on the incident" or "Evidence of justice." More like evidence of injustice.

He was working faster and faster because the bodies were piling up and rotting in the sun. Birds were pecking at them. The smell was unbearable. It clung to one's skin, insinuating itself everywhere, scarring the brain. He was jolted awake at night, covered in sweat.

And the next day, and the day after, more corpses arrived. Long days of this dirty work, finishing late in the evening. Less sleep, more nightmares.

Caesar started to crack. How long before one of these corpses was someone from his own family? He needed to talk. But who do you reach out to in a country that keeps everything tightly controlled and everyone under surveillance? Phones are tapped. His department was becoming rife with suspicion and denunciation. Alawite officers were in charge. He is a Sunni. Many Sunni were defecting. He thought about deserting himself but that could lead to serious trouble—to being found among his photographs.

Finally, one spring evening in 2011, Caesar visited a friend of twenty years, Sami. He decided to unload everything. He wanted to quit. He wanted to leave the country. Sami saw an opportunity to show the world the reality of the regime, it's cruel, systematic administration of torture and death. He convinced Caesar to stay at his post for a while so that they can make secret copies of the photos in his reports. Caesar would smuggle out the photos and Sami would keep them in a safe place. For two years.

Caesar, after that evening, had only one goal. To get the images out, even at the risk of his own life. Release the images so that families can know what happened to their loved ones and mourn. Show them to the whole world so that, one day, justice can be done. Get them out before everything is erased. Immortalize the dead. Although they feared for their lives, Caesar and Sami were committed to this clandestine work.

Finally, September 2013, Caesar fled, seizing the opportunity to tag along with a mission headed outside of Damascus, which he used as a cover to meet an opposition member at a bus stop. It was a bittersweet moment: leaving the world he grew up in, while at the time escaping a life that's had become unsupportable and where each day was a risk.

He jumped into the void, passing through checkpoints in the hands of one smuggler after another, uncertain who to trust. House to house, heading toward the border in a region teeming with informants, militias, armed Islamist groups. In a rebel zone where food is scarce, where sharing is the norm. Then one day, hidden in the back of a car, Caesar crosses the border.

Tens of thousands of photographs had already been shared by activists in low-definition transfers by email and the Cloud. The high-definition hard disk is being smuggled out through the mountains. The world will come to know the filthy, black work of this rotten regime and its intelligence directorates.

The evidence reached Islamic moderates in the Syrian National Council, an Istanbul-based coalition opposed to the government of Bashar al-Assad and committed to bringing peace and democracy to Syria. Its leaders recognized that the photographs could convince the international community of the reality inside Syria and change the dynamic of the conflict, shifting it from military to legal, engaging the forces of international justice.

But not only that. First, families needed to mourn, to recognize their own. So the photographs had to be organized. Caesar's file was divided into several categories: detainees who died in the dungeons of the intelligence services; regime soldiers who died in combat (considered martyrs by the regime); and civilians killed in combat, women, men, and children labeled terrorists by the regime.

The work was done secretly in Istanbul by Sami and others. It was a wretched process, sifting through the succession of grimacing faces. They concentrated on the detainees, of whom the majority were from branches 215 and 227 of the military intelligence directorate. The photos were analyzed to note the age and identifying features of each victim, wounds, style of torture inflicted, the presence of fresh blood, malnutrition, missing eyes, evidence of chemical treatments. About 6,800 victims.

The photos were then published on the Internet by the Association for the Disappeared and Prisoners of Conscience to allow families to identify their loved ones.

There were still unanswered questions.

What became of the bodies?

Buried in trenches? Burned? Hidden in mass graves?

Caesar had taken photos in just two hospitals in Damascus, between the years 2011 and 2013. How many were dead in other parts of the country controlled by the regime?

The photos were next shared with the world. The first country to react was Qatar, which commissioned the London firm Carter-Ruck to authenticate them. Three former international prosecutors were assigned: David Crane, David Crane, former prosecutor of the Special Court for Sierra Leone; Desmond de Silva, former chief prosecutor of the Special Court for Sierra Leone; Geoffrey Nice, former chief prosecutor in the trial of former Yugoslav president Slobodan Milosevic.

In their thirty-one-page report, details of which were published on January 20, 2014, by CNN and *The Guardian*, Crane stated that there was "clear evidence demonstrating that the Al-Assad regime is a killing machine." Prosecutors found Caesar's work convincing. He had been determined in his actions and honest in his approach.

On January 22, Ahmed Jarba, leader of the National Coalition of Syrian Revolutionary and Opposition Forces, held up the photographs at the Geneva 2 conference called to find a peaceful settlement to the conflict in Syria. In response, Damascus claimed that the photographs are fake and that Crane had produced "a politicized report lacking objectivity and professionalism."

The photos were also made public at the Holocaust Memorial in Washington, at the Arab World Institute in Paris, and, later, at the United Nations headquarters in New York.

On April 15, 2014, the UN Security Council held an informal meeting on the Caesar report and declared that it constituted a body of documents of unprecedented importance, systematically demonstrating the practice of war crimes and crimes against humanity. This came in addition to multiple reports produced by the UN Human Rights Council's Independent International Commission of Inquiry on the Syrian Arab Republic, also known as the Pinheiro Commission (named for its chair). The Pinheiro Commission concluded that "certain elements, such as the location identified in some photographs as the military hospital 601 in Damascus, the methods of torture and the conditions of detention, corroborate the commission's long-standing conclusions regarding the systematic use of torture and the deaths of detainees. Investigations are continuing, but the findings will largely depend on the identification of new metadata."

Indeed, since 2011, the commission has collected numerous accounts of torture and deaths in custody in government prisons in the Syrian Arab Republic between March 2011 and January 2015. These accounts support the commission's determination that crimes against humanity in the form of torture and killings were committed. It established that in Damascus the use of torture was widespread and systematic on the premises of various intelligence branches, hospitals, and prisons. Rape and other sexual violence were part of torture. The information gathered indicated that these crimes were a result of a state policy implemented by branches of the government.

Paulo Sérgio Pinheiro stated that "the executions and deaths described in this report occurred with high frequency, over a long period of time. They took place in multiple locations and with logistical support that involved considerable state resources. High-ranking officers, members of the government, all were aware that deaths were taking place on a massive scale."

He continued: "No one can deny it. The conditions in the prison were maintained with the calculated intention of causing mass deaths among the inmates."

The four members of the UN Commission of Inquiry were never allowed by Damascus to visit Syria. Their work is based on the testimony of thousands of documents including the testimony of victims and satellite photos. The commission interviewed 621 people, 200 of whom witnessed the death of one or more of their cellmates.

In short, the policy of exterminating prisoners warranted and conducted by the Syrian regime qualified as a crime against humanity.

In July 2014, Caesar was invited to testify before the U.S. Congress. His photographs were projected. The hashtag #StandwithCaesar began spreading on Twitter on August 11 at the instigation of the Syrian opposition. The photographs were handed over to the FBI, which again authenticated them in June 2015.

What does the International Criminal Court do? Unfortunately, nothing. It is a dead end. Damascus never ratified the treaty creating the ICC, which can only investigate crimes committed on the territory of one of its member states or by one of its nationals. The only other way the ICC can become involved is if the United Nations Security Council refers a case. An ICC prosecutor can then investigate and issue arrest warrants against those responsible for crimes. In May 2014, based on the Caesar report, France submitted a resolution to the security council. Thirteen countries out of fifteen voted in favour. Russia and China vetoed it. Never before has a conflict been so thoroughly documented with photographs, videos, testimony, yet nothing.

While no international jurisdiction can address Syria, the UN nevertheless established a mechanism to facilitate the collection of evidence of atrocities committed by all belligerents in the country since 2011 to ensure that they do not disappear over time and that impunity does not take hold. Catherine Marchi-Uhel, an experienced French magistrate, was appointed to head this structure, M3I, the International Impartial and Independent Mechanism. The mechanism is not allowed to visit Syria but it has collected more than 900,000 documents and testimonies through the Syrian Commission of Inquiry, Syrian civil society, and a number of refugee victims and witnesses.

Despite all this, hopes for justice in Syrian are falling. Its crimes are known but nothing has been done. Confidence in the UN has been lost; at the end of the day, it only reports. Caesar did his part but the world has washed its hands of his work.

I'm reminded of Jan Karski, a real person and the hero of Yannick Haenel's novel which threw me for a loop a couple of years back. With testimonies about death camps falling on deaf ears among the allied powers, Karski chose not to speak again for several decades.

Caesar, too, has gone silent.

Questions arise. What do we do about great powers who for reasons of realpolitik protect criminal heads of allied states?

I forget who said it, "For one murder, you arrest the perpetrator and put him in prison; for ten murders, you arrest him and put him in a psychiatric hospital; for 10,000 murders, you invite him to a negotiating table."

Syria is reaping what it sowed. Bashar released some of his hardest and most radical Islamist leaders from the Seidnaya military prison at the start of the conflict to threaten its opposition. The Islamic State, Islamic Army, and other Islamic groups (some financed by Sunni states) have proliferated, much to the alarm of the West. They use the same means of terror. Imprisonment, cutting throats. One tyrant tries to chase out another, neither better nor worse. They all have the same objective: power and money for the benefit of a minority. Behind the nationalistic, ethnic, or religious veneer you find cash, oil, gold, diamonds. The population is caught in the middle.

The West is paralyzed in the face of these new threats. The crimes are broadcast on our televisions, and exported to the terraces of Parisian cafés, and to our concert halls.

National jurisdictions must step in where universal jurisdiction has failed. In France, Laurent Fabius declared: "Faced with these crimes that shock the human conscience, with this bureaucracy of horror, faced with this negation of the values of humanity, it is our responsibility to act against the impunity of these murderers. The French authorities have received several thousand photographs from the Caesar file. Given the seriousness of the facts, I have decided to transmit these photos to the French justice system to allow it to use them and decide what action to take, including possible criminal prosecution."[4]

On September 15, 2015, the Paris Public Prosecutor's Office and the AC5 section opened a preliminary investigation into multiple charges of crimes against humanity. Camelia B. took on the investigation on behalf of OCLCH. She is a determined woman and vice-prosecutor passionate about international justice and the fight against impunity.

I open one last report on my screen, this one from Amnesty International written in February 2017. The conclusions: from September 2011 to December 2015, between 5,000 and 13,000 people were allegedly summarily executed in Seidnaya prison, thirty kilometres north of Damascus.

The claim was vehemently denied by Bashar Al-Assad in an interview: "This report is based on allegations. Amnesty International is a world-renowned organization, and it is shameful that it is building a report on the basis of mere allegations."

But he refuses international observers permission to visit his country. "No, definitely not! It is a question of sovereignty. Also, the death penalty is legal in Syria. We don't need to hide."

The Caesar case has become a highly-structured investigation. There are no French people among the victims in Caesar's photographs, and no French people among the executioners. But potential Syrian perpetrators are on our territory, some without right to asylum. We have at our disposal the tool of universal jurisdiction and there is no statute of limitations. With the torture being systematic, we can hold to account, say, the leader of a local roadblock with his list of people to arrest, or a general in charge of a branch of the intelligence service if they have fled to France in search of asylum.

Given the scale of the regime's operations, there should be many targets. The Syrian Network for Human Rights (SNHR) reports that between March 2011 and September 2019, at least 14,298 people, including 178 children and sixty-three women, have died by torture in Syria. Investigations conducted by the NGO documented seventy-two methods of torture practiced by the Syrian government in its detention centers and military hospitals. The same source further reports that nearly 1.2 million Syrians have been arrested and imprisoned in the Damascus regime's detention centers, and 130,000 people are still arrested and imprisoned or are missing, since the beginning of the civil war in 2011.

It is our job to collect as much testimony as possible from victims or witnesses who have managed to escape Syria and who are either in France or Europe or countries bordering Syria. To accommodate the workload, the gendarmerie has created an investigative unit called "Sanson."[5] It brings together investigators dedicated to and focused on Syria under the direction of Patrick, who leads the investigation under the auspices of the magistrates, notably Camélia B. We will hear from more than a hundred victims describing similar horrors and establish the facts of crimes against humanity.

Fortunately, as is usually the case, we are not alone. We can draw on our galaxy of partners in the fight against impunity: NGOs, Europol, Eurojust, M3I, European war crime units, etc. As a result of the high number of Syrian refugees wishing to come to Europe and to testify, a coordinated effort between European magistrates and war crimes investigators has emerged organically. We meet twice a year in The Hague to exchange information under the aegis of Eurojust and within the framework of European prosecutors and investigative units dealing with genocide and crimes against humanity.

We are also part of a joint investigative team with our German comrades from the federal prosecutor's office and the BundesKriminalAmt. This means that our investigations are now conducted as a single investigation with the BKA. Our German colleagues can hear our witnesses in France and vice versa. We carry out our interrogations together. The success of such a joint investigation team first and foremost requires mutual trust and friendship. We are lucky enough to have it.

The heat is in my office keeps getting worse. I glance out the window. Scrawny plane trees in the courtyard. Kids playing cops and robbers. We're a long way Syria where children dodge chemical attacks and barrels dropped from helicopters. Another world.

I'm now waiting for our new Syrian witness, Nazim. A freedom fighter whose deposition promises to provide evidence that will further our case. He'll be interviewed by two German colleagues, the federal prosecutor Dieter K. and Marcus N., an investigator of the BKA.

Nazim is a special witness, Camellia warned me. He has endured the worst.

20

FREEDOM FIGHTERS

"There are three types of supervisors and guards, always the same, whether it's a holding cell, a penitentiary, or a concentration camp. These are who can make the lives of the prisoners a hell: the bad, the evil, the treacherous, the brutal consider the prisoner an object on which they can exercise their perverse tendencies. Next to them are the indifferent. Then the benevolent. No former prisoner could claim to have suffered any mistreatment in my establishment."

—Rudolf Höss Commandant, Auschwitz
Concentration Camp, 1947

July 13—Paris, OCLCH, Witness Hearing Room

I look at the man seated in front of me. He is sweating.

This is day two of the heatwave. I slept badly. Apparently, so did he. Maybe not for the same reasons.

In his country, the cops are there to torture. We're here to protect.

In Syria, everything can be bought. Justice. Liberty. In his country, everything is sold. Starting with the soul. Things like that leaves traces on the body and in the mind.

"Good morning, Mr. Al Ahmar."

"Good morning, Colonel."

His attitude is respectful without being ostentatious. Strangely, he keeps his head lowered, eyes fixed on the ground. He's dressed in a navy suit, worn, a little too big. A light blue shirt open at the neck, showing a gold pendant engraved with a verse of the Koran.

He is tall, wizened. About forty years old. His face is dotted with scars. Small but noticeable, especially on his nose, which is crooked. His hair is combed back, probably to hide a bald spot.

Scars visible on the hands as well. A signet ring with an impressive lapis lazuli. His fingers are folded together, the ones on his right hand yellowed from nicotine. The left pinky is crooked. Presumably broken. On the inside of his arm, I see a remarkably fine, slender tattoo that runs up toward his chest.

Suddenly, he straightens up, as if by reflex. His green eyes observe me with a mixture of fear and courage. A reflection of his soul. There's a strange strength to him, as though nothing could touch him. He takes in everything that is happening around him. His eyes search, scrutinize.

A door slams. It startles him and brings a burst of air.

Béatrice and Patrick just entered the room with Dieter K. and Marcus N., who've made the trip by train from Karlsruhe and Bonn, respectively. They are accompanied by Ahmed, our interpreter, who's become a key part of our team. The precision and objectivity of his translations are absolutely essential to the record and the smooth running of the hearings.

Warm greetings with our German colleagues, both Francophones and Francophiles, which is appreciated.

They take their place around the table and introduce themselves to Nazim.

I suggest coffee and fresh water to release a bit of the tension. A habit imported from Bosnia. Coffee first, conversation after. In Bosnia this can last up to two hours. Time is a relative notion in the East. It's fine once you get used to it.

Nazim handles his cup delicately, sipping the espresso and alternating it with fresh water. His gaze wanders outside of the room. His mind seems to follow.

He breaks the silence.

"Do you know Fairuz?"

"No, I don't."

He hands me his cell. His home screen is a picture of a beautiful oriental woman, almond eyes, long hair.

"She's a famous singer in Syria but also in neighboring countries, in Jordan, in Lebanon, where she's from. People living in those countries start the day with coffee and a Fairuz song. It's a stage name, meaning turquoise. You sip your coffee and let her voice sooth you. I always followed that ritual in Syria."

Silence.

"The man who tortured me, too. In my cell, squeezed in with the other prisoners. I always heard the same song. 'Bint El Shalabiya,' one of my favorites. First the guitar, the rhythm, then the languorous voice of Fairuz. My tormentor was drinking his coffee. The accordion, the chorus, then Fairuz again. I would have liked it to last an eternity. She sings about love. Then the song stops. The cage opens. I am pulled out by my torturer. He tortures me twice a day. Since then, I cannot listen to Fairuz anymore."

Silence.

"Why did you set her as the home screen on your mobile?

"So I never forget how angry I am."

Pause.

"Angry at those who destroy my people. And those who let them. A cold anger that comes from afar."

His voice is calm, grave, but his hands are clenched tight, fingers white at the knuckles.

"It was passed on to me by my father. More than fifty years ago, my father was imprisoned in Damascus after making remarks that were considered impertinent. He was then transferred to 'terrible Palmyrae.'"

I wait a moment.

"I thank you for coming to us here to give us your testimony. Many do not do so for fear of the regime and consequences to their families back home, which we understand perfectly."

"I have no more family. All of them are dead or have been murdered. I came because of what I read in the press and learned through the Syrian community. That France and your investigating judges had issued arrest warrants against Syrian officials in the Dabbagh case. I believe in Caesar's work and the work you are doing."

"Our German colleagues do, too."

Everyone looks over, Dieter responds:

"Yes. I issued an international arrest warrant for Jamil Hassan on charges of crimes against humanity in June 2018, and France did the same in November, I believe."

I nod.

Mazen Dabbagh, a person of French-Syrian origin, was a principal education advisor at the French high school in Damascus. He was arrested in Damascus in November 2013 with his son Patrick by Syrian Air Force intelligence officers.

In October 2016, after three years of intense searching, Obeida Dabbagh, Mazen's brother and Patrick's uncle, residing in France, filed a complaint in October 2016 with the special unit on crimes against humanity and war crimes. A judicial investigation was opened for "enforced disappearances and torture, constituting crimes against humanity and complicity in crimes" with the support of the International Federation for Human Rights and the League of Human Rights.

As in many other cases, Syrian authorities issued two death certificates for Mazen and Patrick Dabbagh in 2018. Both were said to have died in detention. Officially, Patrick Dabbagh died as early as January 2014 and his father in November 2017. Of heart attacks. No bodies were returned, and no place of burial was specified.

On November 4, 2018, armed with this new evidence, French authorities issued three arrest warrants against Ali Mamlouk, director of the national security office and a close adviser to Bashar and Jamil Hassan, head of the air force intelligence services, and Abdel Salam Mahmoud, the head of the investigation department at the Mezzeh Military airport in Damascus. They are charged with "complicity in torture," "complicity in enforced disappearances," and "complicity in crimes against humanity."

"You see, finally, things are moving," says Markus.

"Yes. That's why I decided to come."

"We are going to start the hearing. The two investigators sitting at the table are here to take your deposition. If you wish, we can record the interview."

"Yes, no problem."

Patrick and Stéphanie start the computer and video camera. We have decided to modify the way we receive victims, in particular for the Syrian cases. Our former location in an old fort in the Paris region brought back bad memories. So we have created a special room, furnished and equipped for this type of hearing, with a psychologist on standby if the need arises. Two screens are installed outside the room. The second interviewer is in communication with the first through an earpiece through which questions can be advanced. The system translates speech to text automatically.

The camera's red light starts blinking.

"First of all, I would like to tell you how grateful I am to France, and to you personally, as well as the judges of the Paris court for the work you are doing. Without your actions and universal jurisdiction, it would be impossible for Syrian victims, as well as those in many other countries, to obtain reparations."

"I spent about four years in prison and in the intelligence branches where I was brutally tortured. It started with an arrest in Deraa, then I was detained for five months in the intelligence branch of the air force, two months in the Palestine branch, and the rest in Seidnaya prison waiting for my trial, which was a parody of justice. Finally, after the judge was paid a large sum, I was released in June 2015. I fled Syria in December of 2015 and obtained asylum in France in February 2016."

Patrick: "Thank you. Could you tell us about your life before the revolution?"

"My name is Nazim Al Ahmar and I am originally from Douma, a northern suburb of Damascus. I was born on December 21, 1969, into a Sunni family. My mother's name was Basima Shalash. She was a house-wife. She died in a bombardment launched by the regime in 2015. My father, Mohammed Al Ahmar, was an archaeologist and a historian. He did a lot of work at the archaeological sites in Palmyrae. He was also very political. Very active in Syria's communist party which protested the French presence after the Second World War."

Nazim smiles.

"The party was open to everyone, regardless of religion, ethnicity. In 1970, when Hafez al-Assad took power, he established a form of political pluralism and created the National Progressive Front, but demanded the acceptance of the Arab nationalist and socialist policies of the government. Despite those draconian demands, the activists in my father's party decided to join forces. My father disagreed. The future would prove him right. He had no confidence in Assad, especially after 1967 and the war with Israel. We had lost everything and the radio was announcing victory. My father had always fought against the irresponsibility, the vanity, and the hypocrisy of our leaders."

"Then on June 26, 1980, when Hafez al-Assad narrowly escaped an assassination attempt, his brother Rifaat al-Assad, leader of the Defense Companies,[1] had a thousand members of the Muslim Brotherhood massacred in Palmyrae prison."

"My father was officially atheist, but he denounced this massacre as a communist. Then the Defense Companies entered our house one morning in December 1981, on the twenty-first, to be exact. My parents were preparing to celebrate my birthday. They beat my father in front of me and my mother. She tried to intervene but was violently pushed away. Her head hit the corner of the table. One of the officers said to my father, 'Be thankful I am not raping her in front of you and your son.' They were showing us the price of criticizing those in power. I would never see my father alive again. I was twelve years old that day and I understood the direction my life was going to take. My birthday present was that anger that I mentioned, which will never leave me. So I decided to defend the oppressed."

"My father was imprisoned in Palmyre, a city where, precisely for love of his country, he had spent days and nights digging to demonstrate the richness of our country and civilization. Cruel irony of history. His comrades finally managed to find out what prison he had been transferred to after Palmyrae. After paying a large sum of money to a military man that the leader of the communist party knew, we were able to recover his body to give him a dignified burial. His body was marked by reddish stains. We learned later, thanks to the indiscretions of party members, that my father was used as a guinea pig in a chemical weapons experiment."

The German prosecutor interrupts.

"Do you mean to say that in the 1980s, Assad had already been testing chemical weapons on people?"

"Yes. The Ghouta attack did not just fall out of the cupboard one day.[2] All this was part of a rigorous and well thought out plan, directed by high-ranking officials, directors of air force intelligence, members of the government. They used prisoners to verify the effects on human beings."

"OK. What did you do after that?"

"I studied sociology in Damascus and graduated in 1992. I specialized in the defense of prisoners of conscience and their families. In the 2000s, when everyone was caught up in the Damascus Spring, I created the Center for the Promotion of Democracy in Syria, the CPDS, in 2003, to be exact."

"Excellent program."

"As you say. France was our model, of course. Your country and certain NGOs working to defend human rights helped a lot, and not only on the financial level. Of course, we got harassed by the intelligence agencies. But we kept hope. A sort of naive euphoria. Later, when I was arrested for the first time in 2009, the officer who interrogated me, an Alawite, said to me: 'But what are you thinking? That you, the people, will get your freedom?' He laughed hard. I understood then that all of it was lies. The financial interests of government officials and the Bashar clan were such that nothing would change. And that's how things went until March 2011."

"Were you tortured in 2009?"

"No, not really, because they were suspicious of me and my networks, in particular the international ones. It was just intimidation. Flexing muscles and leaving fingernail marks around your neck. We were under enormous pressure. The intelligence services would come in, seize everything we had, and leave. We had to start from scratch each time."

"But I was no longer fighting alone, because it was at CPDS that I met Nadia Hamidou. She was already a writer and had written several successful plays. She wanted to commit herself and put her talent at the service of a noble cause. Freedom. She wanted to give birth to a better world. Her writings became more and more critical of the regime and started to attract attention. But her talent protected her, in a way. She became my wife the same year and gave me two beautiful children, Ghassan and Ahmad, in the years that followed."

"Then from 2011?"

"After the Arab Spring, Nadia and I started to hope again. In March 2011, the fifteenth to be exact, we had organized a protest in Damascus in front of the ministry of the interior with signs showing photos of the prisoners of conscience and our support for their release. Our slogan was, 'Sunnis, Alawites, the Syrian people are one and we want freedom.'"

"How many of you were there?"

"About a hundred in front of the ministry. Through Facebook, others quickly joined, and demands were brought forward, namely for a new constitution, the end of the state of emergency and emergency courts. Things we'd been asking for years, and especially since the Damascus Spring."

"That day, around 4 o'clock, the square was rapidly encircled by security forces. We were arrested, beaten with billy clubs, and thrown onto buses. We were driven to one of the military facilities and put in a large holding cell, the men separate from the women. Nadia, my friend El Tayeb Tassi, a renowned lawyer who was involved with CPDS, and myself were released that evening. The following day, the national newspaper explained that we'd been arrested for drug trafficking. What a joke!"

"Three days later, since I had created a Facebook page where Nadia had posted a pamphlet on the glory of freedom, I was walking in the street when a large Mercedes drove by me. Three men got out, surrounded me, beat me, and threw me in the trunk. I was placed in isolated confinement in military branch 215. The next cell over, I heard a voice and recognized it as that of my old professor, Mohammad al-Chourbago, a well-known Syrian philosopher and opponent of the regime. It gave me courage to know that he was alive. I told him my name, so that the first one to be released could inform our families of our imprisonment. He was released the next day and informed Nadia. In the case of forced disappearances, the regime takes you away without witnesses and your family has no news of you. It is a terrible thing."

"Every hour at night, a guard would open the slot in the cell door to insult me, my mother, my wife. I was instructed to stand up and face the wall. In the morning, they brought me to an officer who questioned me about my Facebook accounts. I gave him fake information, of course. So he asked again, more irritated. He wanted the names of the managers of the accounts. Again, I gave him the names of people living overseas."

"Were you beaten?"

"No, but he was enraged. He yelled insults at me two inches away from my face."

"OK."

"Then he took him to a large, plush office where General Suleiman, the head of the military branch, was sitting. Two plainclothes officers stood in the room beside him. He was smoking a cigar while sipping his coffee. He loved to blow smoke rings and place his cigar in the center. He explained to me that it would be wrong for me to continue in this way. He had no doubt that I would defend my country and that I was a true patriot. According to him, we were being manipulated by foreigners and especially Israel and the United States who want Syria to die. He advised me to learn my lesson and, in the future, not to let myself be manipulated. I was released the same evening. Given this turn of events, we decided that Nadia would keep her voice down so that she could devote herself to the children. We couldn't afford to be arrested together and abandon our sons."

"I understand."

Silence.

"Then there was Deraa and the movement that spread to other cities.[3] Syrians had overcome fear. I admit to being surprised. When we in the CPDS heard that teenagers had been arrested and tortured, we headed south to help the local protests. There was a sense of urgency, I was outraged and found the repression unacceptable."

"Atef Najib, the local chief of the province of Deraa, was a strong supporter of the regime. He did not want to hear anything against it, despite the pleas of families, even after the patriarch of one delegation, as a gesture of submission, put his hatta [Bedouin turban] on his desk."

"Rumors circulated in the country that Atef Najib said to families of those detained: 'Forget your children and go to your wives. They will give you more. And then, if they are not able to give you children, bring us your wives. We will do it for you.'"

"This disturbed the honour of the people of Deraa. And it is why Ahmad Al Zoubi and I got into an old Renault and headed south. Ahmad was my brother in arms, the man with whom I had created the center. He was a human rights lawyer. He was a fiery man, a ball of energy. The fight! Nothing mattered to him more than that. He was an activist who had decided not to leave any family behind, voluntarily. He knew he would sacrifice his life for freedom and his fight."

Silence from Nazim.

I thought of the struggles of those resistance fighters who, in the past, sacrificed their lives to make France a democracy. It is in these moments that you recognize the gap, the abyss that separates a free society from a dictatorship, and at the same time realize how fragile our model of democracy is and how much it needs to be protected.

Nazim breaks my reflections.

"We made it across the army's checkpoints. In Deraa, we met up with other sympathizers and protested alongside the people for several days. Then I was called back to Damas. It was on that return trip that we came across a routine checkpoint asking for identity papers."

"Was it an intelligence check?"

"No, it was military. They made us get out of the car. The man in charged examined our IDs and papers. He had a list of names. Ours were on there. So he took us inside the station for further verification, or so he said. A few minutes later, a pickup truck with men in civilian clothing arrived at the control post, shouting. They made us lie down on the ground and beat us. Then they blindfolded us, and we got into the pickup, with them still beating us. We were driven to the local military security branch. We were laying in the bed of the truck. The soldiers had their feet on our faces. They were smoking and dropping ashes on us. Fifteen minutes later, we were unloaded and pushed into a large room where about forty people were waiting in silence. All men of all ages. Some young people were crying. No one spoke for fear of confiding in a spy."

"Most of them didn't know what they were doing there, nor what they were waiting for them. We did. We stayed there two days. Soldiers would come searching for detainees, calling out their names. We would not see them again."

"Then, it was Ahmad's turn. Two soldiers grabbed him violently. He had time to give me a proud look, his famous mocking smile, as if his destiny to martyrdom was about to be realized. I won't see him again. Alive, that is."

"How do you know that?" asked Patrick.

"I found him in the pictures Caesar smuggled out of Syria. The same ironic smile, frozen in pain, a sort of middle finger to the Bashar regime."

Nazim takes out his phone and shows us a photograph of Ahmad. He grimaces like the Joker in the comic books. Then he takes a document from his jacket and hands it to me. I read the text, written in beautiful calligraphy.

"There is a legend about a bird which sings just once in its life, more sweetly than any other creature on the face of the earth. From the moment it leaves the nest it searches for a thorn tree, and does not rest until it has found one. Then, singing among the savage branches, it impales itself upon the longest, sharpest spine. And, dying, it rises above its own agony to out carol the lark and the nightingale. One superlative song, existence the price. But the whole world stills to listen, and God in His heaven smiles. For the best is only bought at the cost of great pain . . . Or so says the legend."[4]

"Beautiful passage," I say, touched.

"Yes. Ahmad carried that on him constantly. He became that bird. His song was freedom. The only difference is that the entire world didn't stop to listen. On the contrary, it was more like the entire world didn't give a damn. And God, for his part, he turned his back and didn't even look at Syria."

"Yeah. God blinks and forgets to open his eyes again. At least, that's what we see in our files."

Nazim continues.

"Two hours later, the same soldiers came for me. They put the blindfold on me and tied my hands behind my back. Very tight. The blood to me hands was cut off, and the plastic binding cut my skin. We went down several flights of stairs. I could hear screams of pain but I couldn't see anything. Then a long corridor of groans. Sometimes I stumbled over a body, or had to step over someone. I tried to apologize, but was told to shut up. Smells of urine, shit, and blood. Then I was brought into a room. I was put on my knees and the blindfold was removed. A military man, obviously an officer, was sitting in his chair, sweating, with his arms crossed. The room was dark. The shutters were closed. Only two light bulbs dimly illuminated a grimy desk with yellowed paint. On one of the walls was a portrait of Bashar with a cracked gold frame. The officer was in his fifties, with a protruding belly, long greasy hair that fell on the back of his neck, and a moustache that he was constantly smoothing. He smiled and said, 'So you're the famous Nazim? The fighter for human rights? The sociologist as they say! The one who wants freedom!' He burst out laughing."

"I didn't answer. He had an Alawite accent, but his performance seemed forced. I concluded that he was pretending to be one to please his leaders . . . I later met a number of this type. He repeated: 'Freedom! You son of a bitch!' He got up from his chair and spun around. 'Aren't we lucky in Deraa. We have a star! From the capital! We have to take advantage of you before Damascus claims you. But before you confess. We saw you on the videos on Al Jazeera. Did you come from Damascus to piss us off? To organize terrorist actions? Who is financing you?'"

"That was their technique, they would go through the news reports and then go after the people they had identified. I was a public figure. It was not complicated to put me on a list that was circulated to the roadblocks."

"What was the number of the branch?" Markus asks.

"I don't know, I would say that it was more of a military office located somewhere in Deraa. After his tirade, I sensed him position himself behind me. Then I heard him inhale, and he hit me square in the back. I felt like I'd been cut in two. I fell forward. He had a metal pipe in his hands and was pressing it against my head. 'Prostrate yourself before Bashar, star! We'll take good care of you.'"

"He picked up the telephone. Two young behemoths in their thirties came into the room, lifted me up and took me to another room at the end of the corridor. They wore beards, black tank tops, and Reni brand sneakers, the shoes of the intelligence services. In the room, they ripped off my clothes. I was in my underwear. They threw me to the floor on my stomach and asked me to pull up my feet, which they tied with a rope connected to my neck. One of them shouted in my ears: "I am Abu Hitler and this is Abu Himmler." Then they beat on the soles of my feet for many minutes, insulting me. This is called falaka torture. It produces internal bruises and is not supposed to leave any marks. When it stopped, I couldn't walk. They told me to stand. I tried, but couldn't. Then gave me electric shocks but I still couldn't get up. So they said, 'Let's help you!' They chained me up and suspended me using the ghost technique. I found myself hanging by my hands with chains, my feet off the ground. They hit me again with an electric cable. 'Count!' I received sixty-six blows. 'From now on your name is Sixty-Six. You no longer have an identity. Remember it well, otherwise you will be in trouble.' They were laughing."

"Then nothing more for an hour. They left me hanging there. When they came back to let me down, they told me that I would confess my crimes. And they put me back in the cell. For two days, nothing happened. I was with other prisoners. I couldn't move. One of them took care of me, he was from Deraa. We were only allowed to use the bathroom once per day, which was the time to drink as well. They gave us bulgar wheat, and some olives to share. There were so many of us that we had to sleep in shifts, lying head to foot. Sometimes the guards came into the cell. We had to get up, bow our heads, keep our hands in the air, look at the wall, and remain still."

Markus jumps in: "Would you be able to recognize the guards?"

"No. And besides that, they all went by nicknames, things like Abu Hitler, The Phantom, or The Smoker, because he put his cigarettes out on the people's bodies."

"OK."

"After three days, two soldiers took me out and brought me to the officer. He wanted me to give him the passwords to my Facebook accounts and to name members of my organization. He was zealous. He knew that, because I was a public figure, if he got me to crack, he'd be in line for a promotion. I told him that it wouldn't be of any use because, after my disappearance, the passwords would have been changed.

"He presented me a document detailing my charges, which were undermining national sentiment, terrorism, disturbing the public order, and insulting the regime and Bashar al-Assad. I told him that I don't recognize the facts, that I was only fighting to establish democracy in my country, and that I was working to reinforce national sentiment in my country. He ridiculed me, then picked up the phone to order a new torture session with the same guys. This time, I was given electric jolts until I passed out.

"When I awoke, I was in the cell. I stayed there ten days. Then, one night, they took us out, and had us line up blindfolded in the courtyard. There were around twenty-five of us. A truck pulled in. The officer was there. He approached me. 'So, you son of a bitch, you should be happy, you're returning to the capital. You'll find they're happy to have you back. I would have kept you, but orders are order.'"

"We were beaten with the butts of Kalashnikovs as we left. We had to keep our heads between our legs in silence. It was a long ride, which meant that we were returning to Damascus, as the officer had said. Then the truck stopped. I heard the sound of a plane. We were at Mezzeh airport. I knew that the worst was yet to come, because we were now in the hands of the air force intelligence services, the den of the dictatorship. It was still dark, but a welcoming party was there. Thirty men, civilian and military. They beat us savagely while pushing us out of the truck. They called it the welcoming ceremony. Afterward, we were locked in six-by-six-foot steel cages, with seven or eight people per cage."

Suddenly, Nazim stopped. Choked up. He's having trouble breathing. I look at my investigators and realize there's no air flow in the room. Like in prison. Ahmed, our interpreter, suggests we open a window. I propose that we take a break and pick up later. But Nazim refuses, wishing rather to smoke. He quietly gets up, exits the room, and heads for the stairs. Patrick, Stéphanie, and those of our German colleagues who smoke accompany him. Several minutes later, I look down from the fourth floor of our building and see this man in the paved courtyard, smoking his cigarette and exhaling towards the sky.

Questions run through my head. How does one keep it together in a situation like that? How does one stay human? Would I have continued the fight for freedom? Would I have had his courage? And what about the men doing the torturing? How does someone kiss his wife and children during the day, then leave run torture sessions at night?

Impossible to not think of the *Lucifer Effect,* Philip Zimbardo's book elaborating his 1971 Stanford prison experiment.[5] He selected eighty students. All were considered stable and mature, coming from all walks of life and all over North America. Zimbardo randomly assigned them roles as prisoners and prison guards, splitting them into two equal groups. His goal was to study the behavior of ordinary people in a prison simulation in a Stanford basement.

Certain conditions were designed to increase disorientation, depersonalization, and de-individualization. Guards were equipped with wooden batons, khaki military uniforms, and mirrored sunglasses to prevent eye contact.

To start, one morning the prisoners were suddenly arrested for armed robbery by the police. They were fingerprinted, photographed, and read their rights. Once there, they were each given a number. They were striped and cleaned with anti-lice and anti-parasite products. They were clothed in long gowns, no underwear, and rubber flip-flops. Nylon stockings were put on their heads to simulate shaved heads. Finally, their ankles were chained to reinforce the feeling of imprisonment and oppression.

The instructions issued to the guards by Zimbardo were as follows. No violence. The prison and its operation were the responsibility of the guards. They could create in prisoners feelings of boredom and fear, and do so arbitrarily to make it clear to the prisoners that their lives were totally controlled by the system and the guards.

Very quickly, the researchers were able to observe that all the prisoners and guards adapted to the roles they had been assigned in ways that went beyond the limits of what had been planned, triggering psychologically dangerous situations (guards were warned about the potential for this to happen before the experiment began).

The experiment was soon out of control. Prisoners were called by their numbers and tormented with punishments or long periods of forced physical exercise. Some had to endure forced nudity and even acts of sexual humiliation. A third of the guards demonstrated sadistic behavior, while many prisoners were traumatized.

The experiment was stopped after six days. It had been planned for two weeks.

Another glance into the courtyard. Nazim is joking with the investigators. He lights up a second cigarette.

The Stanford experiment demonstrated once more how an individual's behavior can be influenced by an authority or ideology that he or she identifies as legitimate. What people are capable of depends on their situations, not their individual predispositions or genetics. In other words, the situation induces the behavior, not the personality.

The sweet pickle theory holds that a sweet pickle turns sour when soaked in a jar of vinegar.[6] It sits in opposition to the rotten-apple theory, which maintains that some individuals are inherently bad. After the Abu Ghraib prison scandal of March 2004, American military leaders claimed that a few rotten apples were responsible for abuses. They refused to recognize that their problems were due to an institutionalized system of military incarceration that appeared to be using techniques from the Kubark interrogation manual.[7]

Different place, different time, same story.

Nazim puts out his cigarette and looks up toward the windows. He notices me, smiles, and re-enters the building with our colleagues.

A few minutes later, the five of them make it up the stairs, a bit winded.

"Four flights of stairs are tough even for non-smokers," I smile.

Nazim nods, fiddles with his ring, and asks us to continue the deposition.

"You left off at the welcome ceremony . . ."

"Yes, that seemed to be common among the intelligence branches. We were packed in the steel cages. They rotated the prisoners constantly, some were locked in with me, then would leave. I was the only one to stay in that cage for a month. Afterward, I was transferred to a collective cell. The rule was that seniority gave you the right to stand nearest to the wall when the guards came in looking for prey. They mostly picked new arrivals. Like others, I was subjected to two torture sessions per day. To break me. To break me down. The regime wanted to show its strength, its capacity to constrain and kill, known in order to set an example for the public, to control them. Either you bend, you fold, or you die. And it will take a long time. You die a bit with each passing day, with each torture session. Power wants to dominate. It wants to keep people in the anguish of death, in obedience to its tyranny. Wolfgang Sofsky said: "Torture is always a dimension of power, but tyranny makes it the very essence of power."[8]

"And Fairuz, was that during this period?"

"Yes, we mostly had the same guards. One time, I tried to have a conversation with one of them. For him, it was a routine. No doubt he returned home every evening, kissing his wife and children, petting his dog, and then off to torture me again the following day. He was convinced that I was a terrorist. I told him: 'Look, I'm a Syrian like you.' His brain had been washed. I suffered for five months at his hands. The German chair that breaks you in two. The tire. The flying carpet [a device that bends the spine and ribs]. Electric shocks. I never was able to get seniority. There were so many of us that again sometimes we had to take turns sleeping at night. Sickness was common. Dysentery. Torture wounds that didn't heal. We tried not to get close to infected inmates. Sometimes people would shit themselves. The hygiene was sickening. Scabies, insects. Food was sparse. Sometimes you had to fight to get a few crumbs."

Dieter asks: "What were the relationships like among the prisoners?"

"Variable. There was a cell leader appointed by the guards. We were suspicious of him. He was capable of sending you for another round of torture at the drop of a hat. The guards would sometimes place teenagers in the cells to get information about the inmates. We avoided talking because we never knew who we were dealing with. Some inmates looked after the worst among us by placing leftover bread over their wounds."

"OK."

"And then, there were parties . . . The guards would arrive with billy clubs, cattle prods, and enter the cells, swinging at full force. They'd ask a question that didn't have an answer, like: 'Who called their bitch mother this morning?' Obviously, no one had an answer. So they'd take one or two men and beat them to death in the hallway, so that everyone could hear the cracking bones, blows on the skin, and smell the blood and shit. The only time we were let out was to use the toilets, which was once per day, and we had to get there as quickly as possible running through the hallways, which were often strewn with bodies, sometimes corpses. We had to walk over them."

Nazim pauses. Slowly drinks a glass of water.

"After five months, one morning, two guards came looking for me. They called out my name, and my father's and mother's, as well, to make sure I was the right person. They blindfolded me, took me up to the third floor, and pushed me into an office with four generals inside. The guards took off my blindfold. I couldn't see anything. My eyes were no longer accustomed to light. I didn't recognize them. One of them said to me, 'We want you to make a statement on national television.' I was taken aback. 'You want me to do an interview?' 'No, not an interview. A statement where you explain that you have been manipulated by terrorists who are attacking Syria as part of a global plot to remove our president.'"

"I told them that I was no longer photogenic and that I didn't know how to speak in front of a TV camera. The general sitting to the left stood up and yelled, 'Are you kidding us? Do you think your wife would like the smell of other men? Our soldiers wouldn't mind the assignment, judging from the photos I have here.' I said nothing. And the two guards grabbed me, took me down to the courtyard. A car was waiting for me. One of the guards got in the front. The driver asked, 'Where are we going?' A guard answered, 'To the Palestine branch.' Then I understood that they wanted to kill me. I wanted to kill myself."

"That's . . . a particularly terrible branch."

"Yes. The worst was yet to come. After another the welcoming ceremony, I was put in solitary confinement for seven days. No one spoke to me. After that, a guard came looking for me and told me: 'When I go to take a piss, I usually kill someone.' He was colossal. He had Bashar's head tattooed on his chest. He was Alawite with a strong accent. We were his charges. Cooped up like animals. This guy called himself Abu the Killer. The worst bastard I would ever meet. He was imaginative and creative in his cruelty. I had become a piece of flesh that he liked to play with or poke in agony, flirting with the edge of death. I was at the mercy of his perverse joy. He reveled in my fear and shame. I had become the object of his power. My body had finally become my prison, chaining my spirit, muzzling it."

Silence. Nazim breathes heavily.

"This guy was nothing but violence. Violence for the sake of violence, mutated into cruelty beyond the laws of reason and human values. Cruelty for the sake of cruelty. My physical and psychological annihilation was a testimony to his omnipotence. I prayed for death many times. I understood that it was like a drug to him, this cruelty made him master of life and of death. He thought he was immortal. It was his credo."

"I wanted to die. But, no, I kept on living. He always picked up on the moment where life was about to end. Sometimes, his power manifested itself in the form of a violent erection, a symbol of his bestiality that he exhibited at the end of the session."

Silence.

"He had the habit of raping a young fifteen-year-old boy named Firas during torture sessions. He was proud of it. He would have the boy brought to him."

Nazim hunches over and lowers his head, gradually, more and more. Then, in a breath.

"He killed Firas. There was nothing we could do. When they put him back in our cell, it was too late. He was dislocated, open, torn apart."

Ahmed, the interpreter, chokes. Our German colleagues lower their heads, visibly shaken. We have nothing to say, either.

"Would you be able to recognize him?"

"Yes, of course. I will never forget him. But there's no chance of catching him. People like him are too useful to the authorities. Even if he thought of leaving Syria, he would be eliminated before making it across the border."

Silence.

"In fact, I think he was eliminated. By the opposition. In fact, I'm sure of it. The death of the immortal Abu the Killer."

Nazim smiles. Perhaps recalling certain images?

"Did you see other prisoners die?"

"Yes."

"The look of the dying. No one can do anything. Only endure. You hear death coming with velvet steps, on tiptoe, grabbing him and taking him away. First the moans, then the hoarse breathing, and finally the silence. I was often jealous of those that got away, leaving their bodily prisons, this senseless world. But death still scared me. It can't be described what I experienced. I don't know what hell is. But I think it is nothing compared to this. I died every day. I knew I was dead. I saw myself dead. You are not a human being anymore. Not even an animal. You are a thing that's barely alive, and for how long you don't know. I'd tell myself: it would be better to die rather than suffer and be humiliated. But I continued to live."

191

"Then one day, it was out of my hands. The torturer came into the cell and said: 'I have to piss!' He grabbed me, a group of guards circled around, and they beat me to the verge of death. I lost consciousness. When I awoke, one of my cell mates was wiping my wounds, telling me to keep my confidence. Ahmed, he was from Homs. I was disfigured. My toenails were torn off. The next day, the same beating. They hit me even harder. I blacked out again."

Silence.

"I don't remember anything after that, except that my mind was floating in limbo. Between heaven and earth. Then, for a reason that still escapes me, I felt an icy grip. My skin was pressed against a cold body. I picked myself up. I was in blackness, in a sort of storage room, and still with this cold on my skin. I said to myself, 'So this is it. Death.' Either that or I was with dead people. I panicked. I screamed."

"The guards came to the shed. I remember hearing: 'He's not dead, the bastard.'"

"They took me out and put me back into a cell. My fellow inmates treated me once again. Ahmed was gone. He had also been beaten to death. I stayed several days like that. Then they came looking for me, to sign the termination of my interrogation, which was, in the end, a deliverance. I couldn't see anything. My eyes were too swollen. I pressed my finger on the document to indicate that I admit my culpability for terrorism, weakness of national sentiment, etc."

"Why do you think that they let you sign the termination?"

"To tell you the truth, I have no idea. But I was so sick and wounded that I was transferred to the one place I didn't want to go."

"Where?'

"Tichreen hospital. Rumor was that you couldn't make it out of that hospital alive. After signing the admission of guilt, they brought me back to the cell and I lost consciousness. When I awoke, I was at the hospital, attached to two other prisoners with a two-foot chain, lying on a single bed. The doctor came by and gave us two anti-inflammatories to share. Afterward, two nurses came in the room and beat us. The two other detainees were on the verge of death. During the night, a nurse unchained one and took him out into the hallway. He died that night. I don't know what they injected him with. I wanted to get out of that rat hole as soon as possible. It stank of death. When I left the hospital, the white bags with dead bodies were piling up. I asked to be transferred to a prison."

"Which one? Adra or Seidnaya?"

"Seidnaya. The red building. The worst. Adra would have been too nice."

"When was this?"

"February 2013. Do you have Google Maps?"

"Yep, we also have satellite images, if you'd like."

Patrick double clicks on a file to bring up the satellite image.

We turn the screen to face Nazim. Seidnaya prison, shaped like a Mercedes logo. We zoom in. Three buildings appear on the screen. According to certain NGOs, the red building was built in the late 1980s to lock up political prisoners and transfers from Palmyre for rehabilitation. In the 2000s, it collected those who'd joined the jihad in Iraq, activists, opponents of the regime—those who were released in 2011 to spread chaos. Each building has three floors with sixty cells, five by seven meters. No windows, a toilet corner. A door with bars, meager lighting. Around 2012–2013, there were about twenty-five inmates per cell. At the peak, there was an estimated 4,000 prisoners in the building. Underneath, these three buildings are about seventy underground cells of about four-by-six feet, without lighting. They are for solitary confinement as a punishment or as recommended by the intelligence services. According to Amnesty International, since 2011, many of the inmates of this prison have been hanged or otherwise eliminated. Somewhere between 10,000 and 20,000. Prisoners are informed of the sentence a few minutes before it is carried out, usually at night."

Nazim continues:

"I was held in that overcrowded prison nearly a year. First in solitary confinement. Then in a cell with about twenty-five other prisoners. The same horror. The guards wielding the power of life and death over the prisoners. At night, selected candidates were taken to the corridor of death, where they would stand, heads down, facing the wall. The guards beat us for two or three hours, then brought us back to the cells. There was no torture room.

Apart from that, the regiment was the same as in the intelligence branches. The food was as meager. Illness and death as common. Cell leaders were appointed by the prison administrators. Several times I wrote my death warrant for the next day and they would come to get me for hanging."

"The kapos, in a way?"⁹

"Yes. They could denounce you if you didn't obey them."

Pause.

"And then there was a trial. In June 2014. A joke of a trial. In the anti-terrorism court. No lawyer. A judgment rendered in five minutes. I was sentenced to fifteen years in prison on charges of terrorism, weakening the national sentiment, and disrupting the peace. There were ten of us in that batch, if I remember right. The nine others were sentenced to death and hung in prison."

"Can you recall the name of the judge?" Markus questions.

"Yes, Djamel El Keddoub."

"Does he still hold office?"

"No. I think he fled to Europe. Maybe your country, come to think."

"We'll check with our immigration department," Dieter says.

"So, the others were sentenced to death, but not you?"

"Yes. I understood later the reason I received a different judgment. One of my friends from CPDS managed to visit me in prison. He learned the date of the trial and paid off the judge. My colleagues raised one million Syrian pounds, around thirty thousand euros. The judge received fifteen thousand before and he was to receive the other fifteen thousand when I was released. I remained in prison for another month.

"I'll remember for the rest of my life the moment when the guards took me out of the cell. I was expecting another beating. But, finally, no. They took me up the stairs to an office where I received my release order and a stamp on my hand. They returned my personal effects, clothes, watch. It was like a dream."

"I can hardly imagine. What about the fifteen-year sentence?"

"Apparently erased, thanks to an amnesty . . . I can tell you, when that door closed behind me, I couldn't believe it. I walked as quickly as possible without looking back, on the open road, facing the sun. I filled my lungs with air. I only had one fear—that someone would catch up to me. That the dream would end."

"I can imagine."

Nazim gives me an inquisitive look. I backtrack.

"Well, no, of course not. I don't think I can imagine what you suffered. I shouldn't have used that expression."

"I kept going down the road until a car stopped. The man driving was named Anis. He was a taxi driver. Seeing my condition, he took me back to Damascus. We crossed the checkpoints without trouble. I'll be indebted to him all my life. When we parted ways, he didn't want me to pay him. He was touched by my story. Yet he was an Alawite. 'We are all Syrians,' he told me before we parted."

"When the door opened, my wife did not recognize me. I had changed so much. My children, let's not talk about them. I was a skeleton. They couldn't look me in the eye."

Nazim takes out a document indicating the termination of his incarceration. A photograph is stapled to the top of the certificate. His eyes are empty, wide open, lifeless. Desolation and death. His face is deeply marked. Frozen in horror."

"My wife blamed herself for weeks. She'd been sick from it, but she showed a remarkable courage, oscillating from despair of not seeing me again and hope of my return. Some women have extraordinary strength. Nadia was one of them. Sweetness coupled with a relentless will, the kind that can lift mountains."

Silence.

Nazim takes out a photo of Nadia, who is easy to recognize by her black and white scarf, something of a trademark for her.

"She said it symbolized her life. Jumping from one thing to the next, square to square, observing the world and taking risks to better try to save it. This photo was taken before the revolution."

Nazim hands me the photo. Nadia lies on a rock that juts out over the sea, resting on her elbow, mischievous look. The blue in her eyes blends with the sea behind her. Obviously, a woman of character. Very beautiful as well. Committed. I pass it to Dieter, who asks:

"How long did it take for things to get back to normal, assuming it was possible in Syria?"

"At least six months. My wife and kids helped out a lot. It was hard though. We stopped all activity with the opposition. I wouldn't have survived another arrest. The regime won. It had broken me. We stayed in hiding and decided to leave Syria. We couldn't let our children grow up in an open-air prison, and as long as Bashar had Russian support and could reconquer lost territories, he was well position in his fight against the Islamists that he himself had liberated in 2011. So we planned an escape through Lebanon. Ultimately, we were advised against that route. So we left via Turkey. Friends organized everything for us from Damascus."

Silence. Nazim blows his nose. His head sinks.

"My wife didn't want to leave without certain documents she had hidden in Ghouta, important documents she wanted to turn over to European authorities. I begged her not to go back. She didn't want to hear it. To her, it was a counterpart to my commitment, to my suffering. She left in the early morning with two friends to get the documents back, without telling me. When I woke up, I reached over to her side of the bed. It was empty. I ran outside when I heard the sound of the engine. That image is engraved in my memory. I see her, turning and waving with a smile. The kids were still sleeping. It was madness. They never came back. The three were picked up by an Islamic group that controlled the area, six masked men from the Jaysh al-Islam."

One barbaric state replaces another.

"That day, I lost Nadia. By chance or a set-up, I'll probably never know. The worst is not knowing, not having a body to grieve. Nadia had a crazy courage. If she were to choose a way to die, I believe this is how she would have wanted it."

Nazim breaks down. The green of his eyes turns a stormy gray.

The emotion rises in my throat. I look away. Everyone's in the same state.

"Nazim . . . we've exceeded four hours. Would you like to continue?"

"I'm going to smoke another cigarette. Then we'll continue."

"Good idea. We need a break, too."

Everyone heads downstairs, except Dieter who's not tempted to tackle the stairs again. We chat.

"Impressive . . ."

"Yes. And, unfortunately, very common. These depositions are indispensable for us to understand how the system works."

"Of course. They will be translated into German and transferred to the file of the joint investigative team.

"In any case, thank you for having invited us to participate."

Footsteps echo in the hallway. Nazim and the investigators return to the deposition room.

21

RECONSTRUCTION

"The world is a dangerous place, not because of those who do evil, but because of those who look on and do nothing."

—Albert Einstein

Paris—OCLCH, Witness Deposition Room

All help themselves to coffee.

"Those stairs! I really need to stop smoking. Many Syrians smoke. One of the reasons the Islamic State hasn't made a lot of friends there. Everything is forbidden. Especially cigarettes."

"We left off with your wife's disappearance, and the fact that you were unable to find out further information on her whereabouts."

"Yes. The worst was having to leave her there. Resigning myself to the fact that I'd never see her again. I moved heaven and earth trying to find them, in particular through our network. We paid to get information. To no avail. So I decided to permanently leave Syria. I wanted a clean break, to cut all ties. Just to have a normal life, anonymous, free. To save my children from that mess. Maybe one day in the future they'll be able to return to their country. Maybe even a democratic country."

"How did you leave Syria," Markus asks.

"Syrian smugglers. That's all I'm going to say about that though, for security reasons. In Turkey, I was taken in by members of the opposition who wanted me to fight alongside them. But my mind was made up. I was through. Didn't want to hear another word about Syria."

"But, in France, you started an organization . . ."

"Yes. After some time passed, I was seized by a guilt that I was still alive while others had become corpses with numbers scrawled on them by felt-tip pens. Why me? So I told myself that it was time to get back on track. In the end, that's what they all want—the Assads, the Islamists. For us to shut up, to crash."

"This world is much too unjust, and the situation is much too urgent. So I took up the sword or, in this case, the pen to continue the fight for my wife, my children, and all those who have suffered or disappeared. Syria no longer belongs to Syrians. Only death and suffering belong to them. I am here before you so that we can get restitution, so that justice is done. My anger just returned one morning. I rejoined the battle without any political affiliation. Just one idea: justice for all. And to try to understand how humans can massacre others."

"You participated in a treatment program in France?"

"Yes, when I arrived in your country, I was taken in by an NGO for refugees with post-traumatic stress. It took me a long time to rebuild myself. To lift my head up. I had to keep it down for almost four years. Even now, I sometimes have to give myself a shake to straighten up. My friends, and especially my children, tell me: 'Lift your head up!'"

"The NGO helped me a lot. I don't think I would have made it through without them. I couldn't sleep. I had anxieties day and night. I would be seized by tremors, uncontrolled shaking. Irritability. Bulimia. Irrepressible physical pain. I saw certain scenes over and over again, especially the time I woke up on the corpse, when they'd given me up for dead. But I don't complain. I could have gone crazy. Some of my comrades who couldn't take the torture sessions lost their minds."

Silence.

"Human beings are complex machines. The worst thing is that finally, they adapt. They call process cognitive neutralization. Tormentors, victims, witnesses, all adapt themselves to suffering or inflicting suffering on others. Psychologists call the process emotional accommodation. Being able to withstand today what seemed unbearable yesterday prepares us for what will be even worse tomorrow. This process allows you to continually adjust your reference points and survive. It is how, without realizing it, I adapted to my tormentors, to an escalating process of pain and suffering, to my cramped living space, to loss of privacy. Unfortunately, this type of experience tells us a lot about human mechanics. I became accustomed, like my torturers, to horrible scenes. The effect was to dissolve compassion."

"I was fortunate to have participated in the EMDR program.[1] Eye Movement Desensitization and Reprocessing. It helps you to deal with traumatic experiences and to heal post-traumatic after-effects even years after the fact. Through these movements, the memories are erased and the therapist helps the patient to associate a positive, constructive, pacifying thought with the experience.

"We have those types of programs in Germany," Dieter adds.

"To be honest, the therapist doubted that it would work in my personal case. Sometimes it took him several sessions to proves a single memory. An EMDR session lasts between sixty and ninety minutes. The patient can go through intense emotions and, at the end, can generally sense distinct improvement."

"How's it going now?"

"What I can tell you is this. Before, I wouldn't have been able to tell you my story. I wouldn't have been able to be here, sitting in front of you. Now I've restarted my education. Criminology and social psychology. Trying to understand my torturers. In particular my Fairuz fan, and the guy from the Palestine branch."

"We're getting towards the end here. Do you know of any other victims who might be in our territories? Or deserters? Or potential perpetrators?"

"Victims, yes. I founded my organization in part to put the needs of victims of the Bashar regime under a single roof. All the other victims of the, Islamists, as well. Victims of all of those that took over my country. I also decided to get personally involved. I'm starting to participate in TV programs and reports. I have an interview online with Human Rights Watch tomorrow. It will be broadcast on YouTube in a couple days so all Syrian can watch it in wherever they are."

"OK. If that's the case, we'd like to be able to contact other victims or witnesses concerning the crimes committed in Syria."

"I'd also like to contact those now living in Germany. Would you be able to refer them to us?" asks Dieter.

"I'll place you in contact with them if they agree. As you know, some still have families in Syria, many in territories controlled by the regime. They're very cautious about putting their families in potential danger."

"Yes, of course. But please let them know that we can keep their testimonies anonymous. That's the case in both of our countries."

"I'll take note of that."

Béatrice turns off the camera and saves the files. Patrick makes paper printouts of the deposition. The interpreter reads them over. Signatures.

Dieter and Markus give Nazim a warm thank you for his testimony, asking him if they can return later on with further questions. They get ready for their return trip by train. We take a moment to say one final goodbye and set a date for the follow-up meeting the next month in Germany.

Fifteen minutes later, Nazim is ready to leave. I walk him back. We take the stairs in silence. On the landing, just before taking off, Nazim says to me:

"Thank you again for the work you're doing. Without countries like yours, we wouldn't have any hope of one day getting justice and retribution for the horrors we've suffered. The ICC is a dead end. Blocked by Russian and Chinese vetoes. The system needs reform."

"That's why we're here. France and Germany can play their part. We work with other countries, too, in the European Genocide Network. And, as you know, other NGOs and international organizations are working for this as well. It's a long road though, as you know."

"Continue your work. Only justice allows forgiveness."

Before he turns away, I quickly ask:

"How about you? Have you found forgiveness? Seeing that justice hasn't been served?"

"You know, forgiveness is a double-edged sword. You have to start by forgiving yourself before you can forgive others. So yes. I've forgiven myself. I've forgiven others. Those that caused me harm. Those that tried to break my humanity. They didn't succeed."

Nazim is now holding his head straight, looking me in the eyes. Without saying a word, he lifts up his sleeve.

"This tattoo symbolizes everything I've lived through. Everything is here: with Maori symbols, the shark's teeth symbolizing strength, security, and adaptation, and the Enata symbolizing masculinity and energy. Rather than having visible scars, I chose to cover them indelibly, a form of resilience. The pain is still there but I can live with it."

Silence.

"Do you see this symbol?"

I see a tree, deep roots, branches reaching towards the sky.

"When a tree anchors its roots deep within the earth it becomes strong. It can reach its branches higher towards the sky. This tree is the tree of forgiveness, forgiving me for being alive why so many others are dead."

Nazim shakes my hand and invites me to visit his NGO in Marly le Roi. I watch him as he passes through our black gate.

Again, Pierre Soulages and his black paintings come to mind: "That light comes from what is, by definition, the greatest absence of light, causes a disturbance in me."

I'm walking back up the stairs when my cell phone vibrates.

It's prosecutor Camélia B: "So, not too bad, Colonel?"

"It was an extensive interview. We'll have to see Nazim again to get more detail."

"I can see how that would be necessary."

That said, I didn't expect to see Nazim again so soon.

22

COOPERATION

"The only route that offers any hope of a better future for all of humanity is that of cooperation and partnership."
—Kofi Annan UN General Assembly, September 24, 2001

August 22, 2019—OCLCH, Paris

A call on the Signal app. Samia's initials, Nazim's secretary. Her voice is shrill. Then she breaks down in sobs. Something's definitely wrong, but I can't make out her words. I try to calm her. To no avail.

I decide to go to Nazim's house or, rather, to the headquarters of his association, The Center for the Promotion of Democracy in Syria, which is also his personal residence. It's in a building in Marly le Roi. I grab Patrick who was in charge of Nazim's deposition. We jump in the Volkswagen. I turn on the flashers, two tones blaring to clear the way.

Thirty minutes later, we park on Atlas Street in front of a 19th-century building of four floors. The offices are on the first floor. Nazim and his two children live in an apartment on the second floor. The association also has a storage room in the basement with a secure entrance.

The paramedics and an ambulance are already on site. Police as well.

We walk into the building. The door to the right is open. Nazim is stretched out on the ground, lying in a pool of blood. Doctors and nurses are hard at it. Beeps from the electrocardiogram. The works.

Damn.

The gendarme on duty turns toward me. I show my credentials and Patrick explains that we are from OCLCH. With the words "crimes against humanity," the gendarme looks at me with eyes wide.

"Do you know him?"

"Yes, he's one of our witnesses. A Syrian."

"OK. We need to put you in touch with our captain."

I approach the doctor.

"Hello doctor, how's he doing?"

I flash my credentials in front of a dismayed face.

"Good morning. He's lost consciousness and for the moment is in a coma. But he looks strong. He should pull through."

I feel confident that he will after all he's been through.

I turn toward the gendarme and ask for facts.

"The assailant attempted to strangle him and then ran away. Apparently, two people arrived in the hallway and the burglar fled."

Burglar?

We keep outside the apartment to avoid contaminating the crime scene. The police technicians are busy. Photographs, fingerprints, DNA, etc. Nothing left to chance. Two witnesses are being interviewed separately. One woman is visibly in a state of shock.

I catch sight of Samia, eyes puffy, being interrogated by a police officer. Our eyes meet. I signal to her that we'll see each other later.

Nazim is evacuated on a stretcher, unconscious. The gendarme returns with his phone.

"The group commander, for you."

"Hello."

"Hello there. My men have told me that you know our victim."

"That's right. We know him well. He's involved with our cases. A Syrian fella, granted asylum in France. He's a well-known sociologist and created an NGO promoting democracy in Syria."

A deep breath comes through the line.

"Democracy in Syria?"

"Yes, I know . . ."

"OK, you think that this aggression is related to these activities?"

"Hard to say. But certainly likely. In any case, can we help you with this case?"

"Oh dear. We'll see. Let us carry on our investigation. I'll contact you in a few days, sound good?"

"That's fine. Talk to you then."

He sounds like one of those individuals with a big ego get always making a mess of things. I once heard an ambassador say of a cabinet minister: "He has the ability to spread shit like he's doing it in front of a fan."

I hand the phone back to the gendarme. From the corner of my eye, I see Samia coming to toward us, handkerchief in hand.

"I'm confident Nazim will pull through. Sorry for earlier. I couldn't speak. I was holding Nazim in my arms. He took such a hit to the head. He lost so much blood. It was upsetting."

"Don't worry, we understand. What happened?" Patrick asks.

"Nazim told me that he felt he was being watched for the past couple days. Ever since he told his story on the Internet, about being in Bashar's prisons. But nothing for sure. Something else happened, too. He told me that he saw a man just sitting behind the wheel of a car parked on the street. Nazim still has his old Syrian reflexes and watchfulness. Then another time, the same man was with another guy. Never the same car. At 10 o'clock, he called me asking if I was in the office because he heard a noise from his apartment upstairs, which was unusual because our offices are closed on Sundays. I told him no. He said, alright, I'll go check it out. And then nothing. I tried calling him back. I had a bad feeling. I ran over and found him lying in a pool of his own blood. The couple from the third floor were next to reach him. They had called the ambulance. With all the blood, I panicked. I called you."

"That's a bit concerning, that he thought men were following him. Did you explain this to the gendarmes?"

"Yes, of course."

"Did Nazim give you any other information on the individual? Did he take any pictures with his phone?" Patrick questions.

"No, I don't think so. But I could feel he was worried. He wouldn't have told me much, though, to keep me from worrying. I have to go look after the children."

"How are they doing?"

"They don't know yet."

"Our gendarme colleagues, who have a lot of experience with these types of cases, are taking the lead for the time being. But we'll be right there with them."

We leave. In the car, Patrick and I exchange theories. Either a burglary gone wrong (but no, not very likely), or a hit by an intelligence service. Nazim had been compromised by his broadcast.

On the way back to the office, I call Camélia, the vice prosecutor in the crimes against humanity unit, to inform her of the situation. Noticeably concerned, she tells me she will immediately be in touch with the magistrates in charge of the case at the Versailles prosecutor's office.

I send a Signal to Dieter and Markus loop them in.

"Very regrettable," they answer. "Keep us up to date on his condition."

The following day, a Signal from Camélia. After some pushing, the Versailles investigative unit has agreed to get in touch with the local gendarmes. That helps. I'm not confident that I'm going to get much cooperation from them.

I call the colonel at the Versailles investigative unit and tell him we'd like a look at the case file, in particular the photos and video footage of the crime scene.

August 23, 2019—Versailles Investigative Unit

Cleared through the gate, we park in a large paved courtyard.

A gendarme at the entrance conducts us upstairs to the office of the commander of the investigative unit. Tall, lanky, somewhat nervous fellow, shaved head, about thirty years old. He stands up and offers me his hand. A man in a hurry, new to his post.

"Colonel Norbert H., pleasure to meet you. So you are our colleagues from crimes against humanity? Nasty business here. They tell me the guy is in a coma. Apparently, the higher-ups have taken an interest. Coffee?"

"Yes. I really hope he'll pull through. No coffee, thank you."

"We have been asked to give you our full collaboration. Pleased to do so."

"We have to work hand in hand. We can use our sources and networks to make headway for you."

"I'll introduce you to the lieutenant running the investigation."

We get up and head over to the violent crimes team. Norbert H. asks Lieutenant Sébastien M. for the utmost cooperation. Sébastien M. gets up nonchalantly and lets out a sigh. Light clothing, average size, a tattoo representing a dragon on the right arm, hair slicked back. He extends his hand.

"We'll touch base before you leave?" Norbert asks.

"Yes, of course."

The colonel executes an elegant about face and rushes down the hallway. Once he's at a sufficient distance, the lieutenant, suspicious of us, asks:

"What can I do for you?"

I explain the situation and tell him that we'd like to take a look at the photos of the crime scene.

"The magistrates, are they aware of your request?"

"Yes. Mr. Nazim Al Ahmar is a primary witness in one of our proceedings. I've informed the lead prosecutor at the National Antiterrorist Prosecutor's Office who has contacted your magistrate. But please verify if you like," I say, with a little smile.

"No, that works. Follow me."

A few minutes later, we find ourselves in front of Major Maurice B., head of the forensic team. He's surrounded by personnel who all look like they were hired yesterday. The usual introductions. Sébastien M. stands aside, silent, arms crossed. The major grabs his mouse and clicks open the video file of the crime scene.

"Here's the footage we got."

The images roll by. The rooms of the apartment, which have transformed into a makeshift office, appear. Nothing unusual in the of the office. Curtains pulled. Blue walls covered with paper panels displaying Arabic words. Basic furniture, white hallway. Another room. A very ordinary kitchen. Nothing in particular stands out.

Then the camera pans the main room, which is in total disarray. Tourist posters on the wall, snow-capped mountains, white sandy beaches, palm trees. All in Arabic. Lebanon. Syria. Tourism in Syria?

On the parquet floor lie stacks of files and documents. To the right, a 19th-century fireplace of white veined marble, family photos on the mantel.

A beach. Two children. A woman. Nadia, with her firm gaze. Nazim, looking happy. Memories of happier times.

And there is the crime scene. Nazim, wearing a black track suit, lying on the floor, on his side. On his skill, traces of cuts are evident, the source of the blood on the ground. The camera circles around him, back, head, legs, then zooms in on his face and pauses. Zooms in to the wounds, the strangulation marks on his neck.

"What other work has been done?"

The major gives us a rundown.

"We were able to lift some fingerprints, and also got some samples from underneath Mr. Al Ahmar's fingernails. We found skin fragments and sent them over to the DNA lab. We also recovered security camera footage from the surrounding area, which is being analyzed as we speak."

"OK."

"We can update you once the results come in. We also took statements from the neighbors who surprised the aggressor after they heard the shouting. They caught the assailant by surprise and got the scare of their life when he ran out in front of them. A huge fellow, it seems. Our forensic artist worked with them on a composite sketch."

Sébastien M. hands us the image representing the suspect.

"We're looking around the neighborhood, seeing that M. Al Ahmar had the feeling he was being watched."

"Good, we'll keep in touch."

We pass in front of the colonel's office on our way out. He's on the phone, makes a gesture of the see-you-soon variety and slips me his card. We shrug and head back to the OCLCH. Patrick drives and is unusually quiet. Suddenly he pulls over to the side of the road. Other drivers honk at us.

"Can we turn around, sir?"

"Yes, no problem."

"I've got to be sure."

"OK?"

We head back to the Versailles unit.

Soon we're back in front of the computer with the lieutenant and the major. The video plays. The camera focuses on Nazim's body.

"There, stop!"

Patrick takes a photo of the screen with his phone and enlarges the image.

"It looks like a drawing in blood."

The lieutenant leans over. I peer at the image carefully.

"Actually, yes. But of what?"

Everyone is trying to decipher the drawing.

"Yes, something's there, but not necessarily drawing," says Sébastien M.

Silence.

"Sort of like a man in a large cloak. A kind of ghost."

"Yes, you're right," says Maurice. "A kind of ghost."

I turn toward Patrick. We're both thinking the same thing.

"A chabiha!" he says.

"A what?" asks Sébastien.

"A chabiha. It's Arabic for ghost. It refers to a very powerful and violent pro-Bashar militia. They have a reputation for doing the regime's dirty work. Mercenaries. Suspected in numerous massacres during the civil war."

"It could be chance," the lieutenant suggests.

"Yes . . . or more likely," I reply. "In my opinion, it's a useful lead. The Syrian intelligence agencies have a well-earned reputation for operations abroad. We've seen individuals eliminated by foreign agents in our territory. And Nazim is a perfect target."

"Why is that?"

"How about you come to our office. We can play his deposition for you and you'll understand."

"OK."

August 30—OCLCH, Paris

A week later, Samia calls to announce that Nazim is out of his coma. He wants to speak to us. What a relief. I pass the news to Camélia, who's been worried about him.

Patrick and I drive to the hospital and leave a message on the Versailles commander's voicemail.

We show our identification at reception and are directed to room 211. Nazim is there alone, sleeping with one eye open.

"Hello Nazim."

"Good morning, sir."

"How are you?"

"They gave me sedatives. I'm supposed to go for some tests soon. Thanks for getting here so quickly."

"Not a problem. We were worried about you."

"I've been through it before."

No doubt.

A knock at the door. Sébastien M. walks in carrying a briefcase, accompanied by an investigator. Greetings.

"We were hoping that you could answer a few questions."

"That'll be difficult. They're wheeling me out to get a bunch of tests soon."

"One question in particular then. While looking over the crime scene, we noticed a sort of drawing on the ground near your face. Did you make it?" Sébastien asks.

"Yes, I did."

Pause.

"Before I blacked out, I tried to draw a ghost so that Samia would understand. Actually, when I first came down to the office, I saw the guy tinkering with one of the power outlets, the one with the extra sockets. He was surprised, and told me in Arabic, with a Latakia accent: 'I'm going to kill you.' I knew immediately he was a chabiha. Plain as day. That's why I made the drawing. I hoped that Samia would understand."

"Would you be able to recognize him?"

"Everything happened very fast, actually. He had a small beard, shaved head, very strong and muscular, pumped up on protein. A tattoo on his neck. A cross."

"A Catholic-style cross?" Patrick asks.

"Yes."

"Husky, body-builder type?"

"Yes, that's actually what saved me. He was a bit clumsy. He tried to grab me and strangle me, but I was able to break free and yell out. I had left the door open. I heard people coming toward us. Then he cracked me in the head with something and ran out the door. After that, I don't remember much, other than that I made this little drawing with the blood coming out of my head. Did it work?"

"Well, let's say we had our suspicions but wanted confirmation."

"What about Samia?"

"She didn't notice, but she was focused on other priorities."

"That . . . makes sense."

"She told us you thought you were being followed?"

"Definitely. Since the online interviews came out."

"Was this the same guy?"

"Yes, I'm almost positive. He was with other people from our area, the Middle East, I mean."

"Probably scouting."

The door swings open and a nurse arrives to take Nazim for his exams.

"One last thing," asks Patrick. "Where was the electrical outlet? Which room?"

"In the meeting room, with all the computers."

The nurse gets impatient. We say goodbye.

As we're strolling through the hospital hallways, I turn to Sébastien M.

"Have you made any progress with the investigation?"

"Yes, quite a bit. Several witnesses in the neighborhood have told us they saw a dark blue Clio, with two men inside, in the days leading up to the incident. So went through local security camera footage and found the car and the license plate. It's a rental, from Germany, in Munich. That didn't get us anywhere. It was rented with a German ID, obviously stolen, paid in cash. Our German colleagues jumped onboard quickly via Europol. The rental hasn't been returned. Its GPS is disconnected."

"OK."

"But we were able to obtain photos of the suspects. They're wearing hats, but you can still make them out in some of the pictures. It's strange though, one of them seems Asian, his eyes and his complexion. Seems Mongolian, actually."

The lieutenant takes the photos out of his briefcase.

"Yes, seems that way."

"After that, we looked for ATM withdrawals in the city. And bingo! We have a guy matching our composite in front of an ATM on Fontenelle."

He takes out another photograph. The ATM customer fits Nazim's description."

"Bravo, well done."

"Thanks. Another thing, the debit card was issued by an online bank and belongs to a Mohamed Abu Morad, a French-Lebanese man. It hasn't been reported stolen."

"Lebanese? Have we heard of him?"

"No, he keeps a relatively low profile, he does something in cryptocurrency."

"Well, you've got your hands full here."

"We're going to grab the electrical sockets at the apartment. We'll keep you up to date."

"Thank you. See you soon."

September 6—OCLCH, Paris

A week later, Colonel Norbert H. contacts me to announce more good news: they lifted a finger print off one of the outlets, which had a SIM card integrated into it. A remote listening device. The chip hadn't been activated though, the *chabiha* must not have had time. Probably an emissary of the Syrian intelligence services. Norbert adds that his lieutenant will be stopping by the OCLCH tomorrow, as planned, to listen to M. Al Ahmar's deposition, which will also serve as the occasion for new update. I thank him for his diligence.

The following day, Lieutenant Sébastien M. presents himself at OCLCH headquarters. Daniel, our resident police officer, meets him and they review Nazim's deposition. It floors him.

"How can someone make it through all that and go on living? That's . . . insane."

"Yes. Hell of a thing. And the finger print?"

"It was picked up in Eurodac.[1] It belongs to a Syrian man named Samir Sabbagh, born in Latakia, Syria, on August 25, 1989. The interesting bit is that he put in an asylum request to France last year."

"Ah, excellent. We'll check with our colleagues at OFPRA to see the status of his request."

I ask Philippe L., the director of the strategy division, to contact OFPRA. Ten minutes later, he returns.

"Sabbagh is a 1F. His case was transferred to crimes against humanity unit last month. I also called the deputy prosecutor who confirmed he received the file. Given the urgency, they immediately referred the file back to us."

Sebastien's curious. "A 1F?"

"1F designates individuals who've requested French asylum but, after an investigation by the protection officers at OFPRA, have been denied protection on account of suspected involvement in crimes against the peace in their native country. Actually, they still have protection based on the circumstances forcing them to flee their country, which they've revealed to OFPRA. However, if it's discovered that the individual lied or omitted pertinent details about their life at the outset of the investigation, if there are doubts, they're excluded."

"So . . . what does that mean?"

"So he's a *not not*—not protectable and not deportable!"

"That said, OFPRA, ever since the July 2015 reform to the rights-to-asylum laws, is obligated to transfer the case to a judicial authority if it involves suspected crimes against humanity. These cases are referred to us by the public prosecutor for investigation. Currently, 1F cases make up more than 40 per cent of the investigations that we're running. All from countries in crisis, of course."

"Why is your office in charge of these investigations?"

"Because these individuals are potentially perpetrators of atrocities in their own countries, and they come to France trying to take advantage of the asylum system to eventually obtain French citizenship. Many Rwandans, for example, have gone this route. They do everything they can to keep a low profile, stay under the radar. The 1Fs, however, are unique: an initial decision has been made against them, and most of the time they appeal the OFPRA decision to the National Court of Asylum."[2]

"Logical."

"So our investigations protect France's right to asylum from abuse and helps maintain public order."

"I see."

"The prosecutor assures me that we'll receive the case file tomorrow."

"OK. I'll bring our colonel up to speed."

"We'll let you as soon as we have the file in hand. It should contain some interesting information."

The following day, a delivery man arrives with the prosecutor's case file, which contains, among other things, one good quality photograph attached to a copy of our client's asylum request. I set up a coordinating meeting.

The strategy division takes the lead with facial recognition, transmitting information to Europol, and feeding our core international crimes (CIC) database to see if our target has drawn attention to himself in other countries. Open-source intelligence scours social networks. We contact the evidence-seeking NGOs to see if he has come up in their research.

As expected, the head of the investigations division, Captain Bertrand R., appoints Patrick to direct our investigation. He will oversee our first steps, digging through the OFPRA file, requisitioning phone records, and so on.

The results quickly pour in. We schedule a new briefing. Facial recognition reveals a 98 per cent match between the photo of Sabbagh taken in front of the ATM and the one in the OFPRA file.

Patrick reports on the OFPRA file.

"According to what he put in his application, he's living with a French-Lebanese man Mohamed Abu Morad, in Paris. The guy who 'loaned' him his debit card. We have a phone number, but it's likely a fake. However, the email address should be correct, if he was hoping to receive replies from our government. He presented two pieces of Syrian ID, one civilian and the other issued by the military."

Patrick shows me his photograph.

"Obviously, our friend Sabbagh lied all along the line. There are quite a few holes in his story. Questioned by asylum officials about his fears, he said he was from Latakia, born on August 25, 1989, and was of Christian Orthodox religion. His parents, according to him, remain in Syria in Latakia. He is not married and he studied in Damascus. He presented a graduate degree in construction—he's an architect—which he obtained in 2010. Then, when the protests began in 2011, he followed the student movement, was arrested as an opponent of the regime and briefly tortured in Damascus. When the asylum officer asked him for details, he was evasive. He does not know who arrested him, nor which branch of the Syrian government, nor for how long. He says he was imprisoned next to the airport because he could hear the planes taking off. All vague. Then he received a mobilization notice to take up arms in Bashar's army in 2013. He was hired as a guard on barricades around the airport in Damascus. Then, fearing a transfer to the fighting units, he decided to desert. He took advantage of a leave granted for the Christmas holidays in 2014 to exit the country."

"To where?"

"Turkey. There, too, he is vague. Says he stayed there two years, after having passed over the Syrian border north of Al Bab."

"How?"

"Smuggler.

After that, it's the normal route. In 2015, when Angela Merkel decided to offer German asylum to Syrian refugees, he seized the opportunity and made his way up through Greece, Macedonia, Serbia, Croatia, and Austria. Made it to Germany, around Munich. Worked two years as an architect, until he was dismissed. In 2017, he decides to take his chances in France and puts in a request for asylum. He gives the address of the Lebanese man in Paris. OFPRA has him return on two separate occasions before deciding to transfer the case to a public prosecutor. The military ID places him in the ranks of non-commissioned Syrian officers. His story doesn't add up. When pushed, he became uncooperative and evasive."

"I'll ask to our strategy department to check if he's known to our intelligence colleagues."

"OK. I'm starting with the requisitions over the phone, emails, etc."

A few moments later, I stop by the strategy department to ask them to start acting on the new information. Jean-Michel informs me that he's already put in the request to our intelligence agency via an encrypted message.

He launches OSINT and relays the information to WRAP [web research analysis platform], a sophisticated software tool that compiles and analyzes digital traces left by individuals—wrapping them up. I watch as Jean-Michel works on his screen. Night blue background with hexagons, like a honeycomb. Nice design. He clicks and drags different social network icons into the scanner. He enters the email address Sabbagh listed on his application: nemer8908@hotmail.com. Traces it through YouTube, Facebook, VK (a Russian service), Twitter, Ebay, Skype, etc. This quickly brings up our target's Skype profile and username, Nemer89, along with a profile picture representing a tiger, and the name Joni Haddad.

"Tiger is Arabic is Nemer."

"OK."

"Let's check out what this username gives us."

"There's another Skype profile with a similar profile avatar. Nemer8908."

The software goes at it.

"Hang on, I think we've got it. The account is registered under the name Samir Sabbagh."

Jean-Michel drags the icons across the dark-blue screen again.

"Here's a similar username on YouTube. Nemer 8998. With the same tiger avatar. Let's try Facebook."

Jean-Michel types in the two usernames, Nemer89 and Nemer8908. Several profiles appear, under the term nemer, but only one nemer8908. One click on the profile and we have our guy in several photographs posted in 2013, 2014. We see him in combat fatigues, often arm in arm with other individuals, armed with Kalashnikovs and cartridge belts. Some are in civilian clothes, apparently quite happy to be there. Jean-Michel digs deeper and finds another Sabbagh, a guy named Joni. He also has a gun, beard, fatigues, older, with a badge featuring Arabic writing. Google translate gives us: Commandos Special Forces. Joni seems to be Samir's brother.

The various photographs and comments leave no doubt these are the Bashar faithful. Some of the individuals in the photographs have tattoos of Bashar's face on their chest or back.

Samir has posted on Joni's wall a poem about the glory of defending the fatherland. The invincibility of the tigers. Never retreat. Overcome etc.

"Well, I think we have a winner!"

"Yes, but I have to check if he doesn't have another profile. I saw a name on a list with the same tiger avatar."

Indeed, another profile appears, in the name of Johnny Sabbag. The photographs are different. Here, we see him in the company of young women leaning on a BMW. The license plate is Turkish. It was posted on August 25, 2015, and we can see the Aya Sophia in the background, the cathedral of Istanbul. We can follow the rest of his journey from Turkey to Germany. He posted a photo of a piece a paper reading in Arabic: "We are here!" The image went up on November 30, 2017. In the background, behind the paper, we see some kind of store with a sign composed of two eyes, a headset, a white square. Some sort of music, video, or computer store. On the right, another store, with a mill and an inscription in German, "Bäckerei Müller." A bakery.

"I will ask my crowd-sourcing friends if they can geolocate the photograph."

"How long do you think that will take?"

"A few days, probably. Maybe tomorrow, if they move. The really good thing is that his profile is still active and he publishes regularly. He's even got a Snapchat profile. He's posting stories there. Looks like a new user name, but he likes those tigers. Tiger8908."

"Good. Great. So?"

"So I'm going to keep a very close eye on his Facebook and Snapchat profiles."

"OK."

The next day, I contact the colonel at the investigative unit to inform him of our progress. He proposes to meet quickly in the afternoon. In the meantime, we have heard from the intelligence services. The Lebanese is a hawaladar, specializing in hawala type financial transactions—transferring money untraceably through intermediaries who all take a cut. No banks. What's more, he is strongly suspected of being a "super facilitator," laundering criminal money. The services ask us not to get too close as they've been targeting him for a while.

When we arrive, Colonel Norbert H. is waiting for us. He takes us directly to the office of Sebastien M. I explain to them where things are at. The Lebanese is under surveillance and we've been asked to be careful in our movements.

"OK, but our target used his bank card. It's going to be difficult not to follow him," says Norbert H.

"Yes, that's for sure. We'll have to warn them. We've only discussed the 1F part with them."

Sébastien M. tells us that he made requisitions to the four cellphone operators who have relays located around Nazim's apartment for the time periods when the target was seen around there. A German number came up, same one every time. Chances are that it belongs to whoever rented the car in Germany. So, via Siena and Europol, Sébastien asked the Germans to trace the owner of the phone. He is waiting for an answer.

"Perfect."

"By the way, the Germans also told us that the car was found burned, at the end of an alley. Off a street called Bergstrasse or something like that. Guess which town."

We look at him.

"Dachau!"

"No."

"Yes!"

"Have you thought about checking surveillance on the way to Germany?

"We are waiting for the reports."

"So if I've got this right, our targets have left and are probably now in Germany."

"That's what it sounds like," says Norbert.

"I'll notify the German police and the public prosecutor."

"I'll do the same on my side. Think we'll need a European arrest warrant."

"Well, that's it for now. We'll keep in touch. We're still monitoring his social networks. You never know."

Two days later, Jean-Michel walks into my office, smiling.

"I think we know where he's at. He keeps sharing videos on Snapchat coming back from parties with his friends. I set up alerts for when he posts. Last night, it woke me up. Here's what he posted."

Jean-Michel shows me several videos of Sabaggh. It's a birthday party. His. He's celebrating with some friends in a Syrian restaurant in Munich. We can see him with his arms around two individuals. The person on his right looks to be of Mongolian decent.

Then another video.

"'That's the same street where he posted the 'We are here' photograph."

"Yes, I remember."

"See him walking into the building with his friends? My crowdsourcing pals were able to find the bakery. It's located at the corner of K Street and B Street in M."

Jean-Michel zooms in on Google Maps to show me the bakery.

"If you ask me, he can't be far. The video was taken yesterday. His birth-day is August 25. Today is the 26th."

"OK, I'll call the investigative unit commander."

The crowdsourcing results are stunning. People spending their free time geotagging photos and videos around the globe. It takes all kinds to make a world. But it shows how civil society is a growing presence in our investi-gations and often a great help to us.

An hour later, I'm on the phone with Colonel Norbert H. He says that our targets were caught speeding on a highway near Metz. Europol got a phone number, prepaid but apparently still active.

An hour later, he calls me back to say that a European arrest warrant has been issued for Sabbagh. The Germans think they know his location and they might have identified his phone line. They're going to set up a device to pin him down.

September 10, 2019 – Munich

Markus, our colleague, informs us that our target has been located by a police surveillance unit in Munich. The second individual is there as well. The exact same building discovered via WRAP.

They're planning to execute the warrant on September 11, at 6 a.m. local time, accompanied by the Spezialeinsatzkommando (SEK). Markus confirms that he'll be onsite with this partner. He will film the operation.

The night before the arrest, I'm restless, as usual.

At 6:30 a.m., I receive a WhatsApp from Markus confirming that Sabbagh and his partner were arrested in the Munich apartment. He adds a link so that I can watch the video footage using an access code sent over Signal.

I sit down at my computer.

At 5 a.m., the German units charged with executing the European arrest warrant are gathered in the local precinct. Coffees, conversation, updates. Apparently, surveillance held the targets dead in their sites throughout the night to ensure that they'd be where we wanted them in the early morning. The chief gives the signal and they're off. The elite unit has explosive pellets in case it needs to blast its way in. The doors and locks in the building were no doubt cased discreetly the day before.

Everyone piles into vehicles. A few minutes later, they're parked in front of the bakery. They arrange themselves in battle order. They use a key pass to open the building. Quiet steps up the stairs. One officer covers the peepholes of the apartment doors with black duct tape. They cut the lights. Position themselves in front of the apartment door. A specialized hydraulic piston blows open the door. In the blink of an eye, the elite squad has penetrated the tiny apartment and immobilized the two men. Sabaggh tries to fight back, but two officers overwhelm him. The second individual gives himself up without a struggle.

And all is calm. Markus films the apartment. Basic furniture. No weapons found. We learn that the apartment belongs to a Syrian living in Sweden.

Markus sends me a secure message saying that the second individual has also put in an asylum request, but in Germany. He's identified as Sayyed Hassan Husseini, from Afghanistan, Hazara ethnicity. He's a member of the Fatimides division, an Islamic Shiite militia based in Iran— guardians of the Islamic Revolution and Hezbollah. Several thousand Hazara fighters are deployed in Syria, some under the orders of the Al-Qudso force, an elite unit of the Islamic Revolutionary Guard specializing in non-conventional warfare, intelligence, and foreign operations. In short, part of the defense coalition around Bashar and his regime.

Sabbagh and Husseini are turned over to French authorities in the days that follow. Versaille's investigative unit questions them on facts pertaining to their case. They deny everything. But the evidence is solid and sufficient to convict them. OCLCH's investigators are granted visitation permits to hear Sabbagh questioned in Fleury-Mérogis on his participation in crimes committed in Syria. He won't talk. As expected. But the NGO fact finders come through. They find an insider who confirms Sabbagh's participation in several massacres.

Our German colleagues also find a phone hidden in Sabbagh's bathroom. A lot of revealing evidence. Combat videos, executions of Kurdish women, bullets to the head with hands tied behind their back. Finally, photographs of Sabbagh executing a man with a Kalashnikov.

Case closed.

October 30—OCLCH, Paris

Nazim has just been released from the hospital and sends a text, thanking us for the work we've done. He adds an additional comment on the situation in Syria:

"The despots are running out of ideas everywhere in the world. This will send a clear message. They will pay for their cruelty. Ultimately. By the way, the next country on the list is Libya . . ."

I thank him, and point out that the end result was the work of a lot of individuals and agencies, all of whom believe in the work they're doing, fighting for justice, fighting against impunity.

I add: "On the other hand, I'm not sure they're running out of ideas."

23

OPERATION
"COLLINES-955"[1]

"Crimes against humanity are the common marker of all cultures. The mission of human rights is also to preserve civilization for future generations so that humanity remains a promise."

—Mireille Delmas-Marty

May 16, 2020, Paris, Porte de Bagnolet, night

I awake startled. Sweating. Today, we will know. Today, we will know. The sentence runs in a loop in my head through the quiet of the night. I glance at my alarm clock, 3:30 a.m. Every day before a move like this is the same, maximum tension. I think about the action to come, trying to remember ever detail, pondering the imponderables.

Operation "Collines-955" is special for two reasons. It will be the last of my career. I have decided to retire after thirty-eight years of good and loyal service in the army and the gendarmerie. Also, it's a choice target, the Rwandan Félicien Kabuga, one of the most wanted war criminals in the world.

The indictment against Kabuga, filed on April 14, 2011, at the International Criminal Tribunal for Rwanda, lists the most serious offenses committed in Rwanda in 1994: "Genocide, direct and public incitement to commit genocide, attempted genocide, conspiracy to commit genocide, and politically motivated persecution, extermination, and murder, constituting crimes against humanity."[2] A wealthy tea farmer with a range of business interests, Kabuga was closely connected to the ex-president of Rwanda, Juvénal Habyarimana, and the Akazu, the Hutu extremist cell that planned the genocide. He was a primary financier of extremist Hutu media and a contributor to the mass importation of 500,000 machetes in preparation for the attacks.

I look up at the dimly lit ceiling and run the last few days through my mind.

Less than six hours ago, I was still in the south of France supervising work on my earthquake-damaged house, which I plan to move into down the road.

For the past few weeks, my teams have been on the trail of this man who for twenty-five years has eluded the many police forces that have been after him. In other words, we cannot make mistakes. Our Rwandan friends would not forgive us.

Four days ago, we were reviewing the case with our investigators, particularly Estelle, who has been managing the search for Kabuga. We have an operation scheduled several weeks in the future but my intuition has been screaming move faster. I've been doing this long enough to trust my instincts. They've kept me out of trouble, even saved my life.

I'd recently spoken with the general counsel in charge of the case at the Paris Court of Appeal and Serge Brammertz, prosecutor of the International Mechanism to Carry Out the Residual Functions of the Criminal Tribunals, which took over from the International Criminal Tribunal for Rwanda. We walked about a faster timeline but at that moment were still waiting for an answer to one important question.

Two days ago, I got off the train in the south of France and picked up my messages. Estelle left a report that worried me. There has been action on the phones of Kabuga family members. She sent more people to watch entrances and exits to ensure Kabuga didn't not escape.

I suddenly felt like a caged lion, trapped three hours from Paris, bitterly regretting my decision to leave the office. I tapped on my phone, looking at schedules to see if could get back that night.

Before I found anything, I thought better of it. Maybe we were overreacting. An hour later Nicolas, my assistant, called and confirmed that the emergency seemed to have blown over. A relief, but it was clear we could no longer leave things to chance. We needed to move as quickly as possible.

Yesterday morning, we made the decision to force our way into the apartment we've been watching in Asnières-sur-Seine to answer the question that's been bothering us for several weeks: is Kabuga hiding in this residence?

On the station platform, while waiting for the train that will take me to Paris, I called the deputy director of the gendarmerie's judicial police to inform him of the arrest project and the means we intend to use. I looked over the operation order prepared by my deputy, squadron leader Nicolas L.-C., for our upcoming coordination meeting.[3]

I joined our teams in the meeting room at 8 p.m. last night. Estelle was at the table along with officers and non-commissioned officers of the OCLCH and the lieutenant who heads the intervention platoon of the Republican Guard of Paris, which will carry out the operation.

There was a quiet in the room. Everyone understood the exception character of the operations, presuming that our fugitive is indeed in Asnières-sur-Seine. This could be an important moment in the history of international justice.

"Hello everyone. Let me first remind you of the legal framework of this action. This investigative procedure is in search of a person targeted by a request for provisional arrest for the purpose of handing him over to the French justice system. It was opened in application of article 696-9-1 of the French code of criminal procedure and the article 74-2 of the same code. It is conducted under the direction of Mrs. C., general counsel to the Court of Appeal of Paris, who has authorized us to break down the door of the apartment in Asnières-sur-Seine."

The lieutenant nodded.

"If the target is present in the apartment, we will proceed to arrest him in accordance with the warrant issued by the judges of the International Mechanism for Arrest and conduct a search.

I can confirm that the magistrate will join us for this operation, which is rare but an asset. Nobody will be able to accuse us of unwarranted police violence . . ."

Smiles.

"The operation will take place simultaneously on four sites starting at 6:30 a.m.: the first is in Asnières-sur-Seine (92), the main objective. The three others are on secondary targets in the city of Paris. There is indeed a strong probability that the fugitive is present in Asnières, but if for whatever reason he has left the apartment and is at the home of one of his children, we need to have all the sites covered. We cannot risk letting him escape as he did in Germany in 2007."

Nods.

"I want to be clear that I will be operational director with the intervention team in Asnières-sur-Seine, alongside the magistrate and Estelle, the investigation director, and Nicolas, my deputy. Four gendarmes and Kinyarwanda, a few people from the office, and our Rwandan-language interpreter, will accompany us."[4]

I turned to the lieutenant of the Republican Guard platoon.

"The Republican Guard platoon will bring equipment to get us through the door, break down the door, secure the premises, and escort the fugitive to the Nanterre prosecutor's office."

I took another glance at the young lieutenant who commands this platoon. He has a frank and open manner. Enthusiastic. I sensed that he knows he is participating in a major event. More than thirty years separate us, but I saw in him the same passion for public service that animates most of the gendarmes. He continues.

"We have already carried out some discreet reconnaissance of the building. Plainclothes operatives. We know how we'll proceed in the morning."

Back to me.

"That's fine. Regarding the secondary sites, the three other Parisian addresses, the various heads of the OCLCH detachment are charged with ensuring whether or not the fugitive is present. They will search the premises and seize any relevant evidence in accordance with the warrant issued. The four addresses are not located in unfavourable environments for law enforcement, so we will only inform the local police stations of our operations tomorrow at 06:30. The home base will be located in the offices of the OCLCH and directed by JP who will manage whatever requests we get from whichever detachments and prepare for all eventualities and problems."

"Any questions? No? Good evening to all, and see you tomorrow morning at six."

My eyes are still riveted to the ceiling. I'm startled when my alarm clock finally rings at 5:30 a.m. Time to get moving.

May 16, 2020, OCLCH premises, Bagnolet, 6:00 a.m.

Coffee is flowing. Some investigators are standing around joking, others are loading equipment into vehicles—computers, printers, packaging, materials for sealing evidence. It is the usual bustle of a police unit preparing for an arrest. I will miss these moments in the future, but my mind is made up.

From the top of our fourth floor, I watch the gendarmes in charge of the operation down on the street, which is calm at this time of day. They strap on their equipment behind their dark-blue service vehicles. The calmness of experienced troops, as they say.

Our OCLCH investigators gather in the courtyard of our building for one last update. The lieutenant reports on their overnight reconnaissance at the building where Kabuga is supposed to be. Everything was quiet and nobody left the apartment.

I see C., the general counsel. From the east of France, like me. Strong character. She holds out her hand and smiles. I offer her a ride in my unmarked service vehicle to Asnières-sur-Seine. The vehicles move into formation and each team heads to its designated site.

In a few minutes, we will finally know.

I follow the intervention platoon. The column progresses quietly through the still sleeping streets of Paris. Along the way, C. tells me of her personal history with Rwanda. In the past, she had helped a young Rwandan woman, a victim of repeated sexual abuse who had turned to prostitution, get off the street. Probably a coincidence but her involvement in this operation feels like the stars are aligned.

Asnières-sur-Seine, rue du Révérend Père Christian Gilbert, 06.30

When we arrive at the scene, the lieutenant asks us to park in a street out of view of the apartment. The building has two entrances, one at each end. It is not easy to find a spot out of the apartment's sightlines but it's worth the effort. We don't want to be spotted by a cigarette smoker on a balcony, or an insomniac. With Paris still locked down because of the coronavirus, it's uncommon to see so many vehicles moving in the streets.

I finally lay eyes on the building where Kabuga is thought to be hiding. To this point, I have only seen in in photographs or on Google maps. The district is mostly residential.

Without a word, we enter the building's entrance hall one after another, trailing the gendarmes of the platoon who are equipped from helmet to boots, armed, and—a little COVID novelty—wearing face masks with protective goggles.

The intervention squad descends a concrete staircase and heads through the garage to reach the opposite entrance hall. There we rush up a narrow stairwell, one after the other, quiet as possible, to the third floor.

Not a word spoken. I watch as the door-opening team positions its hydraulic jack, ready to burst into the apartment. The lieutenant glances at me. I send a WhatsApp message on the "Big Fish" thread we have created to give the green light to the other three teams positioned in front of other doors.

I receive three thumbs up in return.

I nod to the lieutenant.

Is Kabuga behind that door?

In a few seconds, we'll know.

Without warning, the door shatters and the team of eight gendarmes rushes into the apartment prepared to arrest anyone within. We stay behind. Thirty seconds later, the lieutenant announces that the situation is under control.

I make way for Estelle, giving her the honour of first discovering what's inside. She enters the apartment, inspects the living room and progresses directly to the bedroom. She sees an old man, in his eighties, lying on a bed. She knows this face well. His photo has long been hanging on the walls of the OCLCH with the words: "Wanted for Rwandan Genocide." As she leans in for a closer look, she notices a scar. It is from an operation for a benign throat tumor in Germany in 2007. It is one of his distinguishing marks, described in the Interpol red notice drawn up in Félicien Kabuga's name: "8 to 9 centimetres, on the right side."

Estelle comes back to us.

"It is Kabuga," she says, half-smiling.

It is done.

I venture into the apartment and check to see that the windows are closed. One never knows. The place is clean, rather well decorated, a bit untidy. I approach D. who we've identified as one of the fugitive's sons. He stands silently, stares at me and asks coldly: "Who are you?"

"We are the gendarmes of the Central Office for the Fight against Crimes against Humanity. I guess you know why we are here, right?

"For my father."

A lot is acknowledged in that simple statement.

Kabuga, meanwhile, is still lying down, being questioned by the interpreter in Kinyarwanda. He insists on the identity under which he has been hiding for many years, Antoine Tounga, a citizen of the Democratic Republic of Congo. He speaks in Swahili, pretending not to understand the Kinyarwanda interpreter.

In a few moments, his DNA will be taken and transported to the Institute of Criminal Research of the Gendarmerie Nationale (IRCGN) in Pontoise for comparison with the sample transmitted by our German comrades at the request of Prosecutor Brammertz.

D., the son, his shock wearing off, regains his courage and asks to speak to his father. Of course, we refuse. He looks at us startled: "You are inhuman!"

We look at each other, dumbfounded.

"We are inhuman?" exclaims one of the investigators. "Would you like us to read your father's indictment so we can compare degrees of inhumanity?"

D. does not look down but does not answer, either.

I glance at my watch. It is 7:00 a.m. Magistrate C. tells me that she has to leave to report up her chain of command.

I leave the apartment and do the same. The news will quickly make the media rounds. I also call Prosecutor Brammertz to inform him of Kabuga's arrest. His weekend plans are about to change. After a few rings, he answers me and does not hide his enthusiasm at the news.

I think of our Rwandan friends and in particular of Aisha, one of the GFTU prosecutors in Kigali.[5] I send her a WhatsApp to inform her of Kabuga's arrest so that she can get things moving at her end and report up to her direct boss, John B., and the prosecutor general of Rwanda, Aimable H. She calls me back immediately.

"Eric? Are you kidding? You just arrested Kabuga?"

"That's right. We've just taken the DNA sample to definitively confirm his identity. But I can assure you that he is now under our control and soon to be locked up."

Quiet.

"You are Santa Claus, Eric . . . in May."

"Aisha, I'm really happy that this man can finally be brought before an international court and that the Rwandans will get justice, presuming he is found guilty of the charges against him."

"I'll inform everyone here. Thanks again to the whole team."

She pauses and continues.

"You know, Eric, the worst thing for us would have been if he had died and been buried somewhere in Europe. At least he will be able to be accountable to the Rwandan people. Thank you again."

Aimable H., the prosecutor general, calls me within seconds to congratulate us and to ask for details he can pass on to Rwandan police.

I have one final call to make, to my friend Charles Habonimana, author of *Moi, le dernier Tutsi*.[6] He is speechless when I break the news but recovers to thank us on behalf of the Rwandan people.

Back in the apartment, I take a seat on the couch next to D., who looks at me out of the corner of his eye and asks: "Why don't you ever investigate the crimes of members of the Patriotic Front of Rwanda?"

I hand him my business card and answer: "On this card you will find my contact information and our address. If you have specific information to share with us that we can investigate, you are welcome to use it."

As the team was finishing up, Kabuga asked D. to make him an omelet. I watch the old man swallow the last bite as the investigators inform him that he will be delivered to the public prosecutor in Nanterre. The man who has been taunting officials of the International Criminal Tribunal for Rwanda since 1997 gets up and begins his slow walk toward prison.

Over a quarter of a century, one international prosecutors after another—five in total—have pursued him and dreamed of this moment. Relying on his family, his tribe, his connections, and his wealth, Kabuga remained at large, moving around Africa and Europe under false identities. He was nicknamed "the elusive one."

The United States had been particularly active in the hunt for Kabuga. Ambassador Pierre-Richard Prosper, who handled the war crimes portfolio for President George W. Bush, spearheaded the U.S. effort. Kabuga was their number one target but they couldn't get their hands on him. Intelligence agencies located him in Belgium, the Congo, the United Kingdom, France, Burundi, Kenya, Madagascar, and the Seychelles. He was everywhere and nowhere. They announced a $5 million reward for information leading to his capture under the U.S. Reward for Justice program. In the late 1990s and early 2000s, the hunt focused on Kenya, where he apparently had admirers at the highest level of government. Several informants reported his presence. One of them died for having dealt with the Americans. Another had to be relocated to the United States where he still resides. When contacted by journalists after Kabuga's arrest, he said he was relieved by his arrest.

The trail was lost until 2007 when German police detected one of his sons-in-law: Augustin Ngirabatware, minister of planning before and during the genocide. They weren't able to arrest Kabuga but they did gather important evidence, including a passport application under a false name with a photo of Kabuga, and a sample of his DNA.

For the next decade, the hunt for Félicien Kabuga seemed to be going nowhere. Prosecutor Serge Brammertz, appointed in 2016, upgraded his investigative team and hired more analysts. Informants were always coming forward with news of Kabuga in one African country or another—Gabon, Burundi, Kenya, sometimes in multiple places during the same week. But nothing concrete. Nothing we could verify.

Given that the fugitive was aged, dealing with health problems, and was in Germany in 2007, there were objective reasons to believe that he remained in Europe. But where?

In July 2019, Serge Brammertz made another move. He sent squadron leader Nicolas and chief warrant officer Estelle to The Hague to meet with their counterparts from several other European countries. The idea was to form a European task force that would collaborate and share information on targets of mutual interest. The three key nations were Belgium, Great Britain, and France, where the majority of Félicien Kabuga's thirteen children, biological and adopted, were known to reside.

This was a change in strategy for us. Previously, we tended to be reactive, acting only within the framework of specific requests for international assistance in criminal matters. We were now becoming pro-active.

We also requested that the magistrates in charge of fugitive cases at the Paris Court of Appeal allow us to work more autonomously, broaden the scope of our actions, and improve our ability to conduct searches, record telephone calls, taps wires, and geolocate those of Kabuga's relatives likely to help him and hide him. This allowed us to be more enterprising.

In its first few months of operation, the task force was a tight group of about twenty people, sharing and analyzing information. While this is happening, I make my own visit to the Hague, to Europol, to participate in the 2020 annual meeting of AP CIC (Analysis Project, Core International Crimes). We took stock of current cases—Syria, Iraq, Rwanda, etc.—and I had the opportunity to continue to press for more cooperation and coordination at the European level and the creation of a joint international team including Rwanda and other countries willing to share data. The Kabuga file came up in these meetings. I had let it be known that I was retiring and my friends and colleagues in Great Britain as well as the head of AP CIC remarked that an arrest of Kabuga would be a nice way to end my career. It seemed far-fetched at the time, but why not?

A few weeks later, thanks to information provided by Great Britain, the investigation turned a corner. Our colleagues informed us that one of Félicien Kabuga's daughters lived in London. She periodically commuted between Great Britain and Belgium, passing through France. A close look at the roaming charges on her phone records showed that she was not just passing through France but staying in France for extended visits on multiple occasions. The analysts and our team were able to establish that her cell phone regularly connected to a relay antenna located in Asnières, in Haut-de-Seine.

What was she doing there? We did not believe that anyone in the Kabuga family had an apartment in the vicinity.

On March 17, the pandemic hit and France was locked down. Investigators, too. Estelle, working from home, decided to use the time to scrutinize what was by then a large collection of telephone records belonging to the fugitive's relatives.

She mapped their movements and realized that, over the course of one year, this telephone relay antenna in Asnières was activated by almost all Kabuga's children, roughly three hundred and sixty times. A promising break. Maybe our target was right here in France.

At the end of March, investigators reached out to the tax department and bingo! They discovered that an apartment had been rented in Asnières for several years under the surname of one of Félicien Kabuga's sons. It was a third-floor residence on rue du Révérend Père Christian Gilbert.

This didn't prove that Kabuga was present in the apartment, but it was certainly suggestive.

At the same time, and despite the inconvenience of the lockdown, Estelle was able to access Kabuga family bank statements. She noticed a substantial sum of money had been paid to the Beaujon hospital, not far from Asnières-sur-Seine. It dated from the summer of 2019 and was issued by B., another daughter of the fugitive. She is the widow of one of the sons of ex-Rwandan president Juvénal Habyarimana, and is the head of the Kabuga clan in France.

Question. For whose benefit and for what reason did she write this check? The investigators make inquiries at the hospital.

We are meanwhile monitoring the entrances to the apartment in Asnières-sur-Seine. It is difficult work, with France locked down, the streets almost deserted and the shops closed. We are at constant risk of being exposed. The observation and surveillance group is nevertheless managing.

Two months later, on May 11, we learn that D, the eldest of Kabuga's sons, a Belgian resident who was under surveillance by local police, has slipped away. He is in France. In Asnières-sur-Seine. It occurs to us that with other members of the family in confinement, it fell to him to take care of his father.

On the morning of May 15, another break. The bank check paid for surgery on an octogenarian of African origin. The investigators obtain a photocopy of the passport that was provided to the hospital. The person in question goes by the name of Antoine Tounga. We compare DNA shared by the hospital with investigators to the 2007 sample provided by the German police. Without a doubt, Félicien Kabuga and Antoine Tounga are one and the same.

And this morning we arrest him, bringing to an end one of the longest and most remarkable pursuits in the annals of international criminal justice.

The news of Kabuga's capture hits the media like a bomb. The entire weekend is lost to responding to national and international press inquiries. There are a lot of questions about the famous $5-million bounty offered by the U.S. State Department, but police services are not eligible.

Perhaps the most surprising media request comes from Thomas Zribi, producer of the Netflix series, "World's Most Wanted." He is in a hurry. He has just finished editing an episode on Kabuga. The ending no longer works. He has to shoot a new one and wants the cooperation of the OCLCH.

An appointment is made on Monday morning to shoot his final scene. The director tells me he was shocked to discover that he and Kabuga lived on the same street. When we receive surveillance photos, he spots his own car. "I went around the world to shoot this report on Kabuga and the trail ends right next door . . ."

There are thanks and congratulations, the most enthusiastic coming from Rwanda. In France, the director general of the gendarmerie comes in person to congratulate the team for its accomplishment and to get to know this unusual investigative unit a little better.

The U.S. State Department sends its thanks: "We applaud the government of France and the International Criminal Court residual mechanism for the arrest of Félicien Kabuga, who is accused of having played a key role in the 1994 genocide in Rwanda. We commend the law enforcement officials around the world who contributed to this arrest. This is an important step for international justice, and a message to all fugitives accused of genocide that they will be brought to justice. We hope this arrest will bring some peace to the victims and their families."

The international recognition was fitting. Although Kabuga was ultimately captured in France, it required an international effort. If was only by unprecedented collaboration and sharing of resources that the alleged mastermind of the 1994 genocide of the Tutsis in Rwanda was brought to justice."

Félicien Kabuga is currently in the custody of the International Residual Mechanism for Criminal Tribunals at the Hague, awaiting trial on all of the charges mentioned above.

CONCLUSION

One would think that the 20th century, which gave us decade after decade of atrocity, would have made a serious project of the pursuit for universal justice. And yet, not so. At the beginning of the 21st century, the stench of genocide still hangs in the air. The world is still bloodied by vicious wars, organized massacres, mass rapes, and ethnic cleansing. The latest episodes, whether we're talking about the Islamic State or the massacres of the Rohingyas, are more of the same, in their motives and their mechanics.

My objective in leading you through this black gash in human experience has been to call attention to the work of men and women who make it their mission, day after day, to fight on the side of justice and against impunity. They belong to a galaxy of gendarmes, police officers, magistrates, special investigators, humanitarian workers, psychologists, journalists, NGOs, whistleblowers, and members of international organizations. Collectively, they are committed to investigating, proving, and passing judgment; they seek to repair the world through justice, forgiveness, and reconciliation.

Their targets are those suspected of genocide, war crimes, and crimes against humanity, perpetrators who try to erase their pasts and construct new lives in other lands—in the cases above, France. They need to be unmasked and brought to justice so that our country, the birthplace of human rights, never becomes a refuge for criminals, and so the right to asylum is preserved for those who genuinely merit protection.

In concert with our various partners, the team at OCLCH conducts its investigations in both national and international territories. These investigations differ from traditional criminal cases and demand specific and advanced skill sets because evidence must be collected outside our borders—the sites where crimes were committed and witnesses reside—making our mission extremely complex.

That requires that our investigators be compassionate, curious, humble, and creative. They are aware that their work allows victims to see their torturers denounced, prosecuted, and convicted thanks to universal jurisdiction. The process clears the way for victims to rebuild their lives and for societies to achieve reconciliation. Only justice, by bringing out the truth, allows people to turn the page.

Hence the OCLCH creed. *Hora fugit, stat jus.* Time passes, justice remains.

The fight is far from over. It requires budgets and resources, and it takes time and patience. But it must be fought or the field will be left open to tyrants and their trained killers. They will continue to sow chaos, transform fear into hate, and exploit human flaws and weaknesses to realize their terrible designs. They will insist on exploiting religion, nationalism, ethnicity (sometimes all three at once) for their own narrow profit and gain.

Fighting against impunity means preventing hate from metastasizing, yet again, across entire societies. It means reining in the cynical opportunists who nullify common sense with twisted language, exaggerated fears, and the invention of an "other" beside whom "we" cannot possibly exist.

It is to protect our democracy and freedom. It is also to cultivate the skills of vigilance and lucidity.

Vigilance because, at the risk of bordering on idealism, it is essential to be diligent in vetting those who are brought forth to govern us.[1] Our history of war and genocide shows us that the worst narcissists and psychopaths can attain high office, positions they should never hold. As Steve Taylor explains, power often coincides with selfishness, greed, and lack of empathy.[2] Those in whom the desire for power is strongest are often unscrupulous, cynical, and ruthless, as a glance at the current roster of world leaders attests.

Vigilance cannot be dissociated from lucidity, especially with regard to ourselves. We must be aware of our weaknesses and fragilities, and how easily they are exploited.

As the philosopher Bernard Crevel explains, lucidity is the promotion of mindfulness and the dissolution of the ego. It involves a dedicated effort to overcoming ignorance and base impulses, and liberating ourselves from the disorder we have made or been placed amid. It requires us to let go of our self-centered certitudes. To practice lucidity is to learn to unlearn what we think we know about ourselves and others, freeing the mind of ancient prejudices and dubious teachings, and developing our critical faculties. Only then can we identify fraud and falsity and win freedom from the fears that tyrants feed upon.

As Primo Levi wrote in *If This Is a Man*:

You who live safe
In your warm houses,
You who find on returning in the evening,
Hot food and friendly faces:
Consider if this is a man
Who works in the mud
Who does not know peace
Who fights for a scrap of bread
Who dies because of a yes or a no.
Consider if this is a woman,
Without hair and without name
With no more strength to remember,
Her eyes empty and her womb cold
Like a frog in winter.
Meditate that this came about:
I commend these words to you.
Carve them in your hearts
At home, in the street,
Going to bed, rising;
Repeat them to your children,
Or may your house fall apart,
May illness impede you,
May your children turn their faces from you.

APPENDIX 1

Relevant Infractions

Five infractions are concerned with the gravest international crimes:

Torture

[Art. 222-1 Penal Code (CP); Art. 682-1 Code of Criminal Procedure (CPP); Art. 1 of the 1984 New York Convention against Torture and Other Cruel, Inhuman or Degrading Treatment or Punishment][1]

Statute of Limitations: 20 years [by the law of March 2017 Art. 8 CPP]

This concerns torture or barbaric acts carried out by a public official or any other person acting in an official capacity or at his instigation or with his express or tacit consent for the purpose of obtaining from him or a third person information or a confession, punishing the person for an act that the person or a third person has committed or is suspected of having committed, or intimidating or coercing the person or a third person, or for any other purpose based on discrimination of any kind.

Forced Disappearance

[Art. 221-12 CP]

Statute of Limitations: 30 years [Art. 7 CPP, by the law of August 5, 2013]

The arrest, detention, abduction, or any other form of deprivation of liberty of a person, under conditions that place him/her outside the protection of the law, by one or more agents of the State or by a person or group of persons acting with the authorization, support, or acquiescence of the state authorities, when such actions are followed by the disappearance of the person and accompanied by the denial of the recognition of the deprivation of liberty, or by the concealment of the fate or whereabouts of the person.

Genocide

[Art. 211-1 CP]

Statute of Limitations: Indefinite [Art. 7 CPP]

Genocide is the act, in execution of a concerted plan aimed at the total or partial destruction of a national, ethnic, racial or religious group, or of a group determined on the basis of any other arbitrary criterion, of committing or causing to be committed, against members of this group, one of the following acts:

- willful bodily harm;
- serious harm to physical or psychological integrity;
- submission to conditions of life likely to lead to the total or partial destruction of the group;
- measures to prevent births;
- forced transfer of children.

Genocide is punishable by life imprisonment.

Crimes Against Humanity

[Art. 212-1 CP]

Statute of Limitations: Indefinite [Art. 7 CPP]

The following acts constitute crimes against humanity if committed in execution of a concerted plan against a civilian population group as part of a widespread or systematic attack:

- willful taking of life;
- extermination;

- enslavement;
- deportation or forcible transfer of a population;
- imprisonment or any other form of severe deprivation of physical liberty in violation of fundamental provisions of international law;
- torture;
- rape, enforced prostitution, forced pregnancy, enforced sterilization or any other form of sexual violence of comparable gravity;
- persecution of any identifiable group or collectivity on political, racial, national, ethnic, cultural, religious, gender or other grounds that are universally recognized as impermissible under international law;
- forced disappearance;
- acts of segregation committed as part of an institutionalized regime of systematic oppression and domination by one racial group over any other racial group or groups and with the in- tent to maintain that regime;
- other inhumane acts of a similar character intentionally causing great suffering or serious injury to body or mind.

War Crimes and Misdemeanors

[Book IV bis CP; Law of August 9, 2010]

Statute of Limitations: 30 years [Art. 7 CPP]. Misdemeanors: 20 years [Art. 8 CPP]

According to Article 461-1 of the Penal Code, war crimes and offenses are characterized by the following:

- they are committed during an international or non-international armed conflict;
- they are perpetrated in relation to this conflict;
- they violate the laws and customs of war, or the international conventions applicable to armed conflicts;
- they affect persons or property;
- they are defined in the Penal Code itself.

The material acts of war crimes are for:

International and Non-International Armed Conflicts
[Art. 461-2 to 461-18 CP]

Crimes against the human person: deliberate attacks on the life, physical or psychological integrity, abduction, kidnapping of a person protected by the international law of armed conflict [Art. 461-2 CP]; mutilation or medical or scientific experiments on persons of the opposing party [Art. 461-3 CP]; prostitution, pregnancy, forced sterilization or sexual violence of comparable gravity against a person protected by the international law of armed conflict [Art. 461-4 CP]; humiliating and degrading treatment of persons of the opposing party [Art. 461-5 CP]; infringement of the personal liberty of a person protected by the international law of armed conflict [Art. 461-6 CP]; conscription or enlistment of minors [Art. 461-7 CP].

Conduct of hostilities: ordering that there be no survivors or threatening to do so [s. 461-8 CP]; deliberate attacks against the civilian population [Art. 461-9 CP]; serious bodily harm or killing of a surrendered combatant of the opposing party [Art. 461-10 CP]; serious bodily harm or murder by treachery [Art. 461-11 CP]; deliberate attacks on medical personnel, buildings, equipment, units and means of transport, bearing the distinctive signs provided for by international humanitarian law (e.g., in particular, the insignia of the Red Cross and Red Cres- cent); deliberate attacks against personnel, installations, equipment, units or vehicles employed in the framework of a humanitarian aid or peacekeeping mission of the United Nations [Art. 461-12 CP]; deliberate attacks on buildings dedicated to religion, education, art, science or charity, historical monuments, hospitals or places where the sick or wounded are gathered, provided that these buildings are not used for military purposes [Art. 461-13 CP].

Damage to property: looting of a city or town [Art. 461-15 CP]; theft and its concealment, extortion and its concealment, destruction, degradation and deterioration of property [Art. 461-16 CP].

International Armed Conflicts [Art. 461-2 to 461-18 CP]

Crimes against the human person: employing a person protected by the international law of armed conflict to prevent certain military forces or areas from being targeted for military operations [Art. 461-19 CP]; on behalf of a belligerent power, compelling a person protected by the international law of armed conflict to serve in its armed forces [Art. 461-20 CP]; on behalf of a belligerent power, compelling the nationals of the opposing party to take part in war operations directed against their country, even if they were in the service of the belligerent power before the war began [Art. 461-20 CP]; obstructing the right of a person protected by the international law of armed conflict to be judged regularly and impartially, according to the prescriptions of the applicable international conventions [Art. 461-21 CP]; declaring the rights and actions of the nationals of the opposing party inadmissible in court, forfeited or suspended because of the nationality of the applicants [Art. 461-22 CP].

Conduct of hostilities: using poison or poisoned weapons [Art. 461-23 CP]; using asphyxiating, poisonous or similar gases and any liquids, materials or similar processes [Art. 461-23 CP]; using bullets that easily deform the human body, as well as weapons, projectiles, materials or methods of combat that have been the subject of a general prohibition and have been listed in an annex to the Statute of the International Criminal Court accepted by France [Art. 461-23 CP]; attacking or bombing, by any means whatsoever, towns, villages, dwellings or buildings which are not defended and which are not military objectives [Art. 461-24 CP]; starving civilians, as a method of warfare, by deliberately depriving them of goods essential to their survival, including by intentionally preventing the dispatch of relief supplies as provided for in the Geneva Conventions of 12 August 1949 and their Additional Protocols [Art. 461-25 CP]; participating either in the transfer, directly or indirectly, by an occupying power, of part of its civilian population into the territory it occupies, or in the deportation or transfer within or outside the occupied territory of all or part of the civilian population of this territory [Art. 461-26 CP]; deliberate attack in the knowledge that it will cause incidental loss of life or injury to the civilian population which would be manifestly disproportionate to the concrete and direct military advantage anticipated from the attack as a whole [Art. 461-27 CP]; deliberate attack in the knowledge that it will cause incidental damage to civilian objects or extensive, lasting and severe damage to the natural environment, which would be manifestly disproportionate to the concrete and direct military advantage anticipated from the attack as a whole [Art. 461-28 CP]; improperly using the parliamentary flag, the flag or military insignia and the uniform of the enemy or of the United Nations, as well as the distinctive signs provided for in the Geneva Conventions of August 12, 1949, and their additional protocols, and, in so doing, causing injuries to a combatant of the opposing party that seriously damage his physical integrity [Art. 461-29 CP].

Non-International Armed Conflicts

* displacement of civilian population [Art. 461-30 CP];
* convictions and execution of sentences without a prior judgment, rendered by a regularly constituted court, with the judicial guarantees provided by international humanitarian law

[Art. 461-31 CP].

The responsibility of the individual can be sought by the fact of committing or causing the commission of the offense or that of the accomplice by facilitating the preparation or consumption by aid or assistance, or by provoking by gift, promise, threat, order, abuse of authority or power, or by giving instructions [Art. 121-7 CPP].

The responsibility of the hierarchic superior [Art. 213-4-1] may also be sought by the commanding officer, or the person having the function of a commanding officer whose subordinates under his effective authority and control have committed the above offenses (exception: torture) if he knew or should have known that these subordinates were committing or were going to commit this crime and if he did not take all the necessary and reasonable measures that were in his power to prevent or repress the execution thereof or to refer the matter to the competent authorities for investigation and prosecution.

BIBLIOGRAPHY

Rechtman, Richard. *La Vie ordinaire des génocidaires*. CNRS Éditions, 2020.

Claverie, Élizabeth. "Démasquer la guerre: Chronique d'un nettoyage ethnique Višegrad (Bosnie-Herzégovine) *L'Homme* 2012/3–4," nos. 203–204 (Spring 1992): 169–210.

Claverie, Élisabeth. "Reappearance: Tracing the Bodies of Missing Persons from the Bosnian War." *Raisons politiques* 41, no. 1 (January 2011): 13–31.

La Violence, le procès et la Justification: Scènes d'audience au TPIY. Sens de la justice, Sens critique, Jun 2001, Cerisy, France.

Claverie, Élisabeth. "Techniques de la menace." *Terrain* no. 43 (September 2004): 15–30.

Rwanda

Hatzfeld, Jean. *Dans le nu de la vie: Récits des marais rwandais.* Seuil, 2000.

Hatzfeld, Jean. *Une saison de machettes,* Seuil, 2003.

Hatzfeld, Jean. *La Stratégie des antilopes.* Seuil, 2007.

Dumas, Hélène. *Ce génocide des voisins.* Seuil, 2014.

Reyntjens, Filip. *Le génocide des Tusi au Rwanda,* Presses Universitaires France, 2017.

Vandermeersch, Damien and Marc Schmitz. *Comment devient-on génocidaire ? Et si nous étions tous capables de massacrer nos voisins.* GRIP, 2013.

Liberia

Paulais, Thierry. *Le Liberia: Une singulière histoire.* Le Cavalier Bleu, 2018.

Syria

Seurat, Michel. *Syrie: L'État de barbarie*. Presses Universitaires France, 2012.
Baron, Xavier. *Histoire de la Syrie de 1918 à nos jours*. Tallandier, 2014 (2019 ed.).
Le Caisne, Garance. *Opération César*. Stock, 2015.

Criminological Studies

Sofsky, Wolfgang. *Traité de la violence*. Gallimard, 1998.
Sémelin, Jacques. *Purifier et détruire: Usages politiques des massacres et génocides*. Seuil, 2005.
Thys, Pierre. *Criminels de guerre: Étude criminologique*. L'Harmattan, 2007.

Nazi Germany

Merle, Robert. *La mort est mon métier*. Gallimard, 1952.
Levi, Primo. *Si c'est un homme*. Julliard, 1987; Pocket, 1988.
Browning, Christophe. *Des hommes ordinaires, le 101e bataillon de réserve de la police allemande et la Solution finale en Pologne*. Les Belles Lettres, 2002.

ACKNOWLEDGMENTS

I would like to warmly thank my assistant Nicolas L.-C. for his generosity, the heads of the divisions that make up OCLCH, Laurent P. and Jean-Pierre C., and their assistants, Christophe C. and David G., and all the non-commissioned officers of the gendarmerie and police for the confidence they have shown in me through the years, as well as the surveillance and intervention teams that supported our investigations.

My thanks to the magistrates of the National Anti-Terrorist Prosecutor's Office, the Crimes Against Humanity Unit, the investigating judges, court clerks, and specialized assistants with whom we have shared to many experiences.

To Elisabeth Claverie for her kindness and her passion for Bosnia and Herzegovina.

To Cédric G. for his assiduous proofreading and his assistance during my years in Bosnia and Herzegovina at Nisveta's side.

To Christophe Dubois and Guy Benhamou for their support and encouragement during the writing process.

To the members of international organizations and non-governmental organizations for their participation in the fight against impunity.

To members of Open Facto for their support of OSINT, and the open-source ninja who know who they are.

To the editors at Plon for convincing me to write about our work in the fight against impunity.

NOTES

Preface

1 Preamble to the Rome Statute of the International Crimes Court, July 1998.
2 In French, the l'Office chargé de la lutte contre les crimes contre l'humanité.

Chapter 2

1 Alpine Hunters.
2 L'École militaire de haute montagne.
3 Alpine Guerillas.
4 These sections are grouped together in a structure called Human Research Units of the 27th Alpine Division (URH 27).
5 France's police judiciaire or judicial police operate under the direction of the judiciary, pursuing and interrogating criminal suspects, gathering evidence, serving warrants, and making arrests. Administrative police, under direction of the executive branch, ensure public order, from directing traffic to controlling riots.
6 Jovan Divjak, *Sarajevo, Mon Amour* (Buchet-Chastel, 2004).

Chapter 3

1 Josip Broz Tito was the leader of the Yugoslav Partisans, one of the strongest resistance movements in German-occupied Europe, and later communist president of Yugoslavia.
2 International Criminal Tribunal for the former Yugoslavia.
3 See Claverie, Elisabeth, "Les techniques de la menace," *Terrain*, no. 41 (September 2004): 15–30.

4 Élizabeth Claverie, "Démasquer la guerre: Chronique d'un nettoyage ethnique Višegrad (Bosnie-Herzégovine)," *L'Homme* 2012/3–4, nos. 20–204 (Spring 1992): 169–210.

5 See the Acts of Accusation and Judgment, http://www.icty.org/fr/case/milan_lukic_sre- doje_lukic.

6 Élisabeth Claverie, "Reappearance: Tracing the Bodies of Missing Persons from the Bosnian War," *Raisons politiques* 41, no. 1, (January 2011): 13–31.

7 Jacques Sémelin, "*Purify and Destroy. Political uses of massacres and genocides,*" coll. "The Color of Ideas", Paris, Le Seuil, 2005. Jacques Semelin explored violence in the most extreme, terrifying, and absurd forms, dissecting the complex mechanisms developed by individuals within states or proto-states with the aim of gaining power, but which, I think, most often masks the logic of predation.

8 Formulated by Jacques Sémelin.

Chapter 4

1 Colonel in Bosnian.

Chapter 5

1 For definitions and the rules of jurisdiction related to these offences, see the appendix.

2 Article 689-11 of the Code de procédure pénale modifié par la loi 2019-222 of March 23, 2019, part of the 2018-2022 justice reformation program.

3 Roughly 55,000 snapshots showing the bodies of thousands of tortured Syrians.

4 Article 10 of law 2015-925 enacted on July 29, 2015, relating to the right to asylum as modified by article L722-3 of the code for foreigner entry, visitation, and asylum.

5 To be valid, a civilian complaint concerning crimes of torture committed abroad, or crimes committed in Rwanda or former Yugoslavia, needs to be submitted on the day the accused present in France. It is then up to the investigator to verify the presence of the accused. For other crimes, it must be establish that the person in question was habitually resident in France on the day upon which the complaint was submitted.

6 http://www.revue21.fr/zoom_sur/enquete-sur-le-nazi-de-damas/.

7 This commission was established by the Human Rights Council, through

its "Resolution S-17/1—The situation of human rights in the Syrian Arab Republic," 22 August 2011, A/HRC/S-17/2.

8 Established by UN Security Council resolution 2379 (2017).

9 European Parliament, "Regulation (EU) 2016/794 relating to the European Union agency for law enforcement cooperation," L 135/53-EN.

10 European Parliament, "Regulation (EU) 2018/1727 on the European Union Agency for Judicial Cooperation in Criminal Matters (Eurojust) and replacing and repealing Decision 2002/187/JHA," 21 Nov. 2018, L295/138-FR.

Chapter 6

1 In this case, we can rely on the resources of either Europol or the French financial intelligence unit "TRACFIN" in analyzing the flow of money.

Chapter 8

1 See Hélène Dumas, *Le Génocide au village: Le massacre des Tutsi au Rwanda* (Le Seuil, 2014).

2 See Jean Hatzfeld, *Une Saison de Machettes*, (Le Seuil, 2003).

3 Stanley Milgram, "Experiment on Obedience and Disobedience to Authority," *La Découverte* (2017).

4 The experiment was recently repeated in Poland and fifty years later, Milgram's findings are still relevant. The study, published in 2017 in the journal *Social Psychological and Personality Science* found that seventy-two of eighty participants agreed to administer the highest level of electroshock to their "victim."

Chapter 9

1 Caucasian in Kinyarwanda.

2 Thank you in Kinyarwanda.

Chapter 10

1 Charles Habonimana, *Moi, le dernier Tutsi* (Plon, 2019), 87.

Chapter 11

1 Expressely provided for by article 628-8 of the Code de procédure pénale which concerns investigations and judicial information stemming from infractions releated to organised crime and terrorism.

2 As described in the circulaire de la garde des Sceaux, JUSD 1915381 C of May 27, 2019, an IMSI-Catcher is an "apparatus or technical device that collects technical data that allows the identification of terminal equipment or the subscription numbers of its user, along with data relative to the localisationz of the terminal equipment used." It also allows the interception of electronic correspondence.

3 A secure messaging system.

4 Fichier de personnes recherchées, Wanted Persons Files.

Chapter 14

1 See also Theirry Paulais, *Le Liberia: Une singulière histoire* (Le Cavalier Bleu, 2018).

Chapter 15

1 We will use both traditional investigative techniques and the previously-cited special powers authorized by article 628-8 of the Code de procédure pénale.

2 The UN's International, Impartial, and Independent Mechanism to assist in the investigation and prosecution of persons responsible for the most serious crimes under International Law committed in the Syrian Arab Republic since March 2011.

3 Researching information from open sources on the internet involves not only the collection of clues, but, more importantly, their verification in order that they can be entered into criminal evidence. The work is performed by trained specialists who can be counted on to use the utmost rigor. Facial recognition experts have the tools to identify (or rule out of consideration) persons in photographs. OCLCH has its own specialist in this domain. Like all forms of artificial intelligence, the technology is evolving quickly.

4 The elite police tactical unit of the National Gendarmerie of France.

Chapter 17

1 https://www.msf-crash.org/fr/publications/guerre-et-humanitaire/liberia-derriere-le-chaos-crises-et-interventions.
2 See the BBC report on the practice of Tabay. The members of the NPFL are thought to have been trained in these methods by Libyan forces. They are also common throughout Nigeria (http://www.youtube.com/watch?v=8DESvoJbee0).
3 Pierre Thys, *Criminels de guerre: Etude criminologique* (L'Harmattan Sciences Criminelles, 2007).
4 Christopher R. Browning, *Ordinary Men: Reserve Police Battalion 101 and the Final Solution in Poland* (HarperCollins, 2017).

Chapter 18

1 ULIMO was created in May 1991 in Conakry, Guinea. It was an alliance of three groups formed by former ministers of Samuel Doe, who fled after his death. The organization intended to repel the rebels of Charles Taylor and his allies. After fighting alongside Sierra Leone's army against the Taylor-backed Revolutionary United Front (RUF), ULIMO forces entered western Liberia in September 1991. In August of 1992, ULIMO took control of a major part of northwest Liberia, including the diamond mining sites of Lofa and Bomi counties. But the people were not liberated. Instead, they found themselves with new executioners. Whereas the NPFL had arbitrarily eliminated women and men on the grounds that they might be Mandingo or Krahn, ULIMO did much the same thing, assimilating them to the Mano and Gio ethnic groups.
2 Xavier Baron, *Histoire de la Syrie de 1918 à nos jours* (Tallandier, 2014).

Chapter 19

1 https://www.hrw.org/report/2012/07/03/torture-archipelago/arbitrary-arrests-torture-and-enforced-disappearances-syrias.
2 http://www.leparisien.fr/international/alois-brunner-l-un-des-criminels-nazis-les-plus-recherches-serait-mort-dans-un-cachot-11-01-2017-6554124.php.
3 Garance Le Caisne, *Operation Caesar* (Stock, 2015).
4 Pursuant to Article 40 of the Code of Criminal Procedure, "any constituted authority, any public officer or civil servant who, in the exercise of his functions, acquires knowledge of a crime or misdemeanor is required to give notice

without delay to the public prosecutor and to transmit to this magistrate all the information, minutes and acts relating thereto."

5 After Charles-Henri Sanson, one of the French executioners of Louis XVI.

Chapter 20

1 A Syrian paramilitary force tasked with defending the Assad government and Damascus from internal and external attack, later merged with the Republican Guard of the Syrian Arab Army.

2 See "Report on the Alleged Use of Chemical Weapons in the Ghouta Area of Damascus on 21 August 2013," United Nations, 2013.

3 Daraa was the center of unrest in the 2011 Arab Spring protests in Syria. On April 25, 2011, the Syrian Army began a military siege of Daraa that escalated the protests to armed rebellion and civil war.

4 Colleen McColloughu, *The Thorn Birds* (1996).

5 Philip Zimbardo, *The Lucifer Effect: Understanding How Good People Turn Evil* (Random House, 2007).

6 Pierre Thys, *Criminels de guerre: Etude criminologique* (L'Harmattan, 2007), 155.

7 During the Cold War, the CIA prepared a secret interrogation manual for its agents under the code name "Kubark." This confidential document, written in 1963, was secret until 1997 when American journalists were able to obtain it under the Freedom of Information Act. Many passages were redacted.

8 Wolfgang Sofsky, *Traitéde la violence*. (Gallimard, 1998).

9 Kapos were concentration camp prisoners who collaborated with the Nazis and were trusted to supervise other prisoners.

Chapter 21

1 An American psychologist, Francine Shapiro, discovered by chance this method of stimulating our complex neurophysiological systems.

Chapter 22

1 An information database used by countries of the European Union and containing the digital fingerprints of people that have requested asylum and subsidiary protection, as well as illegal immigrants. Its purpose is two-fold: to determine which country is responsible for the asylum request and to allow

law enforcement agencies of the EU and Europol to consult the database for investigative or preventive purposes.

2 In 2018 there were 123,625 requests and 122,000 decisions with a protection rate of 26.6 per cent, or 35.9 per cent if we add the CNDA protections. In 2019, asylum requests were at 132,614, representing an annual growth rate of 7.3 per cent.

Chapter 23

1 955 is the number of the United Nations resolution that created the International Criminal Tribunal for Rwanda.

2 https://www.irmct.org/fr/cases/mict-13-38.

3 A judicial police operation by the gendarmerie is organized and led by an operational director, generally the head of the unit. He or she assumes responsibility for the success and failure of the operation and collaborates closely with the magistrate in charge of the case.

4 It is important that a target, on arrest, is read his rights in a language he understands.

5 Magistrates specialized in the investigation of the Tutsi genocide.

6 Charles Habonimana, *Moi, le dernier Tutsi* (Plon, 2019).

Conclusion

1 Primo Levi reminds us, "We must therefore beware of those who seek to convince us by means other than reason, in other words, of charismatic leaders: we must weigh our decision carefully before delegating to someone else the power to judge our will in our place. Since it is difficult to distinguish true prophets from false ones, let us beware of all prophets; it is better to renounce revealed truths, even if they transport us by their simplicity and their brilliance, even if we find them convenient because they are free."

2 http://theconversation.com/narcissiques-et-psychopathes-voici-comment-certaines-societes-ecartent-du-pouvoir-ces-personnes-dangereuses-119127.

INDEX

Goma in Congo, 72, 91, 102
GOSIF team, 54
Gospel of Saint John, 107
Grand Mufti of Jerusalem, 43
Grand, Pierre, 35
Greben village, 25
Grellier, Claude, 42
Guinean embassy in Paris, 133

H
Habonimana, Charles, 229
Habyarimana President, 48, 59, 61,
    65–66, 88, 90–91, 223, 232
Haddad, Joni, 216
The Hague, 18, 26, 29, 35
Hamidou, Nadia, 178, 180
Hassan, Jamil, 176
Haut-de-Seine, 232
Haute Savoie, 9
Haute-Savoie highway patrol, 96
Hautes-Pyreìneìes, 9
Herero, 92
Hervèat Open Facto, 128
High Mountain Gendarmerie Platoon
    (PGHM), 8
High Mountain Military School, 7
Himmler, Abu, 184
Hitler, Abu, 184, 185
Hollande, François, 37
Homicides, 9
Hoover, Herbert President, 140
Horn of Africa, 88
Hrvatin Street, 11
Human Research Units of 27th Alpine
    Division (URH 27), 7–8
Human Rights Watch, 47
    report, 161
Husseini, Sayyed Hassan, 220
Hutu Power movement, 90

Hutus, 31, 44, 87–89, 91, 100–101
    government, 48
    President Melchior Ndadayeso, 89
    refugees, 56
    Ruhengeri, in, 100
Hymne-à-la-Joie, 130

I
Ibuka association, 93
Independent Commission for Human
    Rights (ICHR), 47
Independent Commission of Inquiry
    on Syrian Arab Republic, 46
Independent National Patriotic Front
    of Liberia (INPLF), 122
Indigenous populations, 121
Indigenous tribes, 120
Institute of Criminal Research of
    the Gendarmerie Nationale
    (IRCGN), 228
Interministerial Technical Assistance
    Service (SAIT), 77
International Commission for Justice
    and Accountability (CIJA), 47
International Commission on Missing
    Persons in The Hague, 29
International Committee of Red
    Cross, 29
International Cooperation Directorate
    (DCI), 45
International Criminal Court (ICC),
    40, 46, 61, 63, 168
International Criminal Tribunal, 222
International Criminal Tribunal for
    former Yugoslavia, 27
International Criminal Tribunal for
    Rwanda (ICTR), 66, 68
International Federation for Human
    Rights, 176